Energy Time Series Forecasting

Lars Dannecker

Energy Time Series Forecasting

Efficient and Accurate Forecasting
of Evolving Time Series from
the Energy Domain

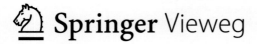 Springer Vieweg

Lars Dannecker
Dresden, Germany

Doctorate at the Technische Universität Dresden, 20.11.2014

Original title: Efficient and Accurate Forecasting of Evolving Time Series from the Energy Domain

ISBN 978-3-658-11038-3   ISBN 978-3-658-11039-0 (eBook)
DOI 10.1007/978-3-658-11039-0

Library of Congress Control Number: 2015947268

Springer Vieweg

Printed on acid-free paper

Springer Vieweg is a brand of Springer Fachmedien Wiesbaden
Springer Fachmedien Wiesbaden is part of Springer Science+Business Media
(www.springer.com)

To my wife Ulrike and my daughter Luisa.

Preface

Continuous balancing of electric power consumption and production is a fundamental prerequisite for the stability and efficiency of electricity grids. This balancing task requires accurate forecasts of future electricity demand and supply at any point in time. For this purpose, today's energy data management systems (EDMS) typically use quantitative models—called forecast models—that already provide accurate predictions. However, recent developments in the energy domain such as real-time intra-day trading and the integration of more renewable energy sources also require more efficient forecasting calculations and a rapid provisioning of forecasting results. Furthermore, today's EDMSs fulfill a number of different tasks, each exhibiting different requirements for the calculation of forecasts with respect to runtime and accuracy. Thus, it is necessary to flexibly adapt the forecasting process with respect to the needs of the current requests. In contrast, currently employed forecasting approaches are rather time-consuming and inflexible. One reason is the very expensive estimation of the forecast model parameters, involving a large number of simulations in a search space that increases exponential with the number of parameters.

We tackle these new requirements by introducing a novel online forecasting process that aims to improve the forecasting calculation efficiency and to provide forecasting process adaptability. For this purpose, the online forecasting process employs forecast model materialization in conjunction with flexible and fast parameter estimation to rapidly provide accurate forecasts that are iteratively improved over time. EDMSs may subscribe to the online forecasting process to retrieve improvements found during the process execution. In addition, they can adapt the progression of the forecast calculation by defining runtime constraints and accuracy targets. With that, we are able to equally server requests that require results in a limited amount of time or that target the best possible accuracy.

The online forecasting process is complemented by further optimizations on the logical as well as on the physical layer. Our optimizations on the logical layer

improve the efficiency of the parameter estimation independently of the data organization and the employed forecast model. As a first approach, we introduce our
context-aware forecast model repository that materializes previously used forecast
models and their parameters in conjunction with information about the time series
context that was valid during the time the model was used. We may then provide
appropriate starting points for future forecasting calculations by reusing models
that produced accurate results in a context similar to the current one. Furthermore,
for some use cases, it is beneficial to consider context information directly within
the forecast models. Especially when predicting renewable supply, information
about the weather are very important. However, including context information typically means to add further parameters to the forecast model, which increases the
efforts for the parameter estimation. To solve this issue, we introduce an integration framework that optimizes the handling of context information and reduces the
additional efforts when considering them. Finally, we improve the calculation of
forecasts in hierarchical environments. Instead of simply aggregating time series,
we propose a forecast model aggregation that eliminates the need for estimating
the forecast model parameters on higher hierarchical levels.

Our physical optimizations aim to directly provide an efficient way for forecast
models to access time series values. For this purpose, we introduce an access-
pattern-aware storage approach that exploits the memory access patterns of the
used forecast models to physically layout the data for sequential access and high
spatial locality. With that, we substantially reduce the negative influence of memory latency and bandwidth, while at the same time improving the utilization of the
different cache levels. In addition, we propose a special parallelization approach
for multi-equation forecast models.

Overall, with the help of our online forecasting process in conjunction with
the optimizations on the logical and on the physical layer, we target to enable
accurate forecasting of evolving time series considering the new requirements of
the changing electricity market.

Acknowledgements

First and foremost, I would like to express my deepest gratitude to my advisor Prof. Dr. Wolfgang Lehner for the opportunity to pursue my dissertation project and for his continuous support along the way. I thank him for the very interesting and challenging topic and for all the advice he gave me. Wolfgang was always available for a discussion and for providing feedback to my ideas. I'm very thankful that I had the chance to leverage his deep knowledge in all areas of data management. Although I was an external member of his research group, Wolfgang never let me feel external, but rather treated me as an integral part. For me, Wolfgang is this kind of advisor who all PhD students should have. I really appreciate all the time and guidance you provided during the last years. Thank you so much for everything.

I would also like to thank Dr. Matthias Bhm for acting as my co-mentor in the first two years. He was deeply involved in shaping the topic of the thesis and creating the first scientific results. Matthias devoted a lot of time for discussions, for providing advice and guidance, and for giving constructive feedback to many papers. I learned so much from him, especially with respect to conducting research, creating publications and evaluating my ideas. Matthias, this thesis would not have been possible without you. I really appreciate your dedication and endless support.

Writing this thesis was greatly supported by the SAP SE and especially the SAP location in Dresden. SAP employed me as a PhD student and thus, gave me the chance to start my dissertation project. I want to especially thank Dr. Gregor Hackenbroich for serving as my mentor as well as for his confidence, his patience, and his belief in me throughout the entire time. In many discussions, Gregor provided me with very helpful input and directions for various aspects of my thesis. Thank you very much, I'm really grateful for your support. Further, I would like to thank my colleague Dr. Philipp Rsch for being a co-author of many papers and the endless discussions about my sometimes strange ideas. With his deep knowledge, he provided great guidance and helped forming several approaches and topics of this thesis. Thank you Philipp for taking so much time and endurance, especially in relation to the second half of my thesis.

Furthermore, I would like to thank Prof. Christian Jensen for co-referring this thesis and for many helpful comments and advice. I really appreciate his great hospitality during my visits in Aarhus and Aalborg. I'm also grateful to Prof. Dr. Dominik Mst for serving as my *Fachreferent*.

Special thanks goes to my students Robert Schulze, Elena Vasilyeva, Robert Lorenz, and Gordon Gaumnitz for contributing to my research and for helping to implement the pEDM prototype. It was a pleasure working with you and I'm very proud that all of you achieved such good results in your final theses.

I am very thankful to all my colleagues at SAP SE and the Technische Universitt Dresden who helped me with their input and discussions. I would especially like to thank: Dr. Gregor Hackenbroich and Dr. Philipp Rsch for proof-reading my thesis and for providing very constructive comments; Dr. Ulrike Fischer for working with me in the MIRABEL project and the fruitful discussions we had; Konrad, Katrin, Andreas, Henrike, and Alexandr for being great roommates; Ines and Annette for helping me with (and enduring) my numerous requests in their role as team assistants; my fellow researchers in the database technology group Dirk, Maik, Martin, Hannes, Tim, Katrin, Julian, Thomas, Tobias, Tomas, Till, Claudio, Kai, Frank, Robert, and Elena for your acceptance and a fruitful research environment; the remaining colleagues at SAP SE especially Kay, Martin, Philipp, Michael, Marcus, David, Robert, Dan, Ivan, and Karim for being good colleagues and for providing a great working atmosphere.

Finally, this thesis would not have been possible without the constant support and motivation from my family and friends. First and foremost, I would like to thank my beloved wife Ulrike for always being there for me, for encouraging me, and for accepting the numerous times I had to work at home. Your love and commitment is what has always motivated me. I also want to thank: My daughter Luisa for cheering me up and for reminding me about the most important things in life; my parents Jutta and Falk as well as my brother Frank for continuously supporting me, for permanently believing in me, and for helping me out of the tough situations where I had a lot of doubts; Kay, Martin, Jan, Gregor, Stefan, and all my other friends for your friendship and the patience you had with me. Thank you! I will dedicate more time to all of you in the future.

Lars Dannecker
Dresden, 12. August 2014

Contents

List of Figures

List of Tables

Chapter 1
Introduction

Time series forecasting is an important statistical data analysis technique used as a basis for manual and automatic planning in many application domains such as sales, traffic control, and energy management [119]. Instead of solely analyzing data of the past, forecasting allows to take a look into possible future developments, which is of great value when making strategic decisions. Thus, it comes at no surprise that forecasting is gaining more and more interest in research and industry [119]. Accordingly, Gartner rated predictive analytics in general and load forecasting in particular in their 2013 hype cycle for analytic applications as "entering the plateau" and "climbing the slope" respectively, which means that both are well-established technologies in the industry and their utilization is steadily increasing. In addition, forecasting is still a field of intensive research, since even small improvements in forecasting accuracy are worth millions of dollars. Hobbs et al. quantify in 1999 the financial loss due to forecast errors in their financial case study of two US American utilities of being between $1.8M and $4.5M annually assuming a forecast error (i.e., the deviation between the actual and the predicted load) of 5% [126]. In another often cited study Bunn and Farmer found that an increase of only 1% in the forecast error caused an operating cost increase of £10M for a single British electric utility company in the year 1984 [39, 216].

In the energy domain, accurate forecasts of electricity demand and supply are a fundamental prerequisite for balancing electric power consumption and production and thus, for the stability and reliability of the electricity grids (see e.g.,[134, 153, 172, 222]). Forecasting employs model-based techniques, where quantitative models—known as forecast models—are used to describe the behavior and development of historic time series. Important forecast model classes are autoregressive models [25], exponential smoothing models [229, 246] and models that apply machine learning [40]. Most forecast model types capture a parameterized relationship between past and future values to express different aspects of a time series such as seasonal patterns, trends, or exogenous influences. These parameters are adapted to the specifics of a time series by estimating them on a training dataset. The goal of this estimation is to find parameter combinations that minimize the forecast error (i.e., the difference between predicted and actual value) measured in terms of an error metric [131]. The estimation of the parameters is typically conducted using local (e.g., Limited Memory – Broyden-Fletcher-Goldfarb-Shanno (L–BFGS) [42]) or global (e.g., simulated annealing [145]) numerical optimization algorithms and is computationally rather complex. The reason is that the parameter search space increases exponentially with the number of parameters, which potentially leads to a large number of simulations. This is especially true for very accurate, but often very complex domain-specific forecast models that exhibit a large number of parameters. The EGRV model [197] (consider Section 3.3) for example may use in one instance 24 sub-models for modeling a single day (given hourly data), where each sub-model exhibits around 30 parameters. Thus, given a coarse-grained search resolution of only 10 values per dimension, we already arrive at 10^{30} possible parameter combinations per sub-model. Therefore, the parameter estimation renders the entire forecasting process very expensive.

The eventually estimated instance of a forecast model can then be used to predict future values up to a defined horizon (e.g., one day). In particular, forecasts with different lead times and horizons are used in the energy domain to support a number of important tasks such as unit commitment, grid regulation, load following, and power scheduling [134]. Previously, with a predominant usage of conventional energy sources, the electricity supply could be almost perfectly matched to the electricity demand by adapting the production schedules of the respective power plants. The reason is that the production of conventional power plants using fossil fuels (coal, oil, gas) or nuclear power is fully dispatchable and controllable [172, 211]. Accordingly, during these times, forecasts where mainly calculated once per day as an input for the production scheduling of conventional power plants for the next day [54, 140, 153]. Hence, the time for calculating forecasts was no major concern. This is also supported by the fact that load forecasting is well researched and provides highly accurate predictions [91, 153, 229]. Furthermore, in most electricity markets short-term fluctuations are compensated using a sophisticated multi-level reserve power system and regulative interventions by the responsible transmission system operators (TSO). When for example a ramping load event is recognized in the demand forecast, the TSOs may induce the start-up of reserve and peak power plants. However, electricity markets worldwide are drastically changing with the goal of providing a more competitive and sustainable market environment. The European Union for example is targeting to create an integrated single European electricity market by 2014 and to provide a substantial share of the electric power production using renewable energy sources (RES) by 2020 [110, 192]. These changes have manifold impact on several areas of the electricity market landscape throughout Europe:

Electricity market changes. First, the electricity market is changing from a static one day-ahead market to a flexible, real-time marketplace that allows dynamic interactions between market participants. In particular, electric energy producers and consumers are free to choose an electricity supplier in a fine-grained manner and the amount of one-time and short-term contracts increases. Competitiveness and reliable power supply are increasingly important, especially since deviations from production commitments are directly penalized using monetary sanctions [23, 153, 193]. The reason is that overcommitment and undercommitment likewise require reactive measures by the producer or even the TSO. This includes trading on the more expensive balancing market (producer) or the activation of costly downwards or upwards reserves (TSO). Thus, accurate forecasts of electricity demand and supply are of utmost importance to limit financial risk and increase market revenue.

Increasing Utilization of Renewables. Second, there is an increasing utilization of renewable energy sources to improve the sustainability and environmental friendliness of the entire electricity production. In the European Union the goal is to provide 20 % of the overall produced energy from renewable energy sources by the year 2020. Globally the International Renewable Energy Agency (IRENA) targets to double the share of renewable energy sources in the global energy mix by 2030 [136]. The increasing share of renewable energy sources drastically changes the conditions for the electric energy production and poses new requirements on the balancing of electricity demand and supply. The final production of the most important renewable energy sources—namely wind and solar power [121]—cannot be planned like for conventional energy sources [10, 157], because their production is influenced by external factors such as the current weather situation [53, 239]. Thus, such intermittent renewable energy sources are subject to frequent and strong fluctuations and their final power output is hard to predict, which means that in contrast to conventional power plants they are not dispatchable [5, 244]. In addition, there are only insufficient electricity storage capabilities available that would allow storing electric power in times of electricity excess and using it later in times of electricity shortage. Thus, electric energy produced by renewable sources must be directly used when it is available [44, 172]. Accordingly, the electricity grid is strained with an increasing amount of excess or scarcity situations that must be compensated. In some countries this even provokes situations close to a wide-spread electricity outage.

As a result, while it was sufficient in the past to plan the electricity production solely with respect to the demand on a day-ahead basis, the current challenges require a much more flexible and fine-grained balancing and grid management in real-time [153, 239]. In particular, it is necessary to improve the ability of power management systems to quickly react on load and supply changes [23, 53, 82]. For this purpose, new technologies such as smart grids and economical measures like real-time electricity trading are increasingly employed [44, 68]. Building upon this, research projects such as MIRABEL [170] and MeRegio [166] develop advanced technologies such as demand response systems, dynamic price signals, and flexible electricity requests [16, 21] to further address the challenges of real-time electricity balancing.

A fundamental prerequisite for these approaches and for a more dynamic and fine-grained scheduling of power consumption and production in the context of real-time balancing is the availability of current and accurate predictions of electricity demand and supply at any point in time. While a lot of research was already done with respect to providing accurate predictions for electricity demand [91, 153, 229], the forecasting of renewable electricity production is recently getting more and more attention in research (e.g., [53, 109, 115, 172]) and industry (e.g., [4, 72, 113]). The reason is that with an increasing penetration of renewable energy sources forecasting their production is an essential aspect to address their variability and uncertainty and thus, to maintain the reliability of the electricity grids [53]. At the same time substantial market opportunities worth millions of dollars arise [10, 191]. IBM states that advanced analytics and with that, forecasting act as "a pivot point for the industrialization of renewable energy" by providing "insights needed to increase system availability, reduce operational expenditure, and improve [unit] dispatch" [113]. Accordingly, previous research with respect to electricity supply forecasting mainly focused on developing highly accurate forecast models, for what reason the current state-of-the art is already able to accurately predict the future electricity production of renewable energy sources [115, 134, 191].

However, the increasing need to tightly integrate forecasting capabilities into energy management systems (EMS) enabling quick, predictive and autonomous reactions on changing load and supply conditions, requires to also optimize the forecast calculation process [18, 24, 251]. The reason is three-fold. First, an increased accuracy often comes with an increasing complexity of the employed forecast models or the utilization of forecast model ensembles. Thus, the estimation and maintenance of the involved models is very time consuming [112, 138, 239]. Second, the forecasting process must be able to fully automatically calculate predictions without requiring human intervention [211]. In addition, an EMS fulfills a number of different tasks each posing different requirements with respect to runtime and accuracy of the forecast calculation [171, 172]. Thus, the forecasting process must be able to adapt with respect to the requirements of the current forecasting request. Third, new measurements of electric power consumption and production are constantly available. They can be seen as a constant stream of updates appended to the respective time series. Accordingly, we call such time series *evolving time series*. These updates bring new information about the most recent development of a time series and possible changes in the time series characteristics. Thus, to maintain a high accuracy of the provided forecasts, it is necessary to automatically pick up those changes and to adapt the employed forecast models accordingly [11, 90, 128, 165]. Such adaptations typically mean to either re-estimate the parameters of the forecast models or even to re-evaluate the used forecast model type and component composition. Hence, the maintenance of forecast models is almost as expensive as the initial forecast model creation [128, 153]. As a result, instead of solely striving for the highest possible forecast accuracy, it is necessary to understand the calculation of forecasts as a two-dimensional optimization problem involving the dimensions runtime and accuracy. Accordingly, besides optimizing the accuracy, we should also consider the efficiency and adaptability of the forecasting process. This is backed by a recent shift in paradigm that some researchers in the electricity forecasting area are proposing. Instead of focusing purely on the forecast error of a forecast model, one should specifically assess the value of a forecast with respect to the consumer and the application [18, 24, 193, 251]. The reason is that a highly accurate forecast is of significantly less value if the employed forecasting system is not able to deliver the prediction in time. Similarly, if the time to apply the optimal measures for a certain situation is not sufficient after providing a forecast, the value of the high accuracy again decreases substantially. According to Crabtree et al. this shift in paradigm from the pure forecasters view to the forecast consumers view [24] can be seen "just as airline pilots know that weather and turbulence forecasts need not to be perfect to be useful" [53]. As a result, consumers and applications should receive a prediction in the accuracy and speed as they require.

In this work we tackle the aforementioned issues by optimizing the forecasting process with the goal of efficiently providing accurate forecasts in an application-aware manner at any point in time. For this purpose, we introduce an online forecasting process that rapidly provides accurate forecasts and iteratively refines them over time. Applications can subscribe to the online forecasting process to receive those improved forecasts. With that, we equally support applications that require forecasts in a limited amount of time as well as applications that need the best possible accuracy. The online forecasting process is complemented with further approaches that target to improve the selection of forecast models and the efficiency of the parameter estimation. To this end, we provide a novel way to efficiently calculate accurate forecasts of evolving time series from the energy domain.

Contributions

This book makes several contributions optimizing the forecast calculation on two layers—the logical and the physical layer. Optimizations on the logical layer refer to improvements that are independent of the data organization, the employed forecast models and the chosen parameter estimation algorithm. They rather comprise optimizations on the forecast calculation, the forecasting process, and the handling of forecast models. The proposed online forecasting process itself is a major optimization on the logical layer. Our further enhancements on the logical layer improve the model identification, the handling of external information and the forecasting in hierarchical environments. Optimizations on the physical layer directly target specific forecast models, estimators, and the data organization. In the course of our research we observed that forecast models exhibit specific access pattern to the data in main memory. During the parameter estimation the data is read multiple times, which means that reducing the memory access frequency by a tailored data organization in main memory poses a large optimization potential. The basic idea is to exploit the access patterns of the forecast models and to organize the data accordingly. This approach can significantly increase the efficiency when estimating forecast models. Overall, in this book we make the following contributions:

- We give an overview about the current developments on the European electricity market as a prime-example for the recent electricity market changes in many countries world-wide. Our study specifically focuses on the improved utilization of renewable energy sources and the resulting challenges all electricity market participants have to deal with.
- We analyze related work about time series forecasting in the energy domain. This comprises an analysis of typical electric energy time series data, the discussion of general and domain-specific forecast models as well as a description of optimization algorithms used for estimating forecast model parameters. In addition, at the beginning of each chapter, we provide a discussion of topic-specific related work.
- We propose a novel online forecasting process that allows an application-aware and efficient calculation of accurate forecasts. The online forecasting process uses forecast model materialization in conjunction with flexible and iterative parameter estimation that refines initially provided forecasts over time. Applications can subscribe to the online forecasting process to retrieve improved forecasts found during the iterative parameter estimation process. In addition, the online forecasting process supports the definition of runtime constraints and accuracy targets to allow applications to directly adapt the progression of the online forecasting process to their needs [59].
- A tight integration of forecasting algorithms directly into the employed data management system is one key aspect to improve the efficiency of the forecast calculation process. The reason is that the used statistical algorithms can directly access the required data without the need for copying the data from the database to an application. We present a high-level concept for integrating forecasting and especially our online forecasting process into database systems [95].

- As part of the online forecasting process we enhance the forecast model selection and the parameter estimation step with the help of a context-aware forecast model repository. The repository preserves previously used forecast models and their parameter combinations in conjunction with information about the time series context that was valid during their usage. For further forecasting requests, we can use the time series context as the selection criterion for the materialized forecast model instances to retrieve suitable starting points for a subsequent parameter estimation [60].
- We present a framework that allows an efficient integration of external information into forecast models for electricity demand and supply. The framework addresses the issue that an inclusion of external information substantially increases the necessary time for estimating a forecast model. By providing the external information as a separate model and by additionally using techniques for reducing the dimensionality of this model, we are able to significantly reduce the runtime of the parameter estimation, while considerably increasing the forecasting accuracy [61].
- We present a concept for improving the efficiency of forecasting calculations in the hierarchically organized European electricity market. Our approach exploits the fact that in the near future smart meters will be widely deployed. Instead of simply providing measurements, we propose to implement forecasting capabilities into the smart meters. Entities on higher hierarchical levels can synchronize with these forecast models to create a forecast model for their entire group without the need for conducting a time-intensive parameter estimation [55, 58, 159].
- We further introduce our access-pattern-aware time series storage that substantially increases the spatial locality of the data within the main memory. This special storage layout organizes the time series data with respect to the access pattern of the involved forecast models. Thus, forecast models can sequentially access the time series values within the main memory greatly improving cache utilization and substantially reducing the impact of memory latency. We further optimized the parameter estimation of multi-equation forecast models by providing a novel parallelization concept [56, 57].

Organization of the Book

The remainder of this book is organized as illustrated in Figure 1.1. We start with an investigation of the current developments on the European electricity market in Chapter 2. Our market analysis specifically focuses on the market liberalization, the integration of renewable energy sources, the implications of these changes for the electricity grid, and the need for improved forecasts. In Chapter 3 we discuss typical data characteristics as well as general and domain-specific forecasting

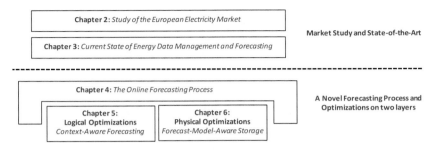

Fig. 1.1   Illustration of the book structure.

and optimization techniques. We conclude our findings from the market analysis (Chapter 2) and our discussion about the current state-of-the art (Chapter 3) with a number of challenges for forecasting in the energy domain.

Our novel online forecasting process is the main topic of Chapter 4. We start Chapter 4 with a general discussion about requirements a forecasting process should fulfill in the new electricity market environment and showcase the issues that occur when employing conventional forecasting approaches. Afterwards, we introduce our online forecasting process in detail, followed by a general concept for creating a forecasting system that complies to the new requirements of the changing electricity market. Our online forecasting process includes several novel optimization techniques on the logical and on the physical layer. We discuss the approaches on the logical layer in Chapter 5. We first introduce our special forecast model materialization technique that uses the time series context as a decision criterion to identify the most appropriate forecast models for the current state of a time series. Afterwards, we present a framework that allows an efficient integration of external information into forecast models, with the goal of substantially improving the forecasting accuracy while limiting the additional efforts. Furthermore, we propose a novel approach to efficiently calculate forecasts in hierarchical environments such as the European electricity market. Following the logical optimizations in Chapter 5, we introduce the physical optimizations included in the online forecasting process in Chapter 6. We start with introducing the different data access patterns of forecast models that are the basis for our access-pattern-aware time series storage. This storage approach specifically acknowledges such access-patterns to improve the spatial locality of the time series data within main memory. We conclude the book and provide directions for future work in Chapter 7.

To assist the reader in following the book and quickly finding the most relevant aspects, we additionally provide a flowchart presented in Figure 1.2. The arrows in the chart highlight whether a chapter or a section is either mandatory, highly recommended, or optional for understanding the subsequent chapters or sections.

Furthermore, we mark the sections of the most relevant contributions of this book with a bold border.

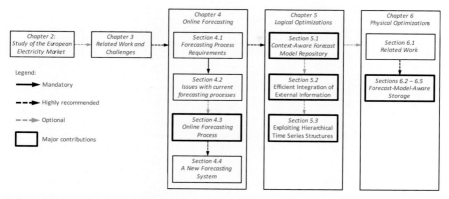

Fig. 1.2 Flowchart for reading the thesis.

Chapter 2
The European Electricity Market: A Market Study

The energy policy of the European Union targets to establish a competitive, ecological sustainable, and reliable pan-European electricity market. This involves the integration and liberalization of national electricity markets as well as new ecological goals. With creating an integrated European electricity market the European Union aims to create a flexible and dynamic real-time marketplace, where market participants throughout Europe are free to directly interact and negotiate. In addition, the European Union set ambitious ecological goals with their EU 20/20/20 target (Directive 2009/28/EC). The directive plans to reduce greenhouse emissions by 20%, to increase the share of renewable energy sources (RES) in the energy mix to 20% and to reduce the overall consumption by 20% until the year 2020 [78, 173]. This results in a strong political and market push towards integrating more renewable energy sources and to reduce the dependence on fossil fuel energy. Unfortunately, the energy production of the most important renewable energy sources, i.e., windmills and solar panels depends on external factors such as the wind speed or the total cloud cover [44, 82]. Hence, RES pose the challenge that their available power cannot be planned like traditional energy sources. In addition, current energy storage capabilities are very limited, thus, renewable energy sources have to be directly used when they are available. As a result, there is a strong need for changing the management of energy consumption and production, which involves a more fine-grained balancing, new market mechanism, grid extensions, and improved information and communication technology [44, 53, 78, 113]. In this chapter we discuss current developments in the European electricity market as well as issues and solutions that occur in conjunction with these developments. In addition, we present MIRABEL, an EU-funded research project dealing with the optimal utilization of renewable energy sources and the avoidance of cost-intensive peak-demand. Please note that for the remainder of this book we always refer to *electric energy* respectively *electricity* when using the term *energy*.

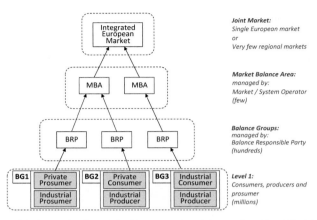

Fig. 2.1 Hierarchical organization of the European electricity market (simplified from [77]).

2.1 Current Developments in the European Electricity Market

The electricity market is changing from a static one-day ahead market to a flexible, ecological and dynamic real-time market place. There are two main reasons for this development: The first reason is the liberalization and the creation of a single European electricity market allowing for free competition and the ability to freely trade between consumers and producers. The second reason is the increased employment of intermittent renewable energy sources such as solar and wind power, which require more fine-grained and short-term trading as well as quick reactions on changing grid situations [53, 113, 239, 241]. We start the discussion about the European electricity market by introducing the current structure and presenting the current development of renewable energy sources. Afterwards, we discuss the issues caused by volatile RES and possible solutions for several aspects of the European electricity market.

2.1.1 Structure of the European Electricity Market

The European electricity market is hierarchically organized [77]. An overview illustration is presented in Figure 2.1. The lowest level of the hierarchy comprises private and industrial consumers as well as industrial energy producers. Some entities might also consume and produce energy at the same time and are therefore called prosumer. Consumers, producers, and prosumer are organized in balance groups, where balance responsible parties (BRP, e.g., utility companies) are responsible for balancing the energy demand and supply within their group. In addition, they buy or sell energy from outside their balance group according to the remaining volume needed or excessed in the case the balancing within the group is not possible. BRP represent the second level of the hierarchy. Multiple balance groups are grouped into market balance areas, with a market or system operator being responsible for the operation of the area and the stability of the transmission grid under their control. Often transmission system operators (TSO) take the role of a market/system operator, which are entitled to take active measures against any imbalances and stability issues that might occur in their market area. Further levels like a single European-wide market organizer are possible enhancements to this hierarchy. Currently, many European TSOs (41 from 34 countries) are organized in a pan-European organization called "European network of transmission system operators for electricity" (ENTSO-E).

This hierarchy is not fix and will change with an increasing penetration and better handling of renewable energy sources as well as a tighter market integration throughout Europe. On the lowest level, for example, previously a small number of big energy producers and some municipal utility companies provided almost the entire energy share using large fossil fuel and nuclear power plants [38]. With the emergence of renewable energy sources small and medium companies as well as even private customers are able to produce and feed in energy; solar panels are the most prominent renewable energy source for them [38]. As a result, the group of prosumers is growing. This development reduces the share of produced energy provided by big energy producing companies. Thus, the market has to deal with a much larger number of energy producing entities with only small to medium production capacity and has to provide suitable ways to integrate their production.

As an example, in Germany the four big electricity producers E.ON, EnBW, RWE, and Vattenfall account for 73% of the available capacity and over 80% of the net production when considering non-renewable energy production in 2011 [17, 38]. However, considering the installed capacity of all energy sources (i.e., RES and non-RES) the share of the four biggest energy producers is much smaller with only 46% (total capacity: 172.4 GW, capacity of the four biggest companies: 79.5 GW) [38, 76, 81, 199, 238]. In addition, their share of both installed capacity and net energy production even in the case of non-RES energy sources is decreasing. This reduction can be mainly accounted to the increasing utilization of RES at the expense of traditional energy sources and the German nuclear moratorium.

2.1.2 Development of Renewable Energy Sources in Europe and Germany

In the last years the amount of installed capacity from renewable energy sources and especially from wind and solar power substantially increased throughout Eu-

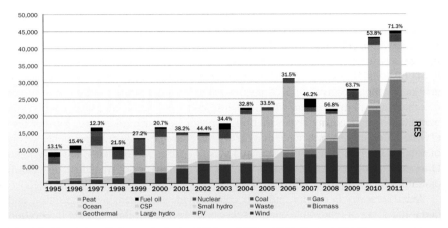

Fig. 2.2 Newly installed capacity in the EU from 1995 to 2011 (Source: [244]).

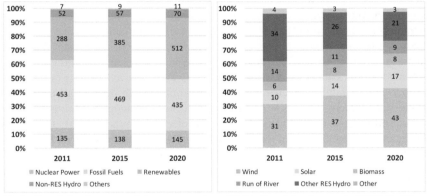

(a) Predicted development of the energy mix   (b) Predicted development of RES (in %)
(in GW)

Fig. 2.3 EU 2020 scenario: Development of energy sources until 2020 (Data from: [78]).

rope, making RES the fastest growing energy source in the European Union [78, 174, 244]. In comparison to the year 2000 the amount of newly installed capacity increased tenfold with a total amount of additional renewable capacity of 32 GW in 2011. This results in a renewables share of 71.3% of all energy production capacity added during the year 2011 [244]. This development of renewable energy sources meant investments of \$101 bn. in 2011 [162]. Figure 2.2 illustrates the amount of newly installed capacities in the European Union from 1995 to 2011 and the corresponding share of renewable energy sources. Here, we see a slightly increasing share of renewable energy sources until 2008, where for the first time the amount of newly installed capacity from renewables exceeded the amount of newly installed conventional capacity. Since then RES show a substantial increase in production capacity, leading to a totally installed capacity of between 280.5 [244] and 288 GW [78] in 2011. With that, RES are already the second largest energy source by installed capacity after energy production from fossil fuels with 453 GW [78]. Following the European Union 2020 scenario [78, 85] the trend will continue for the coming years with a target installed renewables capacity of 512 GW in 2020 as illustrated in Figure 2.3(a). At the same time the installed capacity of fossil fuels will rise marginally until the year 2015 and then starts to decrease. Only nuclear power shows a slight increase of the installed capacity in 2020 compared to 2011 [78].

Among the renewables hydro, wind and solar power exhibit the largest share and thus, are the most important energy sources in the European Union [44, 244]. However, the pace of their growth is different, with wind and solar power showing the strongest increase in installed capacity as illustrated in Figure 2.2. In 2011 9.6 GW of new wind power was installed, summing up to a totally available wind power generation capacity of 93.9 GW at the end of 2011. Solar power showed an extraordinary increase of newly installed capacity with an increase of 21.0 GW in 2011. This results in a totally installed capacity by the end of 2011 of 46.3 GW. In contrast, the available capacity of hydro power only had a marginal increase of 0.6 GW [244]. Following the EU 2020 scenario wind and solar power become even more important, while the share of hydro power declines further. The reason is that suitable installation sites for hydro power are more limited (rivers, mountainous areas) and investment costs are substantially higher compared to wind and solar power installations [78]. This is also confirmed by the prediction of the EU 2020 scenario. The scenario predicts an installed wind power capacity of 219 GW in 2020. Solar power capacity is projected to increase to 87 GW in 2020 [78]. At the same time hydro power exhibits only a marginal increase to an installed capacity of 135.6 GW in 2020. The predicted share of the specific renewables on the total RES production is illustrated in Figure 2.3(b).

When specifically considering Germany, the German government plans to provide 80% of the electricity demand from renewable energy sources by 2050. To reach this ambitious goal, they plan to steadily increase the RES share in the electricity production and provide 35% in 2020 and of 50% in 2030 as intermediate targets [33, 34, 174]. In addition, at the beginning of 2010 the German government released the nuclear moratorium, which resulted in the shut down of eleven German nuclear power plants [38]. Accordingly, renewable energy sources gain increasing importance in the energy supply of Germany, which is especially true for wind and solar power. This leads to the fact that in July 2012 wind and solar power already exhibited the largest installed capacity of all energy sources with around 29 GW and 30 GW respectively when dividing fossil fuel into single sources. In comparison the three largest conventional energy sources hard coal, gas, and lignite exhibit significantly less installed capacity. Hard coal as the most important fossil fuel has an installed capacity of around 21 GW. Besides wind and solar power Biomass and hydro power also play an important role, while all other renewable energy sources exhibit only marginal capacities [38]. This is also true for offshore wind power that however, will get more and more attention in the future due to an increased availability compared to onshore wind energy [78]. Altogether, the installed capacity of renewable energy sources on July 2012 was 71.2 GW compared to 101.2 GW of conventional energy capacity. This is illustrated in the upper part of Figure 2.4.

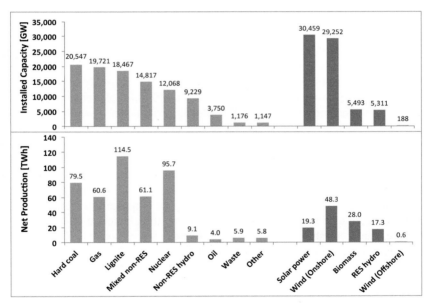

Fig. 2.4 Installed capacity vs. net production in Germany by July 2012 (Source: [38]).

However, Germany is also a good example for the issues when increasing the share of volatile and unpredictable renewable energy sources like wind and solar power. Figure 2.4 shows a comparison between the installed capacity and the net energy generation per energy source for the year 2011. Despite the fact that wind and solar power have the largest installed capacity of all energy sources, their eventually produced output and thus, their contribution to the energy supply is less significant. The largest output is produced by lignite and nuclear power with 114.5 TWh and 95.7 TWh. In comparison the source with the largest installed capacity—solar power—only produced 19.3 TWh and wind power only generated an energy output of 48.3 TWh. The reason is the reduced availability and strong fluctuations of renewable energy sources. While the output of conventional energy sources can be directly controlled, the production of RES depends on external factors such as the weather (e.g., wind speed, amount of daylight). This means that volatile renewables can only produce energy when their primary environmental dependencies match their requirements [53, 82]. In their scenarios the German government assumes an average yearly availability of wind power between 21.7% for onshore and 40% for offshore wind power plants. Even worse, solar power is predicted to be available only 12.6% of the time [33, 34, 173]. As a result, despite a 60% larger installed capacity of photovoltaics compared to lignite, they produce only 17% of the output of lignite. Less volatile renewable energy source like biomass and hydro energy have a much higher availability and thus, produce more power per installed capacity.

Despite the issues regarding availability and volatility the expansion of renewable energy source in Germany continues, especially considering wind and solar power. In 2011 investments of 20.1 bn. € in renewable production of electricity where made, whereof 15 bn. € were accounted for solar power and 2.95 bn. € for wind power. This steadily increasing share of renewable energy source in Germany and Europe will have significant impacts on electricity markets and grids [44]. Thus, it is necessary to specifically deal with the reduced availability and increased volatility of their energy production. Just increasing the installed capacity of RES is not the sole solution for increasing their generated output, reliability, and utilization. Intelligent energy management as well as extending and automating the energy grid, increasing the energy storage capabilities as well as improved forecasting capabilities are required to ultimately remove our dependence on fossil energy sources [23, 53, 82]. In the following section, we further discuss the issues when increasing the share of renewable energy sources and present solutions currently discussed in the research community.

2.1.3 Impact of Volatile Renewable Energy Sources

Beside the positive ecological and economical aspects, the substantially increasing share of renewables also poses new challenges for the electricity markets and transmission grids. While conventional energy sources can be fully planned, controlled, and adapted with respect to the current energy demand, volatile renewable energy sources such as wind and solar power highly depend on external factors especially the weather. Thus, their energy production is hard to predict and subject to strong fluctuations [5, 10, 157, 211]. Current analyses of wind power for example assume a typical fluctuation between subsequent hours of up to 10%. However with respect to offshore wind parks in some cases much larger deviations of up to 20% are possible [111, 173]. In Germany in the year 2011 for example the production capacity varied between 22.656 GW (04.02.2011, 19:00h) and 0.092 GW (05.07.2011, 10:00h), which means a fluctuation of around 66% (22.5 GW) [174, 208]. In addition, the availability of RES is limited. As already stated in Section 2.1.2 the assumed average availability of wind power is between 20% (onshore) and 40% (offshore) and of solar power is around 12.5% [33, 34, 173]. Using wind power as an example, a recent study about wind power in Germany and Spain from the Eurelectric compound [44] analyzed the load factor (ratio of produced wind energy to installed wind energy) for both countries on an hourly basis. They found that in 95% of the time the wind power plants had a load factor of only 4%. This in turn means that only 4% of the installed capacity is reliably available in 95% of the time. Furthermore, only in 5% of the time a load factor between 50% (Spain) and 60% (Germany) was achieved. In addition, the load factor never reached 85%. Combining all results of the Eurelectric study the expected average load factor has a 90% chance to be between 4% and 55% with an average of 22% [44]. Thus, it is only possible to reliably plan with at maximum 22% of the installed wind capacity at all times. In addition, the results also confirm the large fluctuations given the large range of the load factors.

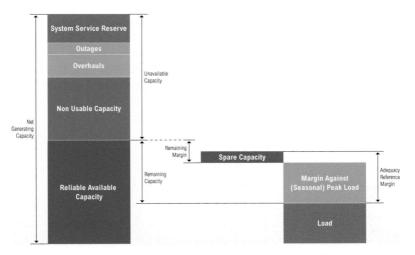

Fig. 2.5 Generation adequacy calculation (Source: [78]).

In principal, the installed capacity can be divided with respect to the generation adequacy as illustrated in Figure 2.5 [78, 174]. In the Figure we see that the net generating capacity (NGC) divides into two large blocks, namely unavailable capacity and reliable available capacity (RAC). Unavailable capacity comprises the currently not usable production capacity, which might be caused by [78]:

- **Non Usable Capacity:** Some capacity might be unusable in the current environmental situation; e.g. no wind is blowing or the sun is not shining.
- **Overhauls:** All power plants are subject to regular maintenance that must be scheduled in conjunction with the TSO.
- **Outages:** Unexpected outages of power plants or parts of the grid.
- **System Service Reserve:** Some capacity is assigned as system reserve to compensate grid fluctuations and thus, does not count as reliable available capacity (compare Section 2.1.4).

The reliable available capacity is used to satisfy the current load. To ensure system stability in most situations, the remaining capacity (RC) as part of the reliable available capacity comprises of an adequacy reference margin (ARM), which is hold available to compensate peak load and generation variations. Thus, the adequacy reference margin accounts for unexpected events regarding load and production. This also includes some spare capacity, which is responsible to guarantee system availability in 99% of the time. The ENTSO-E typically defines 5% of the net generating capacity as spare capacity and distinguishes the following situations [78]:

- $RC \geq ARM$: Some excess capacity is available for export.
- $RC \leq ARM$: Shortage capacity must be imported or grid management must use reserve energy.
- $RC-ARM$ = **positive AND** < **Export Capacity** More export capacity necessary or grid management must compensate for this excess energy.
- $RC-ARM$ = **negative AND** < **Import Capacity** All needed shortage capacity can be satisfied by imports. No grid management necessary.

When using only conventional power plants the reliable available capacity is almost perfectly plannable and can be adapted to the current load. Thus, critical situations did occur very rarely. With an increasing amount of fluctuating renewable energy sources however, the production site is much more volatile and differs much stronger between multiple reference points. In addition, despite large advancements in the last years, forecasting for renewable energy sources still provides a relatively high forecast error [53, 157]. In Germany Moest et al. assume a prediction error for wind power of 7 GW, resulting in a forecast error almost as high as suddenly occurring extraordinary fluctuations [174]. However, further advancements with respect to renewables forecasting are emerging due to intensive research in this area [53, 121]. Overall, the intermittency as well as the still challenging forecasting of renewable energy production, lead to a reduced amount of reliable available capacity and likewise to an reduced remaining capacity. This is illustrated in Figure 2.6, where the remaining capacity for many countries is predicted for the year 2015 (compare Figure 2.6(a)) to be below the average of the ENTSO-E compound (orange and red color). The situation could become even more serious in the year 2020 (compare Figure 2.6(b)), where for many countries

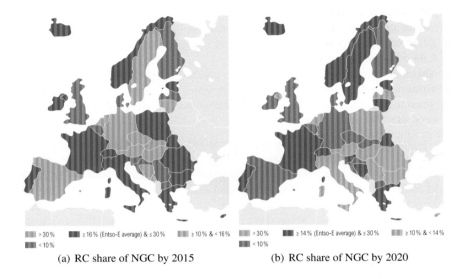

(a) RC share of NGC by 2015   (b) RC share of NGC by 2020

Fig. 2.6 EU 2020 scenario: Share of remaining capacity (RC) of the NGC (Source: [78]).

(including Germany) the remaining capacity falls below 10% of the net generation capacity. This means a critical reduction of this important buffer, leading to more situations, where necessary margins cannot be satisfied and system adequacy is endangered. As a result, TSOs have to intervene with grid management measures more frequently to compensate and ensure the stability of the grid.

To sum up, the fluctuation and uncertain availability of volatile renewable energy sources lead to manifold integration issues and an reduction of the reliable available capacity [17, 36]. One can say that compared to conventional energy sources, RES pose an increased variability on the production site and thus, require an increased flexibility on the grid management and demand side [36]. Overall, when the expansion of renewable energy sources continuous as planned, the challenge to guarantee a stable grid and energy supply will increase in the coming years. Further developments regarding grid management and electricity market as well as especially the development of more advanced forecasting technologies [53, 113, 121] are necessary to foster the integration of renewable energy sources.

2.1.4 How to Keep the Electricity Grid in Balance

Balancing energy consumption and production is a key requirement for the stability of the electricity grid and thus, for the continuous availability of the energy supply. Imbalances are symmetric meaning that to much consumption as well as too much production must be compensated [17]. An increasing share of fluctuating renewable energy sources mean an increasing challenge to ensure this balance [17, 44, 173]. As a first measure the balance is ensured using typical market mechanisms such as higher energy prices at times of energy scarcity and lower prices at times of energy excess. In addition, imbalances in both directions are punished by the TSO [23, 193], for what reason the balance responsible parties are urged to keep the production and consumption balanced within their balance group and the production companies to fulfill their commitments. If the market measures are not sufficient to guarantee a balanced grid, a multi-level reserve system is available in Europe [17, 80]. The main purpose of the multi-level reserve is to maintain the grids 50Hz frequency and to eliminate deviations between different control areas [17]. The control scheme of the reserves used within the pan-European TSO network '"ENTSO-E" is illustrated in Figure 2.7:

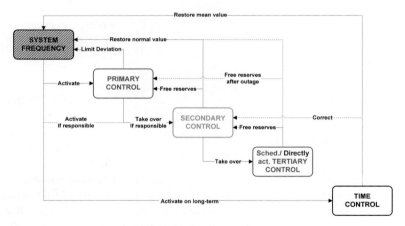

Fig. 2.7 Control scheme of the reserves (Source: [80]).

1. **Primary Control Reserve:** The primary reserve is provided jointly and simultaneously by all TSOs within the control network. It is completely activated within 30 sec and lasts for up to 15 minutes. Its main purpose is to compensate short-term deviations.
2. **Secondary Control Reserve:** The secondary reserve takes over the responsibility of the primary reserve, when deviations are too large or last too long. The purpose of the secondary reserve is to return the grid frequency towards its defined standard and to bring back exchanges between control areas to the target value. It is activated only by the TSO responsible for the respective control area.

The activation is allowed to take 5 min at max and the reserve lasts for up to one hour.

3. **Tertiary / Minute Control Reserve:** The minute reserve can be seen as a long term control reserve. It takes over the responsibility of the secondary reserve when the frequency deviations take longer than the secondary reserve can compensate. It is further responsible to support the system after an outage. The minute reserve is activated by telephone and the complete activation is allowed to take 15 min at max. The duration is destined to last multiple hours.

Figure 2.8 illustrates the described activation, the runtime, and take-over scheme of the three control reserve types described above in the case of a frequency deviation (red dotted line).

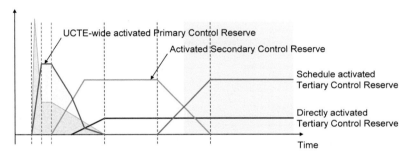

Fig. 2.8   Activation scheme of the reserves (Source: [80]).

To compensate for the outage of at least one of the installed production units, in former times, the secondary and tertiary reserve were sized equally to the capacity of the largest generation unit. However, for systems with a large share of volatile energy sources this system is not adequate anymore [105]. The reasons are again the much higher fluctuations and the increased uncertainty with respect to the eventual net production. A joint study of Frontier Economics and Consentec [105] dealt with the determination of the necessary reserve capacity with regard to the installed wind power. They recommend a probabilistic method for the TSOs to calculate the necessary size for their reserves. The study was based on the German electricity system and assumed a peak load of 70 GW to 80 GW and a installed wind power capacity of 22 GW. Given all circumstances of the systems and typical failure rates, the study revealed a necessary secondary and tertiary control reserve of approximately 7.5 GW positive and 6.0 GW negative control power [105]. Furthermore, they assume a linear increase of the necessary control power with an increasing wind capacity of approximately 0.25 GW to 0.3 GW control power per gigawatt wind capacity. In conjunction with the necessary control power expansions they also estimated the yearly costs for the additional control power needed, when assuming a 94 GW wind power capacity in the year 2020. Given the current prices for the availability and the utilization of the reserves, the yearly costs are estimated to be between 2.5 bn. € and 3.0 bn €. Thus, an increasing share of renewable energy sources, is going to increase the costs for managing the electricity grid.

Currently with the multi-level control reserve in place most of the occurring deviations can be compensated. As a measure of last resort the TSO can also conduct rolling grid shutdowns following a specific plan prioritizing the different consumers by their importance for the preservation of the daily life [38]. In summary, the european TSOs distinguish between three states [36]:

- Green — All market participants can fulfill their plans. Demand and supply is in balance.
- Yellow — Regulation necessity imminent, all measure to stabilize using market mechanisms and afterwards using reserve power should be used.
- Red — The TSOs have to regulate due to an imbalance of demand and supply. Shutdowns of consumers or producers depending on energy shortage or excess.

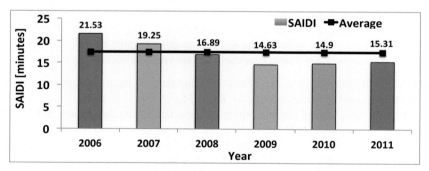

Fig. 2.9 Supply disruptions in german electricity grid (translated from [38]).

Despite the fact that TSOs have to intervene more frequently [17, 37, 44], shutdowns of consumers as a consequence of a red state are very rare. The total nonavailability comprising all kind of outages (e.g., shutdowns, maintenance, damage) is measured in the so called "'System Average Interruption Duration Index'" or short SAIDI. The SAIDI in 2011 for consumers in Germany for example, was only 15.31 min, which is higher than 2010 with 14.9 min, but still lower than the average SAIDI between 2006 and 2010 of 17.44 min [38]. The development of the SAIDI for Germany is illustrated in Figure 2.9, where we see a steady decrease of the value until 2009. From that point on the value starts to rise again, which is a sign for the more complicated situation arriving together with a higher amount of renewable energy sources. However, currently the negative impact with respect to shutdowns of the consumer site is very limited. On the supply site the effect is much larger and rises much faster. A good example for this effect can be observed in Germany due to the German Renewable Energy Act (§§11,12). In Germany TSOs might temporarily down-regulate or shutdown renewable energy sources to ensure the stability of their grid as long as they guarantee that still as much RES as possible is used. However, they have to compensate for the respective regulation work. In 2011 a compensation work of 421 GWh was necessary, which is equivalent to compensation payments in the amount of 33.5 million €. This means a substantial (more than threefold) increase compared to the compensation work of 127 GWh and an equivalent compensation payment of 10 million € in 2010. In 2009—the first year of this rule—the amount of regulation work was only 74 GWh and the compensation payment only 6 million €. This increase is immediately related to the strong expansion of renewable energy sources. Most regulations were necessary due to fluctuating wind (97.4%) and were concentrated on regions with a large amount of wind power [38]. While this is just an isolated example, it still shows the rising effect of increasing the amount of fluctuating renewable energy sources. TSOs have to manage the grid more frequently and regulate the amount of renewable energy sources more often. This results in substantial loss of renewable energy (especially wind energy) and money.

Current research is concerned with finding ways of reducing the negative integration effects and to increase the utilization of renewable energy sources. The following list comprises recent proposals to deal with the increasing issues:

- Intelligent grid management: Short-term and flexible adaptation of production units and regulation capabilities for RES [35, 36, 44, 173, 174].
- Stronger expansion of flexible power sources: Increasing the amount of fast and flexible power sources [44].
- Improving forecasting capabilities: More flexible and accurate real-time scheduling and forecasting [44, 53, 109, 113, 134, 173].
- Increasing energy storage capabilities: Preserving excess energy for later use [17, 44, 174].
- Increasing demand side flexibility: Involving customers using demand side control techniques (e.g., demand response, shifting of demand) [17, 44, 173, 174].
- Extending the transmission grid: Allow for increased exchange between control areas [17, 44, 173, 174].
- Spatial coupling of RES production: Better compensation for local fluctuations and reduced forecast error [44, 173, 174].
- Improving RES technology: Increasing support for resistances against voltage dips and local disturbances [44].
- Adapt the electricity market: More flexible trading in real-time and eliminating the preference of RES in times of electricity excess [36, 174].
- Law adaptations: Balancing responsibility to all producers including RES [44].

Some of the aforementioned proposals are explained in more detail in the following.

2.1.5 Extending the Transmission Grid and Energy Storage

One of the most important measures to allow an increased integration and better utilization of renewable energy sources is the extension and "'smartficiation'" of electricity grids. This involves transmission as well as distribution grids and the further development and extension of energy storage capabilities. The main reason is the decentralized production of renewable energy sources and the high level of strain to the power networks caused by intermittent renewable energy sources [37]. Imbalances in both directions—oversupply and overdemand—cause voltage stability issues, which ultimately can lead to a collapse of the energy grid. In addition, while previously power plants were build close to the consumption side, renewable energy sources require locations with beneficial environmental characteristics. Thus, renewable energy sources are unevenly distributed within Europe and even within European countries, due to different adequacies of its regions for installing RES [17, 38]. As a result, they are often build far away from the consumption side and extensive transmission capacities are needed to transfer the power [37, 173]. The best examples for this decentralization are offshore wind parks, which produce energy on open sea and the entire power needs to be transferred to different consumption sides on the mainland. Another example is provided by onshore wind power in Europe. Production sites are mainly concentrated in the north of Europe and Iberia, but the consumption of this energy is required in entire Europe. Using Germany as an example for the uneven distribution of RES in a single country, Figure 2.10 shows the installed capacity for wind and solar power in the different states of Germany. While wind power is mainly produced in the northern states of Germany, the largest capacities of solar power are installed in the south. As a result, in times where for example the sun is not shining, but the wind is blowing, electricity needs to be either transferred from the north to the south or conventional power plants are required as backup capacity to compensate. Thus, both points—the decentralized production and the intermittency of renewable energy sources—require extensive energy transmission capacities.

Due to the fact that the current transmission grids were not made for extensive and long-range energy transportation, three typically options exist to overcome the increasing transportation requirements posed by renewable energy sources [44, 173]:

- Distribute load geographically
- Movement of production to shortage regions
- Expanding and enhancing the electricity grid

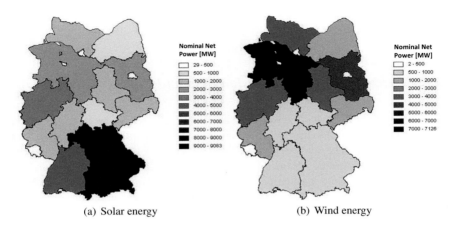

(a) Solar energy   (b) Wind energy

Fig. 2.10 Distribution of renewable energy sources in Germany (Source: [38]).

The first option is very impractical, because it would mean a movement of people and industry, which would be very hard to achieve. A better option to control the demand side in this regard is the usage of demand-response systems [173] (as discussed in Section 2.1.6). The second option, would involve the extensive installation of new production capacity in regions with energy shortage. However, RES cannot be installed in all regions and just installing further conventional power plants would endanger the ecological long-term goals. The third option means an accelerated expansion of transmission and distribution grids to increase the overall grid capacity and thus, to allow a more extensive and long range electricity transportation between regions. Expanding the grid brings some major advantages such as an increased spatial coupling of RES production to create portfolio effects, which allows the compensation of local fluctuations and a reduction of the prediction error [44, 171, 173]. In addition, it would help to optimize the electricity market by increasing the market's flexibility and evening out energy prices between regions; energy could be transported from regions with low prices to regions with higher prices. As a result, the third option is the current focus within Europe. The final goal would be to create an integrated European-wide energy grid, allowing a comprehensive pan-European energy exchange and enabling a joint and demand-oriented cross boarder usage of renewable energy sources [73, 88, 250]. One could for example interconnect all offshore wind parks using an offshore super grid that is connected to central mainland grid points in multiple countries [44]. As a result, the current and future investments for expanding the transmission and distribution grids are very high. Currently, investments of around 100 bn. € are planned for pan-European transmission grid expansions until 2020 [74, 79]. From this 100 bn. € an amount of 30.1 bn. € planned investments are coming from Germany [79]. In the year 2011, in Germany investments targeting the extension of the transmission grid were 847 million € and investments for the distribution grid were 6,281 million €. For the year 2012 even higher investments of 952 million € for the transmission grid and almost the same amount of investment (6,288 million €) in the distribution grids are planned. However, comparing these number to the overall target investments, German lags still behind [38].

Expanding the grid does not solely mean to build up new power lines, but also to convert conventional grids to smart grids and the installation of additional and flexible buffer capacities. The goal of smart grids is the optimal usage of grid capacities and an increased average grid utilization. This corresponds to the core reliability of all grid operators to provide, maximize, and optimize grid capacity. The creation of smart grids means to enhance conventional grids with advanced communication and measurement capabilities, more comprehensive regulation techniques as well as advanced and tightly integrated forecasting technology [16, 21, 193]. With that, smart grids allow a constant real-time monitoring of the system status and automated fine-grained and appropriate regulations of grid capacities. In addition, they provide the possibility to change energy flow directions and hence, to dynamically relocate production and load on the grid. Furthermore they are capable of balancing the grid using automatic grid control [239]. This means that smart grids can autonomously detect and react upon changing capacity situations of local grid sections. As a result, smart grids provide a more intelligent and automated grid management, which results in a better utilization of existing grid capacities. In this way, they allow grid extensions in more economic reasonable ways.

The increasing implementation of smart grids also comes with the need for more balancing, reserve and backup power. The realization of more flexible buffer capacities, can be realized using two different options. The first option is to provide more flexible production sites that serve as buffer capacity and the second option means increasing energy storage capabilities [35, 36, 174]. Due to the fact that renewable energy is preferred politically, economically, and on the market, conventional power production has to change significantly. Conventional power plants will mainly serve as backup capacity with reduced hours of full utilization, many adjustments with respect to their production, and a larger amount of startups and shutdowns [35, 44, 174]. Such backup power plants basically step-in in cases the renewable energy production is not able to satisfy the current load and to compensate large fluctuations of renewable energy sources. Thus, conventional power plants must be enhanced to support quicker and autonomous responses to load and renewable production changes. In addition, they are required to allow faster ramp-up speed and more flexible minimum operation levels [44]. As a result, while it is important to reduce fossil and nuclear power production, these power plants are still necessary to provide the respective buffer capacity to address large deviations and to ensure the stability of the electricity grid. This means that instead of shutting down conventional power plants, they should be restored in a way that they fulfill the requirements for serving as flexible backup capacity. In addition to establishing more flexible backup capacity, increased energy storage capabilities are needed. The idea of energy storage is relatively simple. In times of excess energy, the additional energy is stored and used later in times of energy shortage [36, 44]. This also works for optimizing electricity market pricing, by storing energy when energy prices are low and feeding this energy back, when energy costs are higher [36]. Typical established and new storage technologies comprise among other things:

- Hydro reservoirs
- Pumped storage facilities
- Compressed air storage
- Gas storage
- District heating systems
- Electric cars with bi-directional grid connection

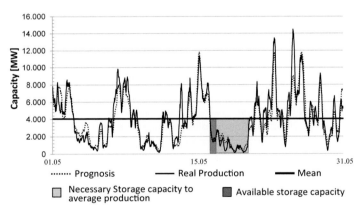

Fig. 2.11 Available vs. necessary energy storage capabilities (Source: [174]).

While storage is a promising technology that greatly helps to integrate renewable energy sources, currently the energy storage capabilities are limited. For this reason a large amount of renewable energy sources must be directly used when they are available, leaving most excess energy wasted. In Germany an energy storage capacity of 40 GWh was available in the year 2011 [36, 174]. In comparison, in Germany the total energy consumption on one day is 1440 GWh [36]. Thus, to compensate large fluctuations or power outages new and larger storage capacities are required [174]. Moest et al. presented an example for the storage capacity in Germany [174], which is illustrated in Figure 2.11. Here, the amount of storage capacity necessary to average the wind power fluctuations and guarantee a constant supply is compared with the available pump storage capacity. The installed storage capacity is by far not sufficient to even average the small area shown in the Figure. Schiffer [208] assumes that a 70-fold storage capacity is necessary by 2030 to only compensate for the wind fluctuations. However, currently the storage capacity is planned to only increase to 55 - 60 GWh in the year 2020, which means that it will not reach considerable amounts in the near future. As a result, energy storage is a necessary component to help integrating renewable energy sources, but cannot serve as the sole solutions to solve the balancing issues that come with an increasing amount of RES [36].

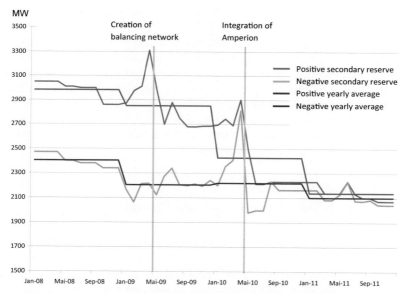

Fig. 2.12 Development of needed reserves when combining regulation zones (Source: [38]).

Overall, to enable the integration of an increasing amount of renewable energy sources throughout Europe while at the same time ensuring the stability of the energy grid in the future a joint implementation of all introduced measures—grid expansions, smart grids, and flexible buffer capacities—is needed. However, this comes with the need for coordinated measures of all players in the market: producers, consumers, prosumers, transmission system operators (TSO), energy service providers etc. to avoid contrary actions on the grid [36]. The following example clearly shows the advantages of coordinated measures and motivates a tight European-wide collaboration between all affected companies. Starting from May 2009 the three German TSOs—Tennet, Transnet BW, and 50 Hertz—started to create the German grid regulation compound. Within that compound the TSOs jointly determine the amount of grid management electricity for the entire group, coordinate the use of grid management measures and aim for a cost optimal usage of control energy [38]. Figure 2.12 shows the effect of creating and extending the regulation compound on the usage of the secondary reserve. As illustrated in the figure, the implementation of the compound and the later integration of Amperion resulted in a substantial reduction of the used secondary reserve energy, especially for the usage of the positive secondary reserve. In addition, after all German TSOs joint the compound, the fluctuations of the used control reserve power were considerably reduced, which leads to a better predictability and lower overall costs for using reserve power. A first European-wide step in this direction is the creation of the TSO network ENTSO-E in 2008 [84] and the regulator agency ACER in 2010 [83].

To facilitate a broad integration of renewable energy sources grid reinforcements and enhancements are one key aspect. Besides the expansion of the grid itself, this also involves the conversion of conventional grids to smart grids and the establishment of flexible buffer capacities. All measures should not be implemented on their own but need European-wide coordination to guarantee the best possible effect and the lowest possible costs. Grid reinforcements and especially smart grids enable and very well cooperate with measures to increase the flexibility of the demand side that are discussed next.

2.1.6 Demand-Side Management and Demand-Response

Currently, the energy supply side is getting more and more flexible with the power of smart grids and the creation of flexible production and buffer capacities. This leads to an increasing share of energy production that can be regulated flexibly and partially autonomously based on market signals and grid situations. In contrast, today the demand side is rather inelastic and inflexible. Most private and industrial consumers use their energy as they wish, without thinking about possible consequences on the grid [173]. However, as mentioned in Section 2.1.3 renewable energy sources exhibit strong fluctuations, due to their dependence on external environmental factors. In addition, currently the capabilities to store energy from those sources is very limited (compare Section 2.1.5), for what reason they must be consumed when they are available. This strongly motivates to also increase the demand side flexibility and to shift the demand in accordance to the amount of available energy from renewable sources [17, 44, 173]. Furthermore, more flexible demand would greatly integrate and cooperate with other measures used to solve the RES integration issues such as more flexible production sites and smart grids [36].

Consumers and especially private persons typically do only need their maximum amount of energy in some time of the day and not at every point in time.

In addition, some applications in private households and the industry are non-time-critical or non-process-critical and could thus, be subject to demand shifts. This means, that consumers have certain flexibilities they could offer in exchange for monetary incentives, increased comfort (e.g., intelligent home management) and special quality of service agreements. Some examples for flexible applications from private households are dishwashers, washing machines, heat pumps, (micro) cogeneration equipment and storage heaters. Industrial consumers could offer flexibilities by allowing shifts of their production or flexible temporary reductions/increases of their load factor. Furthermore, public utility companies could flexibly apply public lightning in accordance to grid requirements. As a result, private, industrial and public consumers should be integrated in the process of balancing energy demand and supply, which can be achieved by using demand-response or demand management systems [17, 36, 44, 173]. Large consumers could even be integrated into the electricity market, to actively interact with energy providers, which means a shift from pure TSO oriented grid management to a more market-oriented grid management [36].

While in current demand management projects relatively simple monetary approaches such as variable tariffs, contractually agreed demand flexibilities and voluntary disconnections prevail, more advanced solutions are planned in the future [36]. One of the most promising solutions deals with the management of electric cars. With an increasing market share in the future, electric cars will be responsible for a considerable amount of energy consumption. However, they also offer possibilities to balance the energy grid. Currently, charging cars is done in the evening, when the grid is overloaded anyway [173]. The idea is to use an demand-response approach for electric cars, where TSOs or BRPs might control the car loading. In many cases, for example, car loading is done at the evening and over night, which leaves a certain flexibility when the actual loading is done during that time [173]. In addition, cars can be used as energy storage, providing buffer energy, when critical situations occur on the grid [75, 143, 170, 234]. However, in all cases the car must be fully available at predefined times.

Overall, an extensive amount of renewable energy sources requires an increased flexibility of all players participating in the electricity market. With smart grids and highly adjustable buffer capabilities, the generation site is substantially increasing its flexibility. To complement and fully utilize this new production flexibility, it is also necessary to increase the demand side flexibility. Thus, demand management and demand-response systems will become even more important in the future and will become a key prerequisite to reach the ambitious goals of the European Union.

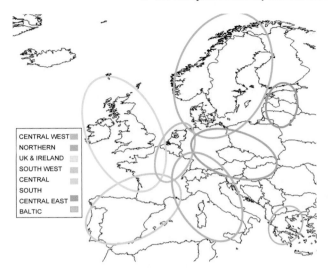

Fig. 2.13 The regional markets of the European Union (Source: [52]).

2.1.7 Changes on the European Electricity Market

With the liberalization of the electricity market in the late 1990s, the European Union started to create a free, competitive, and transparent European-wide electricity market, where customers and producers are free to choose their energy provider in a fine-grained manner. The ultimate goal is to trade energy on a single integrated European wholesale market, which is expected to lead to an increased supply security, a better handling of renewable energy sources and finally, an energy price reduction [13, 196]. As an intermediate step to reach the final goal, the European Union created several regional markets, which comprise the European countries as follows [141]:

- **Central-West:** Belgium, France, Germany, Luxembourg, and Netherlands
- **Central-East:** Austria, Czech Republic, Germany, Hungary, Poland, Slovakia, and Slovenia
- **Central-South:** Italy, Austria, France, Germany, Greece, and Slovenia
- **Northern:** Denmark, Finland, Germany, Norway, Poland, and Sweden
- **South-West:** Spain, France, and Portugal
- **Baltic:** Latvia, Estonia, and Lithuania
- **France-UK-Ireland:** France, Ireland, and the United Kingdom

The current regional markets following the "'Electricity Regional Initiative'" are also illustrated in Figure 2.13. The European Union aims to complete the integration and with that, the creation of a single European market by 2014 [110, 192].

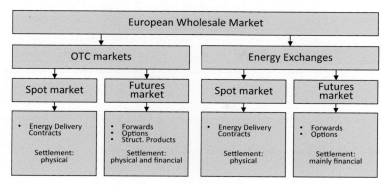

Fig. 2.14 Products offered on the European wholesale market (Source: [196]).

Within the wholesale markets of the European Union, typically two different market models are used: over-the-counter (OTC) markets and energy exchanges. OTC markets deal with direct, bilateral contracts between two parties. The trading is typically conducted using a broker and both involved parties are known to each other. The second market place are energy exchanges, where electricity contracts are handled like shares on a stock exchange. The main goal of exchanges is to facilitate the trading of energy contracts, for what reason settling deals is often faster, cheaper, anonymous, and happens at a neutral market place [196]. In general, on both market places players can trade the same products. The first kind of products are spot market contracts, which allow market participants to directly offer available energy (produced energy of producers or surplus energy of consumers) in terms of physical energy delivery contracts. The spot market products are traded on the day-ahead and the intraday market and thus, concern energy delivery up to one day ahead. Second, there are derivates including forward, option and structured product contracts. They allow the trading of energy delivery contracts fulfilled in the future up to multiple years ahead. While the futures on an energy exchange are in most cases settled financially, on OTC markets also physical settlements are common. A typical product structure on European markets is illustrated in Figure 2.14.

In addition, Figure 2.15 illustrates the temporal distribution of the different trading options. The futures market, as already mentioned, targets long-term contracts with a lead time of up to multiple years. Its main purpose is the long-term determination of the energy demand and supply. They offer planning security for both the consumer as well as the producers. The day-ahead and intraday trading are flexible possibilities to compensate short-term supply and demand deviations from the long term planning. It is hard to plan multiple years ahead, for what reason it is necessary to adapt the energy production with respect to recent demand and supply forecasts and changing production capacities. In addition, with an increasing share

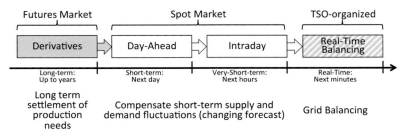

Fig. 2.15 Temporal illustration of the different energy trading possibilities.

of fluctuating RES, the forecast accuracy is decreasing and energy production is subject to more frequent short-term changes. Thus, these flexible trading options become more and more important. Finally, the TSO offer the trading of balancing energy to ensure the stability of the grid and with that, the security of supply.

With an increasing share of renewable energy sources the market conditions are changing. The volatility and unpredictability of RES endanger the suitability of long-term contracts and increase the volatility of energy prices. In particular, it is hard to predict the eventual RES production multiple years ahead and to estimate the resulting profitability of such long-term contracts. In addition, with an increasing share of RES the costs for ensuring agreed quality of service measures are rising. As a result, while previously long-term future contracts exhibited the by far highest trading volume, currently their importance is declining in favor of short-term products traded up to 45 mins before delivery [67, 86, 87]. In 2012 on the power market of the largest energy exchange in central Europe—the German EEX (European Energy Exchange)—derivatives in the amount of 931 TWh were traded. This is a significant decrease compared to a trading volume of 1208 TWh in 2010. In comparison, the trading volume of the spot market increased over the last years from 279 TWh in 2010 to 339 TWh in 2012 [86, 87]. Also within the derivatives, contracts with shorter lead times were favored over long-term contracts [87]. However, even the relatively flexible spot market products with small lead times of up to 45 mins have to deal with an increasing uncertainty about the eventual production and the profitability of the short-term operations [44]. Thus, there is a strong need to reduce the lead times even further and allow real trading (besides balancing energy) close to real-time [17]. All of these changes and especially the emerging need for real-time trading, requires advanced forecasting technology that is capable of providing accurate forecasts in a short amount of time. Adopting such new developments in forecasting technology significantly reduces the risk and costs of market participants [23, 53, 172].

A further issue of the European electricity market are changing energy pricing characteristics. The determination of the energy prices will be less dependent on the current load (i.e., day and seasonal fluctuations) than on the fluctuating produc-

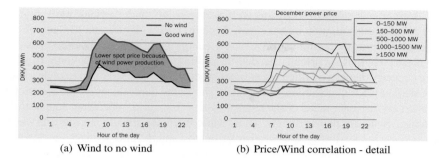

Fig. 2.16 Correlation between wind energy and market price (Source: [150]).

tion of renewable energy sources [174, 248]. This effect is increased by the fact that many countries placed their electricity markets under the obligation to favor renewable energy sources over conventional energy sources. This means that first the production of renewable energy sources has to be used, before conventional power can be fed-in. As a result, two effects on the electricity market prices are conceivable. First, an increasing amount of RES might lead to energy price reductions as soon as a considerable amount of wind energy is available [44, 150, 174]. This is illustrated in Figure 2.16. As a result, nowadays even negative prices occur, when a large amount of energy is produced from RES, but the consumption is relatively low. The reason is that due to the favoring of RES, conventional power plants producing more expensive energy cannot sell all their produced energy. However, instead of shutting down (parts of) the power plant the operating companies use negative prices to still sell their excess energy which is cheaper than frequent shutdowns and restarts [44].

The second effect are increasing energy prices caused by the so called merit order effect. The merit order effect means that high-cost power plants are displaced by low-cost energy sources like renewables. While this in the first place reduces the market price for the electricity, the displaced power plants now work in a backup mode or as peak power plants. Such backup / peak power plants have far higher costs due to frequently changing the plant output or shutting down / restarting the power plant. Thus, they charge extra fees for keeping their service available and to balance the fluctuations of renewable energy sources. Finally, this might lead to an increase of the market price [44, 150, 174].

The biggest issue is that it is very hard to predict whether the extensive support of RES eventually leads to a strong price reduction or a substantial price increase. This leaves some kind of uncertainty for investors about the profitability of their investments in transmission grids and balancing / peak capacity. The market has to find ways to decrease this uncertainty and thus, to encourage more investments, which are necessary to reach the final goal of the European Union [44, 150].

Both effects, negative prices as well as increasing market prices, are a sign of (1) missing consumption management through market signals and (2) lack of exchange and transportation capacity on the energy grids to transmit excess energy to places where it is currently needed. In addition, a considerable amount of storage capacity that can be filled-up in times of excess energy would help to decrease the market price fluctuations. This greatly shows the dependency of the electricity market on the other areas of the energy system (e.g., grid, balancing, forecasting, storage, customer management). Thus, while there are already measures in place to increase the flexibility of the transmission grid and to better manage the demand side, it is also necessary to increase the flexibility of the electricity market [36, 44]. A first and very important measure of mitigating the issues coming with an increasing amount of fluctuating RES is to increase and facilitate an active cross-border energy exchange. This includes an active market coupling and a cross-border balancing resulting in the possibility for a continuous cross-border trading of energy [44, 150]. With that, energy could be transmitted from regions with an energy surplus to regions that are in need of additional energy. Until 2050 the European Union plans an extensive grid extension to exactly allow a very active cross-border trading and a european wide balancing of energy demand and supply [88].

In addition to a European-wide trading, it is also necessary to provide suitable market signals for influencing energy demand and likewise energy production [36, 44]. Thus, demand is controlled with respect to the current energy situation, flexibly increasing the demand in excess situations and flexibly decreasing the demand in scarcity situations [36]. Approaches to do so are presented in Section 2.1.6. However, in addition to the demand also the supply (RES and non-RES) should be managed in a similar way. This first and foremost means that after a grace period, RES should be controlled like any other energy source, meaning that it should be subject to forecasting, scheduling, and balancing as well as penalty payments when their production deviates from their commitment. Thus, RES production could be cut to avoid for example extensive negative prices or a large amount of excess energy. In addition, it would also help operators of conventional power plants to better predict and plan the profits of their business and investments. This in turn would encourage further investments in grid and power production. A positive side-effect of applying the same rules to demand and supply is that it is expected to stimulate improvements in forecasting, balancing, and scheduling [44].

Finally, to eventually increase the flexibility of the electricity market, the trading itself should be improved. This means to reduce the lead times as close to real-time as possible and to offer more flexible energy products. The ultimate goal would be to allow a continuous trading of energy production and consumption close to real-time. Similar to increasing the flexibility of smart grids, electricity markets likewise require improvements in forecasting calculations to enable more detailed and automated interactions with respect to the current situation on the electricity market and the grid. The reason is that a major prerequisite for real-time trading as well as any kind of automation approaches is to have up-to-date and accurate forecasts available at any point in time. Especially in this area improvements with respect to accuracy and flexibility of calculating forecasts are necessary. Finally, consumers, producers, and prosumers of any size could directly interact on the electricity market in a fine-grained manner offering for example their flexibilities in exchange for reduction of their energy costs.

As a result, to support a full integration of an increasing amount of renewable energy sources it is necessary to complement changes on the energy grid and demand side management with an increasing flexibility of the electricity market. This includes to facilitate an active cross-border trading throughout Europe, a more market- and situation-oriented handling of renewable and non-renewable energy sources and the transformation of the trading to a continuous trading close to real-time. A major prerequisite to do so is to improve forecasting technology allowing more autonomous reactions on market situations. The following section discusses these improvements in detail.

2.1.8 Improvements in Forecasting Energy Demand and Renewable Supply

Forecasts of future energy consumption and production are a fundamental requirement for the stability and the day to day operation of the electricity grid. While demand forecasts are well-established since years (consider e.g., [91, 153, 229]), the increasing amount of renewable energy sources substantiate the need to also provide accurate forecasting for renewable supply. The reason is that renewable energy sources cannot be planned or dispatched like conventional energy sources, since they strongly depend on environmental conditions and most importantly on the current state of the weather. In addition, we already pointed out that current storage capabilities are insufficient and renewable production must be directly used when it is available (compare Section 2.1.5). As a result, forecasts are the only option to get an insight into the potential future production of renewable energy sources and hence, enable their planning and scheduling as well as their trading on the electricity market [53, 82, 193]. In particular, accurate supply forecasts are a key aspect to address the growing variability and uncertainty in the renewable energy production [23].

In todays electricity market, forecasts with different horizons serve as input and decision support for many tasks within grid operation and electricity market handling. The following list provides the typically used forecasting horizons including some of the connected tasks [128, 193, 251]:

- very short term (seconds to minutes): turbine control

- short term (minutes and hours up to day-ahead): power plant operations, grid balancing and scheduling, real-time unit dispatching, automatic generation control, operating reserve planning and control, real-time electricity market trading and administration, peak load analysis, load following
- medium term (days) pre-dispatch, unit commitment, day ahead trading, and maintenance planning
- long term (weeks) maintenance planning, improving balance area control, system planning, investment planning

The large amount of tasks that involve the calculation of forecasts emphasizes the importance and the need for predicting future energy demand and supply. Depending on the task and on the horizon different forecast models are employed. Load forecasts typically use statistical forecast methods that try to estimate a statistical relationship between different characteristics of a time series as well as potentially included external information. Statistical models distinguish classical approaches such as Box-Jenkins models (e.g., ARIMA) [25] and exponential smoothing [229] as well as approaches from machine learning such as most importantly artificial neural networks [40]. Forecast models from this category are introduced in more detail in Section 3.2. Besides statistical models forecasts for renewable supply additionally employ physical models that describe the physical relationship between variables distinctive for the production of a certain renewable energy source. In particular, they model the physical process of converting the driving force of a production unit to power considering the given physical circumstances. The considered physical variables include among other things atmospheric conditions, weather movements, and local topography [23, 92, 128]. A typical prerequisite for physical models is to determine the power curve of each production unit, since each unit provides a very specific production profile. The power curve is then combined with the current physical coherences at the installation site of the production unit. Physical models are typically employed for forecasts targeting a longer horizon, since in this setting employing the physical coherences and phenomena provides a clear accuracy advantage over pure statistical approaches mainly based on historic measurements [155, 171]. However, they are typically very complex and their creation needs a lot of computational power [128]. In contrast, statistical models are used for short-term predictions, since they provide a very high accuracy on shorter horizons [82, 134, 171]. Recently, approaches were suggested that combine physical and statistical approaches [155, 171]. The goal is to create forecast models providing accurate predictions for a wide-range of forecasting horizons. The type of integration largely varies between the approaches and reaches from a simple model chaining over an ensemble approach to a very deep interconnection between both model types.

Currently, research and industry are focusing on the short-term horizon, since short-term forecasts are of highest importance for the day-to-day grid management and trading on the electricity market [128, 251]. Accordingly, they play a key role when it comes to integrating renewable energy sources and increasing the flexibility of several areas of the current energy system. As a result, for the remainder of this book we likewise focus on the short-term horizon and thus, on statistical forecast models for both predicting energy demand and renewable supply.

To address the intermittency of renewable energy sources new technologies are employed that specifically target to improve the flexibility and the real-time capabilities of the grid, the demand-side, and the electricity market. In particular, these changes target to enable quick, automatic, and autonomous reactions on changing consumption and production situations. Since forecasting is involved in a substantial amount of tasks within all of these areas, it is likewise necessary to improve the calculation process and accuracy of forecasts. While previously the focus was clearly on improving the forecasting accuracy, recently the efficiency of calculating forecasts is gaining increasing importance [18, 193, 251]. The reason is that lead times for calculating forecasts were significantly reduced especially due to the emerging need for real-time balancing of energy demand and supply. In particular, while it previously was sufficient to provide day-ahead demand forecasts once per day, an increasing share of renewable energy sources requires accurate forecasts of energy demand and supply at basically any point in time. This includes to continuously consider the most recent measurements of consumption and production as well as up-to-date external information such as the weather [82, 128, 207]. Considering most recent information is of special importance for predicting renewable production, since the most variable influence—the weather—is changing frequently. Accordingly using outdated information means to base the calculations on wrong assumptions, which consequently leads to a reduced forecasting accuracy. Furthermore, providing accurate forecasts also means to continuously adapt the employed forecast models with respect to the most recent values to pick up potential changes in the time series developments and characteristics [11, 92, 165]. On the contrary, increasing the forecasting accuracy, often means to increase the complexity of the involved forecast models, which results in more computational efforts for creating and adapting the model. Thus, a very complex forecast model might provide very accurate forecasts, but it might not be possible to calculate the forecasts within a limited time frame as required by a certain task or application. This is especially true given the reduced lead times and the need to always consider the most recent measurements. As a result, in general the worth of a forecast should not be assessed solely on pure accuracy measures, but also with respect to the value for the requesting consumer (application or consumer) [24, 53]. Hence, calculating forecasts should be threaded as a two-dimensional optimization problem, where accuracy and runtime are two important dimensions. This means that an application should receive its requested forecasts in an accuracy and runtime as it requires them. Accordingly, forecasting systems employed in the current and future electricity market environment should be capable of efficiently calculating accurate forecasts while considering specific requirements of requesting applications.

Furthermore, autonomous reactions on changing grid and market situations requires to tightly integrate forecasting into the employed energy data management systems (EDMS) [18, 24, 239]. Such a tight integration means that the forecasting process including the selection of forecast models and the estimation of parameters must work fully automatically without requiring human intervention during runtime. In addition, the efficient and tightly integrated forecasting must be complemented with improved data processing capabilities of the employed data management system. They are required to support an automated recording, processing, and analysis of large amounts of measurements in real-time throughout the entire grid. Moreover, smart grids allow a fine-grained control of the energy flow through the different segments and hierarchy levels of the energy grid. This requires to separately consider the various grid segments in even larger detail, which increases the complexity of the data analysis even more [36].

To sum up, forecasting is a key-enabling technology used as decision support for many tasks in the day-to-day grid operation and the electricity market business. Accordingly, improvements for the grid, the demand-side, and the electricity market always come with the need to likewise improve the forecasting technology. This especially includes to improve the efficiency and application-awareness of forecasting calculations in addition to the focus on providing highly-accurate predictions.

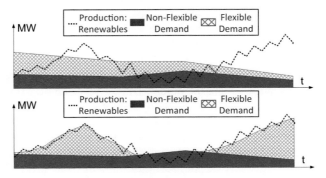

Fig. 2.17 Balancing with and without the MIRABEL concept (Source: [21, 170]).

2.2 The MIRABEL Project: Exploiting Demand and Supply Side Flexibility

One project that addresses the need for a more flexible balancing of energy demand and supply in real-time is the EU-funded research project MIRABEL (Micro-Request-Based Aggregation, Forecasting and Scheduling of Energy Demand, Supply and Distribution). The project aims at developing a conceptual and infrastructural demand/supply response approach to enable a better utilization of renewable energy sources and a more flexible demand management in an ad-hoc fashion. The core idea is that market players may express acceptable flexibilities for their energy demand and even specific supplies in terms of so-called micro-requests. The execution of these so called flex-offers can then be scheduled within their given flexibilities to allow fine-grained balancing. With the help of this concept, renewable energies can be better utilized by executing demand requests when energy from RES is available. Also, utility companies can smooth cost-extensive peaks or execute demand requests while cheap energy is available. Thus, they can substantially reduce their operational costs by which means they could offer more attractive energy prices. Furthermore, one could use the flex-offers to more efficiently schedule energy storage facilities and backup power plants to situations with energy scarcity [16, 21, 170]. Figure 2.17 illustrates the advantages of the MIRABEL system. There, we see the energy consumption situation without (top Figure 2.17) and with the MIRABEL flexibility concept (bottom Figure 2.17). The dark grey and shaded areas visualize the non-flexible and flexible demand respectively. The dotted line depicts the renewable energy production. With the help of the MIRABEL flex-offers, renewable energy sources can be better utilized by shifting energy demand through time to positions of large renewable production [21]. In the following we explain the main concept of the MIRABEL project—the flex-offers— in more detail and discuss the target architecture of the employed energy data management system. Afterwards we present to use-cases for the approaches developed in MIRABEL.

2.2.1 Flex-Offers

The basic concept of the MIRABEL project are micro-requests of energy demand and supply, called flex-offers. These flex-offers exploit the fact that some demand and even some supply is flexible in the time of their execution. Examples for flexible demand and supply are:

- **private consumers**: Electric car charging, dish-washer, washing machines, night storage heating
- **Industry**: Non-time critical production, cold storage houses, public lightning

- **Supply**: Pumped-Storage, backup power plants

In contrast, non-flexible demand such as private lightning, cooking, and time-critical industry processes cannot be shifted through time and must be satisfied directly at the time it is demanded.

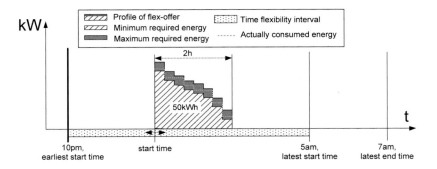

Fig. 2.18 The definition of flex-offers (Source: [21, 170]).

Flex-offers are flexible in their execution time, but also in the amount of consumed energy as well as in their duration. As illustrated in Figure 2.18 a flex-offer exhibits the following definitions: The earliest start time defines the earliest time a flex-offer might be scheduled. Similarly, the latest end time defines the time the flex-offer must be finished at the latest. In conjunction with the additionally defined duration of the flex-offer, the latest end time can be used to calculate the latest start time of the flex-offer. Furthermore, the flex-offer defines a specific energy consumption (or production) profile in a certain granularity. In the MIRABEL project the granularity of each interval is 15 minutes. The profile comprises of a maximum required energy and a minimum required energy for each of the comprised intervals. The eventual consumption (production) is then required to be in between these defined limits.

In Figure 2.19 we show the lifecycle of a flex-offer from its definition to its execution and beyond. A flex-offer as defined above is submitted to the utility company and depending on its capacity, the utility company might accept or reject the flex-offer. In the case of acceptance the utility company starts to schedule the flex-offer and as the time of execution is approaching assigns a fixed execution time slot. After the execution the billing is conducted and depending on the benefit of the flex-offer for the utility company, an incentive is provided to the consumer, producer, or prosumer. In general one can say that the larger the temporal flexibility, the longer the flex-offer was defined in advance and the smaller the difference between minimal and maximal consumed/produced energy, the higher the bene-

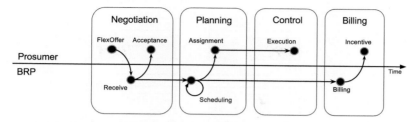

Fig. 2.19 Flex-offer lifecycle (Source: [170]).

fit of a flex-offer. First, a large time flexibility increases the number of options to schedule the flex-offer and thus, allows utility companies to better adapt the final execution time to their needs and to the current grid load situation. Second, the longer the lead time of a flex-offer definition, the more time is left for the utility companies to find a suitable execution time for the flex-offer. Third, a small deviation between the minimal and maximal energy consumption/production, reduces the uncertainty for the utility companies and thus, allows a better planning.

Overall, the presented flex-offers represent an important tool for utility companies to flexibly balance their demand and supply. Renewable energies can be better utilized by facilitating the consumption of energy when they are available. In addition, the concept even helps to reduce peak demand and with that, to flatten the overall energy demand curve.

2.2.2 Architecture of MIRABEL's EDMS

To realize the developed concepts, the MIRABEL project involves the design and implementation of an energy data management system (EDMS). The EDMS exhibits a hierarchical architecture that is based on the hierarchy of the European electricity market. This architecture is illustrated in Figure 2.20. The lowest level comprises the smart meters of energy consumers, producers, and prosumer (entities consuming and producing energy at the same time). All the data from these lowest level entities are collected and processed by the balance responsible party (BRP—second level) accountable for the respective balance group. Further on, on the third level, the transmission system operators (TSO) or the market operators collect and unify the data of all balance responsible parties and use the information to balance their grid segment respectively their market area. A further level could be managed by a European-wide market organizer that employs an EDMS combining all data of the system.

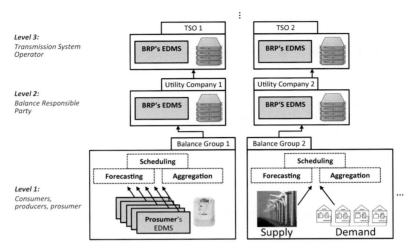

Fig. 2.20 The EDMS of the MIRABEL project (Source: [21, 170]).

Each level of the hierarchy requires specific data in a certain granularity. For this reason, between each hierarchy level the data is aggregated to a granularity that serves the needs of the higher level entity. The consumption of the consumers, for example, is aggregated to a unified demand of the entire balance group. The balance responsible party then just submits this unified demand to its higher-level entity. Furthermore, the entity on the next level is responsible for calculating and providing a consumption and production forecasts of its lower level entities and for the entire group it is responsible for. The unified forecast for the entire group is then communicated to the next level, while single forecasts are used to eventually determine a scheduling of the necessary energy consumption and production. The goal of the scheduling is to balance energy demand and supply for the entire group of lower level entities [21, 170].

The EDMS is designed to work as part of a single European electricity market, spanning the system over all European countries [21, 170]. Employing such a large-scale system poses some challenges. Among other things one has to cope with high-availability and fault tolerance as well as wide-area distributed systems. In addition, near real-time data integration and flexible data analytics are required [21]. In this book we specifically discuss the design and implementation of flexible forecasting as one of the most important data analytics components of the MIRABEL EDMS.

2.2.3 Basic and Advanced Use-Case

The basic goal of the MIRABEL project is a flexible balancing of energy demand and supply in real-time. In the following we present two use-cases for the MIRABEL concepts.

Basic Use-Cases: Charging Electric Cars

A driver of an electric car comes home at 10:00 pm and and needs the car charged until the next morning. The duration for fully charging the car is two hours. Upon plugging-in the car he specifies the exact time he needs the car, which might be 6:00 am in the morning. His smart meter creates a flex-offer with the specified times and the energy profile of charging the car. Assuming sufficient capacities his utility company accepts the flex-offer, which would give them a flexibility of six hours for actually executing the request (10:00 pm earliest start time until 4:00 pm latest start time). At 2:00 am in the night a large amount of wind energy is predicted, for what reason, the utility company schedules the charging of the electric car at this time. A message is sent to the smart metering device of the customer, acknowledging the acceptance and specifying the time of execution. At 2:00 am the electric car starts charging until the batteries are fully loaded. During this process the smart meter monitors the actual energy consumption and ensures that the consumption is always between the defined minimal and maximal defined values. After the loading is complete, the utility company starts calculating the benefit of the flex-offer compared to an open contract consumption. Parts of this benefit are then accounted to the consumer that now saved money while charging its car. In addition, with the help of the MIRABEL concept the average share of renewable energy sources consumed by this consumer increases [21, 170].

Advanced Use-Cases: Utility Company

A public utility company in a city is active in trading flex-offers from the balance group it is responsible for as well as with other energy traders. The scheduling of this utility company is based on forecasts concerning the energy consumption as well as the energy production from renewable and conventional power plants. At 6:00 pm the local steel plant issues a flex-offer (execution between 8:00 pm earliest start time and 6:00 am latest end time) about starting their second smelting furnace. Due to the current wind forecast, a large amount of renewable wind energy is expected to be produced starting from 2:00 am, were currently some energy would be wasted. As a result, the utility company schedules the execution for the furnace flex-offer at 2:00 am, which however, would now lead to a scarcity situation of renewable energy. To compensate the utility company reschedules some private household appliances as well as the charging of electric cars to 4:00 am. Now, the predicted amount of renewable energy sources is completely utilized at 2:00 am and almost utilized at 4:00 am. Unfortunately, the weather forecast was somewhat inaccurate, for what reason at 1:00 am new weather information are provided. The utility company already uses the flexible forecasting of the MIRABEL system that we are introducing in this book. The system continuously considers current measurements and weather informations and thus, provides the most accurate forecasts at all times. The forecasting system predicts a smaller wind energy production between 2:00 am and 4:00 am and a larger wind energy production between 4:00 am and 6:00 am. To address this issue, the utility company shifts the flex-offer start of the melting furnace from 2:00 am to 4:00 am and informs the steel plant accordingly. At the same time the execution of the city-wide car charging is moved to 2:00 am. Afterwards, all flex-offers could be executed as planned and the energy was provided as scheduled. With the help of the shifting, the utility company was able to avoid critical grid situations, while at the same time maximizing the utilization of fluctuating renewable energy sources. In addition, they avoided to pay penalty payments due to causing imbalances that would require the TSOs to issue positive or negative reserve power. Accordingly, the utility company also saved a lot of money.

2.3　Conclusion

In this chapter we provided an overview about the current developments on the European electricity market as well as the challenges that come with an increasing utilization of renewable energy sources. Especially their intermittency including strong and sudden fluctuations present a major issue for the stability of the energy grids. These challenges and issues are currently addressed by new developments in several areas of the energy system. Grids are more and more converted to smart grids to automatically and autonomously react on changing grid situations. Likewise, electricity markets allow for trading close to real-time and autonomous reactions on market signals. Finally, demand can be managed using demand-response systems flexibly activating or deactivating appliances with respect to the currently available energy supply.

In addition, there are major research projects such as MIRABEL that target to provide a more flexible and fine-grained way of balancing energy demand and supply. In the MIRABEL project a new energy trading object called flex-offer was designed that allows market participants to express acceptable flexibilities within their energy consumption or production request. This means that energy consumption and (non-renewable) production can be shifted to positions, where their execution is most appropriate. As a result, with the help of flex-offers, it is possible to substantially increase the utilization of renewable energy sources and at the same time avoid or reduce consumption peaks.

For many of the aforementioned measures and research projects accurate forecasts of energy demand and supply are a key requirement. To acknowledge the increasing flexibility of the energy system, it is necessary to adapt the way forecasts are calculated and provided accordingly. Especially the efficiency, flexibility, and the adaptability of the forecasting process are major areas for improvements. In the course of this book we propose a new forecasting process that is capable of working in the face of the new requirements posed by todays electricity markets.

Chapter 3
The Current State of
Energy Data Management and Forecasting

The different actors and companies in the European electricity market use specific systems to manage their data, called energy data management systems (EDMS). Beside the pure collection and storage of energy-related data, EDMSs typically include a forecasting component that is responsible for calculating predictions of energy time series. In such systems forecasts are calculated using a distinct process as defined by Box and Jenkins [25]. It comprises two different main phases: (1) the actual calculation of the forecast and (2) the monitoring and maintenance of the forecast model. Figure 3.1 illustrates this process:

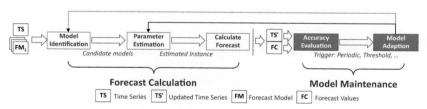

Fig. 3.1   Steps of the forecasting calculation process.

First, it is necessary to identify the most appropriate forecast models for the time series at hand. Second, to exactly capture the specific development of the time series, the parameters are estimated on a training dataset. Third, the most accurate forecast model instance is used to calculate forecasts that are provided to the application. Afterwards, it is necessary to continuously evaluate the forecast model accuracy and provide this information to the consumer allowing him to assess the quality and confidence of the forecast. To maintain a high accuracy a forecast model is continuously adapted to the most recent time series developments. This adaptation is conducted by either re-estimating the forecast model parameters or in some cases by even by re-evaluating the forecast model identification.

In this chapter, we use the calculation phase of the presented forecasting process as a blueprint for discussing general as well as domain-specific forecasting and estimation techniques. We start with presenting characteristics of time series from the energy domain. This analysis is the basis for identifying appropriate models for forecasting energy demand and supply. Afterwards, we present common general-purpose forecast models and their application to the energy domain. This ultimately leads to the introduction of two domain-specific forecast models that we are exemplarily using throughout the book. These models are adapted to exploit the data characteristics of the energy domain and thus, substantially increase the forecasting accuracy compared to general-purpose approaches. Subsequently, we discuss the estimation of forecast models using numerical optimization algorithms. This includes an in detail presentation of the optimization algorithms we employ exemplarily in this book. We close the chapter by presenting the most important challenges for forecasting in the energy domain, that we use to formulate requirements for an advanced forecasting process introduced in Chapter 4.

For the remainder of this book we refer to the following metrics for determining the forecast error, i.e., the deviation between predicted and actual value:

- Mean Square Error (MSE) [25]
- (Symmetric) Mean Average Percentage Error ((S)MAPE) [131]
- Mean Absolute Scaled Error (MASE) [131]

3.1 Data Characteristics in the Energy Domain

Forecasts are based on time series of historic data. The employed mathematical models reason future values based on the characteristic of the historic time series behavior. Datasets from the energy domain exhibit some specifics, where some can be utilized to increase the accuracy of the forecast models, while others are

Dataset	Type	Aggregation	Partitioning	Resolution
D1: National Grid [176]	Demand	Nation	Train: 2002 - 2008 Eval: 2009	30 min
D2: MeRegio [166]	Demand	Household	Train: 11.2009 - 04.2010 Eval: 05.2010 - 06.2010	1 h
D3: CRES Office [47]	Demand	Test Site (Office Building)	Train: 01.2008 - 09.2008 Eval: 10.2008 - 12.2008	30 min
S1: CRES Solar [47]	Supply	Single Appliances	Train: 01.2008 - 09.2008 Eval: 10.2008 - 11.2008	30 min
S2: CRES Wind [47]	Supply	Single Appliances	Train: 2002 - 2008 Eval: 2009	30 min

Table 3.1 Datasets used throughout this book.

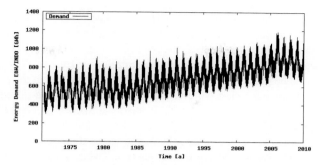

Fig. 3.2 Dataset D1 – Linear trend of total energy demand in UK.

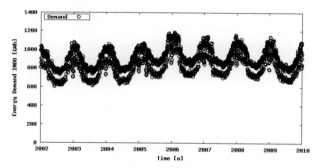

Fig. 3.3 Dataset D1 – Annual season of total energy demand in UK.

challenges that have to be taken into account. In the following we present the specific energy data characteristics and the resulting research questions. For this analysis we used five datasets (compare Table 3.1), where three datasets contain historic demand time series and two datasets contain historic supply time series. All datasets are obtained from real energy demand and supply. They are either publicly available or they are provided by MIRABEL consortium partners.

3.1.1 Seasonal Patterns

An analysis of the main characteristic and general patterns of the data at hand is the prerequisite for discussing forecasting in the energy domain. We first discuss specific reoccurring patterns observed when dealing with data from the energy domain.

Figure 3.2 illustrates the temporal development of the energy consumption of the dataset D1 aggregated per day. Besides annual fluctuations, we observe a weak

linear increase over the last 40 years. Within the last 5 years, this trend flattens
such that the differences between days of subsequent years are almost negligible.
This also corresponds to the general trend of omitting trend components in forecast models used for predicting energy consumption in Europe [229, 231]. Figure 3.3 displays the progression of the dataset D1 over the last eight years, where
we observe a yearly repeating pattern forming an annual season. In addition, demand data exhibits a daily and a weekly season as shown in Figure 3.4. First,
Figures 3.4(a) and 3.4(b) compare the intra-week season for the summer and the
winter. The demand at the weekend is typically lower than during working days.
This difference is invariant to the annual season. There is also an intra-day season shown in Figure 3.4(c) and 3.4(d), showing different behavior between typical
summer and winter days due to the yearly season. Typically, the energy consumption during winter days is significantly higher and exhibits a peak in the evening
hours (4pm to 8pm). To summarize, aggregated energy demand time series comprising the energy consumption of multiple entities (e.g., city, country) exhibit a

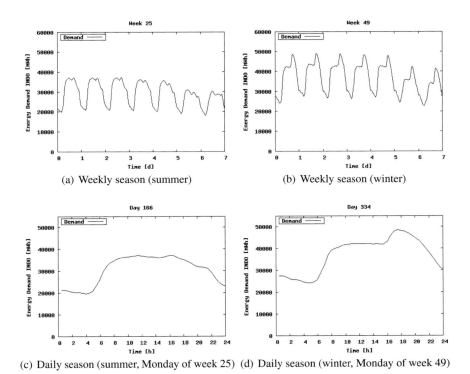

(a) Weekly season (summer)   (b) Weekly season (winter)

(c) Daily season (summer, Monday of week 25) (d) Daily season (winter, Monday of week 49)

Fig. 3.4 Dataset D1: Weakly and daily season of total energy demand.

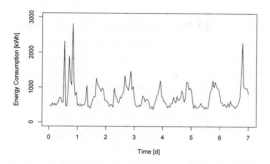

(a) Aggregated energy consumption of all MeRegio customers

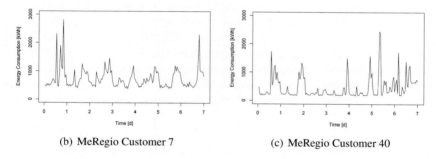

(b) MeRegio Customer 7   (c) MeRegio Customer 40

Fig. 3.5 Dataset D2: Energy consumption of single customers.

weak linear trend over the years and three different seasonal components that influence the total energy demand. An appropriate forecast model should cover all seasons.

3.1.2 Aggregation-Level-Dependent Predictability

Regional resolution

Besides a trend and seasonal pattern, the predictability of energy demand and supply greatly depends on the regional aggregation level. In general, the more entities are aggregated the better the predictability. This is exactly the reason for the portfolio effect (compare Section 2.1.5) and the consolidation of multiple renewable energy production sites. The more entities are considered jointly, the better the compensation of single fluctuations. The aggregation dependency of the predictability is not limited to the regional dimension, but is true for all aggregation dimensions such as time, customer profile, and product (type of supply or demand). Figures 3.5(a) and 3.5 illustrate three time series of the MeRegio dataset, where Figure 3.5(a) shows the aggregated demand of all customers and Figure 3.5 shows the consumption of two single customers (customer 7 (Figure 3.5(b)) and customer 40 (Figure 3.5(c))). We can see that the time series of the single customers are subject of large fluctuations with customer 7 being more regular than customer 40. Both time series do not exhibit the typical daily and weekly patterns, but abrupt and large peaks. We account this to the typical human behavior that is not constant from day to day, but subject to sudden changes. However, observing the aggregation of all 83 customers in Figure 3.5(a), the described typical patterns are clearly recognizable. The collective compensates the fluctuations of single households, smoothing the aggregated energy curve. As a result, while forecasting the single customers exhibits a large forecast error (for this dataset between 10% to 20% average forecast error), the aggregated time series exhibits a much better predictability and a much lower forecast error (for this dataset around 4%). Similar results were observed in several research studies in the area of supply forecasts that commonly concluded that including multiple renewables power plants into an aggregated forecast, substantially increases the forecasting accuracy [109, 128, 171]. Some even state that forecasts of single sites (e.g., wind turbines) makes only very limited sense [121].

Temporal resolution

As a second example, we show the dependence of the predictability on the temporal aggregation level for energy demand and supply. For this purpose, we used the datasets D3 and S1 that exhibit a resolution of 1 min, aggregated over time. Figure 3.6 illustrates the energy demand and supply of February 1st 2008 (Friday). Column 1 illustrates the heat pump demand (for cooling and heating) of dataset D3, column 2 shows the additional demand of the building (e.g., illumination, technical appliances), and column 3 shows the supply of the dataset S2. Each column shows, in detail, the influence of increasing the aggregation level with respect to the temporal resolution. First, the heat pump at 1 min resolution exhibits the characteristics of many short peaks, which is reasoned by fuzzy temperature control. Only when aggregated to 15 min or hours, we can obtain a predictable time series. Second, the aggregation of the additional demand to 15 min intervals leads to a smoothed time series. Third, the photovoltaic grid also shows a typical behavior. The energy supply is only provided during daytime, with a peak around noon. In addition, at the day of measurement, scattered clouds led to fine-grained breakdowns. When aggregating this series to hours we obtain time series with much better predictabil-

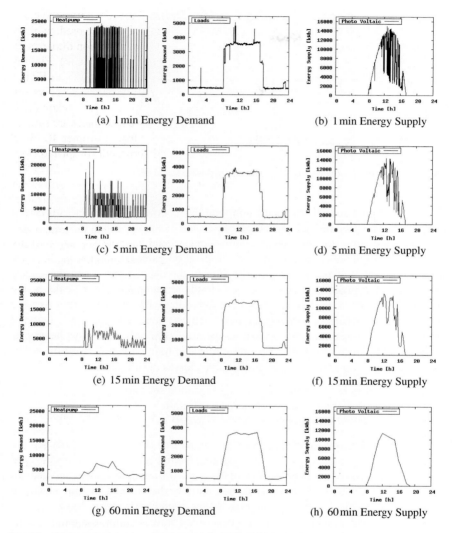

Fig. 3.6 Dataset D3 and S1: Aggregation-dependent predictability (temporal).

ity. In addition to the issue of aggregation-dependent predictability, this column shows the high importance of additional external input in the form of weather data or weather forecasts (e.g., daylight duration, sunlight intensity, cloud movements) to improve the forecasting accuracy.

3.1.3 Time Series Context and Context Drifts

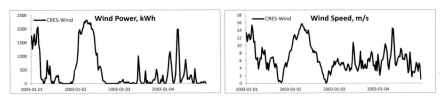

Fig. 3.7   Time series of wind energy production and wind speed [61].

In many application domains the temporal development of time series is driven by a conglomeration of background processes and external influences. This is also true for the energy domain, where energy demand and especially energy supply from renewable energy sources strongly depend on external influences [53, 121, 172, 211]. For solar power we already showed the dependence when discussing the temporal aggregation. There, scatter clouds led to many short peaks in the photovoltaic time series that are very hard to predict without considering weather information. Furthermore, energy demand exhibits some correlation to external information, for example, the current temperature. On very cold days heating is activate, while on warm days air conditioning is running. Overall, for time series from the energy domain, we distinguish three classes of influences:

• Calendar: Special days, public holidays, vacation seasons
• Meteorological: Temperature, cloudiness, rainfall
• Economic: Local law, special events (e.g., sport)

This classification is supported by a study of Crabtree at all, that similarly see the biggest influence on energy time series coming from weather, demand history, and major events [53]. While in general all of these factors are independent and take individual states at any point in time, in their entirety they form a specific influence conglomeration that we refer to as *time series context*. The term *context* in this sense was coined in machine learning describing influences on the temporal development of data streams [235, 254]. There, they assume that hidden background processes and influences are the key driver for the development of a data stream. In general it remains unknown how the hidden contexts influence and interact with the values of a data stream, since they cannot be directly observed. Observations are only possible through the development of the data stream itself. However, a specialty of the energy domain is the fact that most of the influences and their interaction with the main time series are actually observable. In Figure 3.7 we show two example time series from the dataset S2. There we see a wind energy production curve and the corresponding wind speed. The wind power production

time series itself does not have any regular patterns and exhibits very irregular behavior. For this reason, an accurate forecast is hardly possible. However, we can
clearly see a strong correlation between both time series, without even considering
intensive data analysis techniques. This means that the wind speed is an influence
factor for the wind energy production. As a result, we can exploit the observable
external information by incorporating their measurements and developments into
our forecasting calculation. This leads to a substantially increasing predictability.
This is also backed by several research studies in the domain of forecasting energy
demand and supply (consider e.g. for supply: [128, 134, 171, 191] and for demand:
[90, 123]).

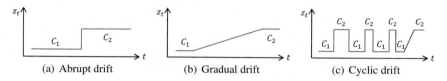

Fig. 3.8   Types of context drifts (based on classification in [254]).

The states of the influence factors are not static, but rather change over time and
with that, the entire time series context. These changes are called *context drifts* and
can influence the behavior and further development of a time series. Zliobaite distinguishes between three types of context drift based on their duration, abruptness,
and occurrence patterns [254]. We illustrate the three types in Figure 3.8. There,
abrupt drifts mean a sudden replacement of the current influencing factor state with
a new state. In the energy domain such a drift could be caused by a power outage
or a popular sporting event. However, in most cases abrupt drifts return to their
current state after a short time frame; e.g., when the outage is fixed or the sporting
event is over. Gradual drifts are a slow transformation from one factor state to a
new one. This could be caused for example by an increasing population in a city,
aging power transmission and distribution equipment, or an increasing ecological
awareness by the consumers. Finally, there are cyclic drifts where the context constantly iterates between two or more states. Examples for cyclic drifts are general
seasonal patterns (long term, e.g., summer, winter), reoccurring hot/cold spells in
summer/winter (short term) or production cycles in the industry. Since changes in
the time series context can also lead to changes in the behavior and characteristic
of the influenced time series, it is necessary to continuously detect those changes
and adapt the forecasting model accordingly to avoid inaccurate forecasts.

3.1.4 Typical Data Characteristics of Energy Time Series

To allow for accurate forecasts, all the identified characteristics should be considered within a forecast model. In particular, we identified the following three characteristics:

Multi-Seasonality: The behavior of energy demand exhibits multiple seasons. First, there is a typical daily season, which shape the common time series progression of the day according to winter and summer days. Second, there is a weekly season, where a time series exhibits the typical working day and weekend pattern. Third, there is a long-term annual season, caused by exogenous influence (especially the weather). Following the analysis of Taylor, forecast models used in the energy domain should at least consider the daily and the weekly season. Additionally including the yearly season leads to further but rather marginal accuracy improvements [229].

Aggregation-Level-Dependent Predictability: When comparing the behavior of energy demand of single households against regionally aggregated behavior, we observe that the lower the aggregation level, the lower the accuracy of forecasts because of higher diversity and unpredictable behavior. This is true for all aggregation dimensions such as time and region. One important effect of the aggregation level dependence is that combining multiple supply sides for calculating a forecast, leads to an ensemble effect. This means that deviations of a single side are compensated by other included sides. This also substantially increases the forecasting accuracy. Thus, increasing the aggregation-level allows for more robust forecasts (similar to the law of large numbers). However, if the aggregation level is too high many effects are hidden and cannot be precisely estimated. As a result, forecasting energy demand and supply should be designed with aggregation-awareness [94].

Exogenous Influence: Both energy demand and renewable energy supply strongly depend on exogenous influences. The supply side is mainly influenced by environmental factors especially the weather (wind energy: wind speed; solar power: daylight intensity, cloudiness), but also influences like the installation terrain. As shown in the data analysis section, for the supply side it is of utmost importance to include external information into the forecast model. Without considering the environmental factors accurate forecast are almost impossible. In addition to the energy supply, the demand side can benefit from including these additional information, which can increase the forecasting accuracy. However, for the demand side the inclusion of external information is not a prerequisite as for the supply side.

3.2 Forecasting in the Energy Domain

Forecasting the future energy demand and supply is one of the key analysis techniques used in electricity management to balance energy consumption and production. For this purpose mathematical models—called forecast models—are used. Forecast models reason the future development of energy demand and supply based on the behavior and characteristics of historic time series. To do so, most forecast model types capture a parameterized relationship between past and future values to express different aspects of a time series such as seasonal patterns or the current energy output. Typically one can distinguish between two forecast model categories: multi-purpose general forecasting approaches and energy domain specific forecast models. While the first are universally employable basic models, the latter typically are adaptations of the general forecasting approaches and catch up the specific data characteristics of the energy domain as described in Section 3.1.1. Thus, domain-specific forecast models often yield better forecasting accuracy than general-purpose models. In the following we start describing basic general forecast models in the context of forecasting in the energy domain. The general forecast models can be divided into three large classes namely: models with autoregressive structures [25], exponential smoothing [127, 246] and approaches from machine learning [40].

3.2.1 Forecast Models with Autoregressive Structures

Models with autoregressive structures describe the characteristics and behavior of time series using an autoregression process. They have been introduced by Box and Jenkins [25]. To simplify the following mathematical notations, we use the Backshift Operator $Bx_t = x_{t-1}$ and $B^j x_t = x_{t-j}$ [25].

Mathematical Basics

The base form of models with autoregressive structures comprises two different parts: The autoregressive model (AR) and the moving average model [25, 29]. The autoregressive model uses a weighted linear combination of previous stochastic process values (x_t at time t) combined with a random shock out of white noise data (a_t). A stochastic process is the mathematical description of an ordered set of random variables, whose future evolvement exhibits indeterminacy. The model is described by the following equation:

$$x_t = \phi_1 x_{t-1} + \phi_2 x_{t-2} + \ldots + \phi_p x_{t-p} + a_t = \sum_{i=1}^{p} \phi_i x_{t-i} + a_t. \tag{3.1}$$

With the help of the backshift operator $B^j x_t$ we may rearrange the equation to the final form:

$$a_t = \left(1 - \sum_{i=1}^{p} \phi_i B^i \right) x_t. \tag{3.2}$$

The number of included previous values is determined by the order p of the AR model.

The moving average part (MA) describes a time series as a weighted linear combination of several previous values of a white noise process (a_t at time t); i.e., a set of uncorrelated, normal-distributed, random variables with an assumed equal variance. The notation of this model is:

$$x_t = a_t + \theta_1 a_{t-1} + \theta_2 a_{t-2} + \ldots + \theta_q a_{t-q} = a_t + \sum_{i=1}^{q} \theta_i a_{t-i} = \left(1 + \sum_{i=1}^{q} \theta_i B^q \right) a_t.$$
$$\tag{3.3}$$

The sum is weighted by the parameters θ_q, which are absolutely summable weights, where *absolute summable* refers to the associative relationship of sum and expected value. It is important to note that the weights of a moving average process describing the function cannot be estimated as easily as with the autoregressive part, because the random shocks are not directly observable even though they are chosen from a fixed distribution. For this purpose non-linear fitting methods are necessary (compare Section 3.4). The number of white noise random shocks is described by the order q of the model.

The direct combination of both models—AR and MA—was introduced by Box and Jenkins [25] and is called the Auto Regressive Moving Average model (ARMA). It is is denoted as:

$$\left(1 - \sum_{i=1}^{p} \phi_i B^i \right) x_t = \left(1 + \sum_{i=1}^{q} \theta_i B^q \right) a_t. \tag{3.4}$$

The ARMA model is referred to as ARMA(p, q) where p is the order of the AR part and q is the order of the MA part. The values of p and q can be estimated using the (partial) autocorrelation function ((P)ACF). However, real time series do not behave like perfect autoregressive models and thus, the estimations provided by the ACF and PACF can only be seen as a hint.

Trend Component

The ARMA model as well as its individual components only supports stationary time series. Here, the term *stationarity* means that the probability distribution of a stochastic process does not change upon shifting time (e.g. from t to $t+1$). However, time series often exhibit a certain trend, which means that they behave non-stationary. To express such time series, the Auto Regressive Integrated Moving Average model (ARIMA) has been introduced [25]. The model adjusts for the non-stationarity by applying an ARMA process to a modified time series obtained by subtracting values, e.g. $x'_t = x_t - x_{t-1}$. Taking these differences into account addresses trends and non-stationary behavior. The resulting ARIMA model takes the form:

$$\left(1 - \sum_{i=1}^{p} \phi_i B^i\right) (1-B)^d x_t = \left(1 + \sum_{i=1}^{q} \theta_i B^q\right) a_t. \tag{3.5}$$

The incorporated trend of the ARIMA model is denoted with $(1-B)^d$. We refer to an ARIMA model as $\text{ARIMA}(p,d,q)$, where the parameters p, d, q describe the order of the ARIMA model (each representing the order of its respective part). The ARIMA model counts as one of the most general time series models available, since all formerly introduced models are in fact special cases of the ARIMA model.

Season Component

In addition to non-stationary behavior, many time series exhibit seasonal behavior, which means reoccurring structural patterns after certain periods in time. As described in Section 3.1.1 energy demand data typically show an intra-day, intra-week and intra-year season. The standard approach for autoregressive models is the SARIMA model or $\text{ARIMA}(p,d,q) \times (P,D,Q)_s$ [25, 29]. The SARIMA model is a combination of two ARIMA models, one for the base time series and one describing the seasonality. The seasonal part can be described by:

$$\left(1 - \sum_{i=1}^{p} \Phi B^i\right)^s (1-B^s)^D x_t = \left(1 + \sum_{i=1}^{q} \Theta_i B^q\right)^s a_t, \tag{3.6}$$

with Φ, Θ being the known weights of the components and s being the length of the season. The seasonal part is combined with the standard ARIMA model:

$$\left(1 - \sum_{i=1}^{p} \phi B^i\right)\left(1 - \sum_{i=1}^{p} \Phi B^i\right)^s (1-B)^d (1-B^s)^D x_t$$

$$= \left(1 + \sum_{i=1}^{q} \theta_i B^q\right)\left(1 + \sum_{i=1}^{q} \Theta_i B^q\right)^s a_t. \tag{3.7}$$

Here, all Greek and Latin capital letters belong to the seasonal part, whereas the lower-case letters represent the non-seasonal part. Further seasons can be incorporated into the model, by adding additional seasonal components.

Some alternative techniques for including seasonal behavior exist next to the classic SARIMA approach. Since seasonality is a periodically reoccurring behavior, it can also be represented by a periodic function. Thus, Taylor introduced a periodic AR model that is illustrated in the Example 3.1 below [227]. In this example he uses a Fourier representation to model periodic seasons.

Example 3.1. Periodic AR Seasonality Representation: This example represents the calculation of the AR model parameter ϕ with the intra-day season as a Fourier function.

$$\phi_p = \omega_p + \sum_{m=1}^{h}\left\{\lambda_{pm} sin\left(2m\pi\left(\frac{d(t)}{48}\right)\right) + \nu_{pm} cos\left(2m\pi\left(\frac{d(t)}{48}\right)\right)\right\}.$$

The parameters ω, λ and ν are the parameters of the Fourier function. A quantification of the intra-day periodicity is denoted by the repeating step function $d(t)$ (e.g., $d(t) = 1, 2, ..., 48$ for half-hourly load data).

A similar approach called Two-Level Seasonal AR Model (TLSAR) was introduced by Soares et al. [216], which models the periodic behavior as a sum of waves of sine and cosine like in a Fourier decomposition. The advantage of forecast models that use a periodic function to describe seasonalities is that the parameters change with the seasons and thus, they reduce the number of parameters compared to non-periodic forecast models [227].

The question about the number of seasons highly depends on the application domain and the use case. For energy demand forecasting, Talyor et al. conducted a study comparing models with two and three seasons [229]. In particular they included double and triple seasonal ARIMA in their comparison using: (1) a double seasonal configuration (intra-day and intra-week), (2) a second double seasonal configuration (intra-week and intra-year), (3) a triple seasonal configuration (intra-day, intra-week, and intra-year). The evaluation was performed on British and on French data. Thus, Taylor's study is highly relevant for forecasting within the European electricity market. The results show that the triple seasonal configurations outperform both double seasonal variants. However, in this specific analysis, the accuracy of the triple seasonal configuration increased the accuracy only marginally by less than 0.5% (MAPE). However, even this slight accuracy advan-

tage might still be of interested. Bunn and Farmer stated that an increase in the
forecast error of just 1% would also mean an increase in the operational costs for
a single utility company in the UK in 1984 of 10 million pounds [39].

Integration of Exogenous Influence

As shown in Section 3.1.1 energy forecasts and especially supply forecasts depend
on exogenous influences. Thus, to allow accurate predictions, it is beneficial to
include these dependencies with the goal of increasing the accuracy of a forecast
model. The Box and Jenkins models allow the integration of external influences
by extending the AR(I)MA model to the AR(I)MAX model [25, 29]. The ARI-
MAX model allows the inclusion of exogenous variables by additively or multiplicatively adding a term for the exogenous variable to the equation. The model
ARIMAX(p,d,q,b) then describes a time series under the influence of another exogenous time series. The following notation describes the ARIMAX model with
an additively included external time series.:

$$\left(1 - \sum_{i=1}^{p} \phi_i B^i\right)(1-B)^d x_t = \left(1 + \sum_{i=1}^{q} \theta_i B^q\right) a_t + \left(1 + \sum_{i=1}^{b} \eta_i B^b\right) d_t. \qquad (3.8)$$

where η_i are the parameters of the exogenous time series d_t and b is the order of
this time series. More influences can be added by including additional exogenous
terms.

An alternative to the inclusion of an additional time series, is the integration using boolean variables as described by [197]. Boolean variables are binary variables
that indicate whether a certain effect exists. In combination with weight parameters, they are used to integrate dependencies by quantifying their influence on the
specific data. Boolean variables are especially useful in conjunction with external
influences that exhibit only the state of currently existing or not existing as well as
influences where not dedicated historic time series is available.

3.2.2 Exponential Smoothing

The exponential smoothing technique uses a weighted linear combination of past
observations to smooth erratic time series and to predict future values. The weights
of the linear combination are decreasing exponentially with the progression of the
time series, meaning that recent observations are given more weight in relation to
older values. The initial values of the weights can be set manually, yet to get optimal values they should be estimated (compare Section 3.4). Exponential smooth-

ing is a common model class to describe time series from multiple application domains and can be enhanced to also support non-stationarity and seasonal behavior. Some very accurate forecast models from the energy domain base on exponential smoothing.

Mathematical Basics

Simple or single exponential smoothing (SESM) [107, 179] is mainly used for stationary time series. It includes a parameter, called smoothing constant α that determines the influence of the current value compared to the last smoothed value:

$$\bar{x}_t = \bar{x}_{t-1} + \alpha \left(x_{t-1} - \bar{x}_{t-1} \right) \text{ (Smoothing)}.$$
$$\bar{x}_{t+m} = \bar{x}_{t+m-1} + \alpha \left(x_t - \bar{x}_{t+m-1} \right) \text{ (Forecast)}. \tag{3.9}$$

In equation 3.9 $\bar{x}_t$ is the smoothed value and x_t is the current value of the time series. When calculating a forecast, the last known value x_t is used for the whole forecast horizon m. This is called bootstrapping. The exponential characteristic of this approach can be revealed by a repeated use of the algorithm as shown in the following example:

$$\bar{x}_t = \alpha x_{t-1} + (1 - \alpha)[\alpha x_{t-2} + (1 - \alpha)\bar{x}_{t-2}]$$
$$= \alpha x_{t-1} + \alpha(1 - \alpha)x_{t-2} + (1 - \alpha)^2\bar{x}_{t-2}.$$

Trend Component

The single exponential smoothing does not deliver accurate results for non-stationary time series containing a trend component. For such time series, the exponential smoothing can incorporate a trend component. The exponential smoothing is then called double exponential smoothing (DESM) [179]. The trend incorporation can be realized in a multiplicative or additive way. This includes the introduction of an additional trend factor β within the trend component. Due to the fact that time series can exhibit a damped trend it is also possible to include an additional damping parameter [107]. The following equation shows a possible additive integration of the trend component without a damping parameter.

$$\bar{x}_t = \bar{x}_{t-1} + b_{t-1} + \alpha \left(x_t - \bar{x}_{t-1} - b_{t-1} \right) \text{ (Smoothing)},$$
$$b_t = b_{t-1} + \beta \left(\bar{x}_t - \bar{x}_{t-1} - b_{t-1} \right) \text{ (Trend)}, \tag{3.10}$$
$$\bar{x}_{t+m} = \bar{x}_t + m \cdot b_t \text{ (Forecast)}.$$

Season Integration

Seasonal behavior like observed for energy demand time series, requires a further extension of the exponential smoothing. There, a component describing the seasonal behavior can be added multiplicatively or additively [107]. This leads to the triple exponential smoothing (TESM) [179]:

$$
\begin{aligned}
\bar{x}_t &= \alpha \frac{x_t}{I_{t-L}} + (1-\alpha)(\bar{x}_{t-1} + b_{t-1}) \text{ (Smoothing)}, \\
b_t &= \beta(\bar{x}_t - \bar{x}_{t-1}) + (1-\beta)b_{t-1} \text{ (Trend)}, \\
I_t &= \gamma \frac{x_t}{\bar{x}_t} + (1-\gamma)I_{t-L} \text{ (Season)}, \\
\bar{x}_{t+m} &= (\bar{x}_t + m \cdot b_t) \cdot I_{t-L+m} \text{ (Forecast)}.
\end{aligned}
\tag{3.11}
$$

where b_t is the trend component and I_t is the seasonal component. The index L represents the period of the seasonal component. The trend in this example equation was included multiplicatively.

As with the autoregressive models the question about the number of seasons that should be integrated arises. With respect to the energy domain and the study of Taylor et al. (compare Sec. 3.2.1) [229], the results remain the same like for models with autoregressive structures . The integration of a third season improves the forecast accuracy by around 0.5% (MAPE). However, the best overall results were achieved by combining the forecasts of the triple seasonal exponential smoothing and the triple seasonal ARMA.

Integration of Exogenous Influence

Exponential smoothing approaches do not directly integrate exogenous influences. As a result, effects of exogenous influences are modeled by specifically adapting the final forecast values. Souza et al. [220] describes such an option for the inclusion of holidays and temperatures. Holidays are included by multiplying the forecasts of the holiday, the preceding day and the following day with load reduction factors that are based on statistics about the percentage variation in load between holiday and weekday. For the inclusion of the temperature a special model for the relationship between load and temperature was used.

3.2.3 Machine Learning Techniques

In addition to autoregressive models and exponential smoothing, it is also possible
to use approaches from the area of machine learning to calculate forecasts. The
most important examples for machine learning techniques used for forecasting
are: Bayesian Networks, Artificial Neural Networks (ANN) and Support Vector
Machines (SVM). Several studies such as for example conducted by Bunnon et
al. [40], Ahmed et al. [6], and Krollner et al. [151] investigate the use of machine
learning techniques for time series forecasting in several application domains. The
studies show that many machine learning techniques can be enhanced to calculate
forecasts. Additionally, there are also some evaluations that show the applicability
of machine learning techniques in comparison to classical statistical techniques
(autoregression, exponential smoothing) when forecasting in the energy domain.
Taylor et al. for example compared an ANN against multi-seasonal ARIMA and
exponential smoothing models [232]. Similarly, Darbellay et al. evaluated ANNs
against standard ARIMA and ARIMAX forecast models, when forecasting electricity load [63]. The study of Taylor et al. favor the statistical forecast models,
while the study of Darbellay et al. see ANNs in front. Furthermore, in several
research studies that evaluated the use of artificial neural networks and other machine learning approaches for forecasting energy supply and demand the results
are likewise controversial [2, 114, 125, 213, 242]. Some even argue that there is
no clear advantage of using ANN especially when considering the high computational efforts they require. This shows that the advantage of one over the other
modeling technique highly depends on the use-case and on the existing data. In
this book we clearly focus on statistical forecasting using exponential smoothing
models and models with autoregressive structures. For this purpose, we only give
a brief overview over the most important machine learning techniques used for
forecasting in the energy domain.

Bayesian Networks

Bayesian Networks are decision networks used to represent knowledge about an
uncertain domain. The domains are typically represented as an n-dimensional set
of stochastic observations, which can be correlated among each other. The main
goal of inference in Bayesian networks is to estimate the values of hidden nodes,
given the values of observed nodes. This ability of Bayesian networks is used in
the forecasting domain to predict future values. In general forecasting can be seen
as an inference problem of the Bayesian network, describing the dependencies between different values of a time series. It partitions the variables and estimates the
optimal value of a variable using the minimum of the mean squared error (MSE)

[253]. Bayesian networks are employed for weather forecasts [46, 48] and are also used in the energy domain [51].

Artificial Neural Networks

An artificial neural network (ANN) is a computational model that is inspired by the functional aspects of a biological nervous system. ANNs are highly adaptive systems that learn to process information or to perform a function directly from the data. An ANN is a one to multi layer set of artificial neurons N interconnected through a number of network edges E. A network edge E is formally defined as a mapping between the output of a neuron to the input of a neuron on a subsequent layer. Edges are often assigned with weights that are used to modify the forwarded value. Each neuron in an artificial neural network typically comprises three functions [27, 149]:

1. The *propagation function* modifies the input to the neuron; e.g., it applies the weight of the edge to the forwarded value.
2. The *activation function* decides upon the degree of activation of a neuron and transforms the input of the neuron to its output. Common activation functions are for example the binary, sigmoid, hyperbolic, or pice-wise linear function.
3. The *output function* creates the final output of a neuron. In most cases the identity is used.

ANNs are adapted using observed or unobserved learning techniques. During the learning phase the weights on the network edges are adapted and new edges between neurons are created to solve the given task in an optimal sense. ANNs further create their own organization or representation of the given information and the computations can be carried out in parallel [27, 223]. ANNs are also used for forecasting in the energy domain [187, 212]. The advantage of ANNs in this context is that they can capture non-linear dependencies between load and exogenous influences. For this reason they can quickly react on abrupt changes in the behavior of a time series. However, ANNs tend to be very complex and the training is very time consuming. In addition, the accuracy potential of an ANN highly depends on the selection of suitable input variables. Solutions like the automatic input selection proposed in [212] have to be considered to overcome some of the problems.

Support Vector Machines

Support Vector Machines (SVM) are an approach in the field of machine learning for classification, pattern recognition, and regression. In the simplest case, an

SVM is used to divide a set of data points into two classes. The goal is to find a dividing classifier that maximizes the distance between the classes. In general, an SVM is not limited to a binary deviation. Using a transformation to a high-dimensional feature space, more complex and non-linear classification problems can be solved. Furthermore, SVMs can also be used for regression. The basic idea is to map a time series to a high-dimensional feature space and to perform linear regression in this space. Thus, linear regression in a high-dimensional space corresponds to nonlinear regression in lower-dimensional space [102, 122, 175, 215]. One approach for forecasting in the energy domain using an SVM is introduced in [185]. The advantage of SVMs is that they minimize the upper bound of the generalization error instead of the training error as it is done in traditional forecast models. In addition, solutions found by an SVM are always unique and globally optimal, since they are equivalent to solve linear constrained programming problems. Thus, SVM emerge as a very important technique for calculating forecasts in the energy domain. However, similar to other artificial intelligence methods, SVM have to be understood as black-box models. Therefore, it is hard to examine the modeled relationships and to interpret the results. In addition, the development of an SVM model is rather complex and requires very sensitive decisions such as the selection of an appropriate kernel function [147].

3.3 Forecast Models Tailor-Made for the Energy Domain

When forecasting in the energy domain, the general forecast models introduced in Section 3.2 are typically adapted to match the specific data characteristics of the energy domain. Surveys such as presented by Alfares et al. [8] discuss the applicability of different general and domain-specific forecast models for forecasting electric load and supply. Similarly, Taylor et al. compared several forecast model that they specifically adapted to match the characteristics of electric load and supply time series [228, 231]. In this section, we discuss some of these energy domain-specific forecast models, with focusing on two approaches that we will specifically use exemplarily throughout this book. First, we present the multi seasonal exponential smoothing (MSESM) model as introduced by Taylor et al. [229] that is a energy-domain-specific adaptation of the general Holt-Winters exponential smoothing model [246]. Second, we discuss the EGRV model as introduced by Ramanathan et al. [197]. The EGRV model is a multi-equation model that uses individual sub-models with respect to the daily data granularity; e.g., a separate sub-model for each hour of the day. The sub-models itself combine an autoregression of lagged values and errors with boolean variables describing the current state of the time series (e.g., the day of the week, the current month). The EGRV model was the winning model in the Puget Sound Power and Light forecasting competition [197]. With both models in place we cover a large space of forecast models typically employed in the energy domain, with considering single and multi-equation models as well as exponential smoothing and autoregression.

3.3.1 Exponential Smoothing for the Energy Domain

Exponential smoothing models are used in many application domains for describing historic data, smoothing time series, and predicting future values. Typically the model is adapted to match the requirements of the respective domain. With respect to the energy domain Taylor et al. as well as the data analysis in Section 3.1.1 revealed up to three seasonal patterns (daily, weekly, yearly) for energy demand time series. Accordingly, Taylor et al. proposed an exponential smoothing derivative for multi-seasonal energy demand [229] that we refer to as MSESM. A double seasonal variant of the model is denoted as:

$$
\begin{aligned}
\text{Forecast} \quad & \hat{x}_t(h) = l_t + d_{t-s_1+h} + w_{t-s_2+h} + a_{t-s_3+h} \\
& \quad + \phi^m(x_t - (l_{t-1} + d_{t-s_1} + w_{t-s_2}) + a_{t-s_3}) \\
\text{Level} \quad & l_t = \lambda(x_t - d_{t-s_1} - w_{t-s_2} - a_{t-s_3}) + (1-\lambda)l_{t-1} \\
\text{Saison 1} \quad & d_t = \delta(x_t - l_{t-1} - w_{t-s_2} - a_{t-s_3}) + (1-\delta)d_{t-s_1} \\
\text{Saison 2} \quad & w_t = \omega(x_t - l_{t-1} - d_{t-s_1} - a_{t-s_3}) + (1-\omega)w_{t-s_2}
\end{aligned}
\tag{3.12}
$$

In the model, l_t denotes the base level of the energy load. The variables d_t and w_t represent the daily and weekly seasonal patterns respectively. Taylor also included a first-order error autocorrelation term denoted by ϕ, which improves the accuracy of the forecast model [226]. Additionally, the model can be adapted to the specifics of the actual data at hand, by simply adjusting the number of considered seasons. This can be achieved by simply adding or removing seasonal components. The forecast model presented above is the additive version of Taylor's exponential smoothing model MSESM. However, they also described a similar multiplicative version that however typically leads to similar results [226, 229].

Besides the model presented above, there are more exponential smoothing variations used for forecasting in the energy domain. Taylor et. al for example proposed an intra day cycle model [231], a multi-equation forecast model [232] and a singular value decomposition model [230] based on exponential smoothing. Also some exponential smoothing approaches were introduced that include external information such as the one from Souza et al. [220]. Similarly, Song et al. proposed an electric load forecasting method that uses a combination of fuzzy linear regression and exponential smoothing to better describe the differences between weekend and working days [217]. They also incorporate temperature sensitivities that model the relationship between daily load and temperature. However, in this book we exemplarily focus on the multi-seasonal exponential smoothing (MSESM) model from Taylor as one of the most accurate forecast models for describing energy demand and supply for the European electricity market [229].

3.3.2 A multi-equation forecast model using autoregression

There are two ways for forecast models to describe time series from the energy domain. First, the *single-equation* models describe the behavioral aspects in a single forecasting model, which tends to be very complex. Second, *multi-equation* models use individual forecasting models for specific time periods (e.g., one hour). In particular, each sub-model typically follows the same equation, but is instantiated with individual values for the comprised parameters. The reason for splitting up the forecast model is to ease the time series behavior a sub-model has to describe and thus, to increase the forecasting accuracy. The underlying assumption is that time series values corresponding to a specific time slot fluctuate only very slightly over the selected season and thus, the relationship between past and future values is easier to model. Besides decomposing the time series with respect to a single season, it is also possible to provide separate sub-models for multiple seasons. A typical example for considering multiple seasons is to assign different sub-models to weekends and working days (weekly season) in addition to the hourly models decomposing the daily season. Additionally, multi-equation models tend to have an increased reactivity to intraday changes, because subsequent sub-models can be adapted based on the accuracy of preceding sub-models. A very promising multi-equation model that is the EGRV forecast model introduced by Ramanathan et al. [197]. They use one separate regression model for each hour of the day and different models for weekdays and weekends resulting in a total of 48 hourly models. Seasons and external information are included using independent variables for each hourly model, representing for example the current day of the week or the current month. These variables reflect reoccurring events in the forecast model. Additionally, the EGRV model supports the inclusion of further external information such as the current temperature. The notation for a single hour sub-model with coefficients grouped into several components is as follows:

$$HOUR_i = BASELOAD + \alpha DETERMINISTIC$$
$$+ \beta TEMPERATURE$$
$$+ \gamma LOAD + \delta PASTERROR$$

Each component has an assigned group of parameters (α, β, γ and δ), which comprises of multiple individual parameter values assigned to the individual coefficients of the components. The component DETERMINISTIC contains exogenous coefficients like the day of the week or the month or the year, which are represented by boolean variables. The model also allows the inclusion of additional temperature coefficients, which are described in the TEMPERATURE component. The TEMPERATURE component is typically related to a single temperature time series, but contains multiple coefficients representing different temperature aspects (e.g., current temperature, average temperature). LOAD and PASTERROR represent the actual auto correlated time series values reflecting the load at a specific time, respectively the last forecast errors or lagged values. The component BASELOAD is a special component, due to the fact that BASELOAD itself is a single parameter without any coefficient. BASELOAD is used to determine the average amount of consumed or produced energy.

The multi-equation approach and the EGRV model was adapted and enhanced by several other approaches such as the first order stationary vector regression developed by Cottet and Smith [51], the PCA based forecast method proposed by Taylor and McSharry [232] and a variant specifically suited to account for changes in customer and production behavior introduced by Dordonnat et al. [69]. In addition there are some model adaptations specifically suited for a certain country and energy provider such as the adaptation for the Spanish system operator RED Electricia [45] and the specialized forecasting model for an electricity utility company in Brazil [216]. Typical enhancements are to model short term time series values using a more advanced processes (e.g., ARMA in Cancelos approach, Vector Autoregression (VAR) in Cottets approach) instead of a residual autocorrelation adjustment [45] and modeling the remaining seasonal cycles in alternative ways (e.g., annual cycle as Fourier decomposition [216]). Furthermore, some approaches discuss improvements regarding the model estimation by reducing for example the number of involved parameters or employing alternative estimation methods [51, 69, 232].

While multi-equation models like the EGRV provide very accurate forecasts in most situations, they also tend to be very complex, due to multiple sub-models and a large number of coefficients. One typical EGRV sub-model for example contains around 30 parameters and for predicting the next day, 24 of such models (assuming hourly data granularity) have to be estimated. Thus, calculating forecasts using multi-equation models and in particular the EGRV model is very time consuming. This contradicts to the requirements of the changing electricity market as discussed in Section 2.1. As a result, in this book we specifically target to increase the efficiency of multi-equation forecast models, with using the EGRV model as an exemplarily representative of this class.

3.4 Estimation of Forecast Models

To allow the calculation of accurate forecasts, the parameters of the forecast model are adapted to the specifics of the corresponding time series. For this purpose numerical optimization algorithms are used that determine the forecast model parameters by minimizing the forecast error, i.e., the deviation of the forecast values to the real values. Accordingly, a naïve estimation approach is to span a logical d-dimensional grid (d = number of model parameters) and sequentially evaluate all possible parameter combinations in a given discrete resolution. While this solution guarantees to find the optimal parameter combination given a sufficient search resolution, it fails for complex models that involve a large number of parameters due to an exponentially increasing search space. Even a relative simple forecast model, e.g. the triple seasonal exponential smoothing model with only five parameters (each within the interval from 0 to 1), leads to a solution space of 20^5 solutions given a search resolution of 20 steps per parameter. Thus, typically more sophisticated optimization algorithms are employed that use heuristics to better anticipate possible solutions.

	Local Optimization	Global Optimization

Derivable	- Gradient Descent
	- (Gauß-) Newton Approach
	- Quasi-Newton Approaches
	  - LBFGS
	  - Levenberg-Marquardt Algorithm
	- Least Square Estimation
	- Maximum Likelihood Estimators
		Not available

Non-Derivable	- Hill Climbing (Hook-Jeeves) - Downhill Simplex (Nelder-Mead) - Secant Method - Bisection Method	- Simulated Annealing - Swarm Algorithm - Genetic Algorithms - Random Restart Local Algorithms - Monte Carlo

Fig. 3.9 Categorization of optimization algorithms.

The optimization algorithms can be classified along two dimensions. The first dimension distinguishes local and global optimization algorithms. Local algorithms typically use a directed search approach trying to find an optimal solution in the surrounding of a given start point. In contrast, global algorithms consider the entire search space, meaning that they avoid getting stuck in local sub-optima. However, they need a lot more time to find a final solution, therefore they are typically used in conjunction with a time budget. The second dimension classifies the optimization algorithms into approaches that rely on derivable functions and approaches that can be used in conjunction with arbitrary functions. In the context of forecasting the optimization function depends on the employed forecast model and the error metric. Figure 3.9 presents a classification of important optimization algorithms with respect to both dimensions.

In the following we describe local and global optimization algorithms grouped by their characteristic of supporting only derivable or arbitrary functions. In addition, we describe a third option called incremental maintenance, which can be seen as an application of local algorithms that are directly incorporated in the forecast model. Thus, the parameters of a model are automatically adapted with respect to the output of a forecast model. Afterwards, we introduce some example algorithms that we are using for our evaluations in this book.

3.4.1 Optimization of Derivable Functions

Algorithms that pertain to this algorithm class need a derivable error function. By following the gradient of a derivable function, we can quickly find local minima of that function, which means an efficient way to estimate the optimal forecast model parameter combination. The most common example for this algorithm class is the Newton approach [100]. The Newton approach in its original form tries to find the root of a function by iteratively enhancing the result starting from an initial guess x_0. In more detail, starting from x_0 we iteratively determine the intersection of the tangent at the given point with the x-axis, which is a new approximation of the root. This can be formalized to:

$$x_{n+1} = x_n - \frac{f(x_n)}{f'(x_n)} \tag{3.13}$$

When using the first $f'(x_n)$ and second $f''(x_n)$ derivation we can use the Newton approach to also find minima and maxima of a function. Several other algorithms base on the Newton approach and further enhance it. The Gau-Newton approach [100] for example avoids the need of the second derivative that might be hard to calculate, but the approach can only be used to minimize a sum of squared function values. Furthermore, Quasi-Newton approaches [65, 101] replace complicated second derivative calculations by successive gradient evaluations. Common quasi-Newton methods are the Broyden-Fletcher-Goldfarb-Shanno (BFGS) algorithm [31, 99, 118, 210], the Levenberg-Marquardt algorithm [156, 161] and Berndt-Hall-Hall-Hausman [14]. Besides the Newton-based approaches this class also comprises other algorithms such as the gradient descent, which can be seen as an adaption of Euler's method for solving differential equations to sequences of gradients. Further algorithms base on the least square approaches such as ordinary (OLS), weighted (WLS) and generalized (GLS) least squares [25, 161], and maximum likelihood estimators [137, 163, 164].

The algorithms of this class are directed approaches that are able to converge to a solution relatively fast. However, they are also local optimization algorithms, for what reason they cannot guarantee to find the global optimal solution. Furthermore, some of the algorithms—especially the Newton approach and its derivations—are less robust with respect to the distance of the start point to local optima and the general appearance of the function. For this reason, it is possible that these algorithms even do not converge to a solution at all. Some algorithms such as the Levenberg-Marquardt algorithm [156, 161] try to avoid these drawbacks by combining techniques from several algorithms. In this case the Levenberg-Marquardt algorithm combines the Gauss-Newton approach with the gradient descent method. However, even using these combinatory approaches does not guarantee to find a solution. Another solution to increase the chance of converging to a solution is to combine the algorithms with Monte Carlo grid sampling. This means that all algorithms re-iterate with different start points and thus, multiple areas in the solutions space are considered. As a result, the introduced local algorithms are enabled for global optimization. However, this solution also increases the execution time for those algorithms. To conclude, the presented algorithm class highly depends on the position of the given starting point. Starting points that are already close to the optimum provide a high chance to finally converge to this solution, whereas distant starting points pose the risk for the algorithms to starve in local optima. Thus, providing a good initial guess is crucial for the success of the local optimization algorithms.

3.4.2 Optimization of Arbitrary Functions

Algorithms in this class are more general and flexible, because they can be used in conjunction with arbitrary error function and forecast models. Most common for a local optimization algorithm for arbitrary functions are algorithms that follow the hill climbing technique. They start from a given starting point and iteratively evaluate the neighborhood trying to find a better solution. Thus over time they iteratively move in a direction of better solutions and converge when they reach an optimum where no further improvements are possible in the near surrounding. A first example for a hill climbing algorithm is called the Hooke-Jeeves algorithm [130]. This algorithm evaluates the surrounding of a given point in the solution space, calculates the direction and step length, and takes the best available solution in the surrounding as long as better solutions exist. Thus, it is following a path to an optimum. An alternative is the Nelder Mead or downhill simplex algorithm [177]. It also belongs to the category of hill climbing techniques. Nelder Mead uses a $(d+1)$-dimensional simplex, where d is the number of variables (e.g., the dimensions of the solution space). A detailed description for the Nelder Mead algorithm is provided below in Section 3.4.4. Neither the Nelder Mead nor the Hook Jeeves algorithm can be seen as generally advantageous over the other one. It highly depends on the problem at hand whether one algorithm dominates the other one [178, 243]. In general, the Nelder Mead algorithm counts as more robust towards noise and numerical precision, because the simplex is only ranked by the relative order of its elements. However, for some special function the simplex of the Nelder Mead algorithm might collapse, which means that the algorithm fails to converge. Like local optimization algorithms for derivable functions, the local algorithms for arbitrary functions converge relatively fast and their final quality and performance highly depends on the selection of a good starting point. In addition, they have difficulties with respect to robustness for difficulty shaped functions. Thus, they also require the provisioning of good starting points to converge to the optimal solution.

Besides local optimization algorithms this category comprises algorithms that try to find the global optimal solution. Global optimization approaches consider the entire solution space, which means that they need more time compared to local optimization algorithms. Global optimization algorithms are the aforementioned grid search and nature-inspired algorithms such as simulated annealing [50, 145] or genetic algorithms [117, 219]. Nature-inspired algorithms exploit the character of natural processes. Simulated annealing for example is inspired by the annealing process in the metallurgy domain. The annealing process in metallurgy involves controlled heating and cooling of metal to allow the atoms to randomly take positions in states of higher energy levels. The simulated annealing algorithm replaces a current solution with a randomly selected neighbor solution that is chosen with respect to a calculated acceptance probability. This probability does not solely rely on the result of the solution but also on a pre-defined variable that is decreased during the whole simulation called the temperature. Thus, it is also possible that solutions with worse results are accepted allowing the simulated annealing algorithms to avoid the starvation in local optima, which is a clear advantage of this algorithm. However, given a large search space simulated annealing has either a long runtime compared to local search algorithms or a low chance to find the global optimal solution. For this reason it is possible to cap the runtime of simulated annealing by means of the temperature variable and intermediate results of the algorithm can be used during the optimization process. Genetic algorithms simulate the evolution and mutation of living organisms. This means that from a starting population of solutions the solutions with the best results evolve further and thus, enhance over time. In doing so, genetic algorithms also avoid the starvation in local minima by allowing random mutations during the runtime of the process. However, in average genetic algorithms are slower or deliver worse solutions compared to simulated annealing [154, 160].

3.4.3 Incremental Maintenance

In addition to heuristic, numerical optimization algorithms, there is also the approach to incrementally maintain forecast models. Incremental maintenance tries to adapt data models to new developments of the underlying data by involving the feedback of the model or characteristics of the data development. Thus, the parameters of the model are adapted without employing costly parameter estimation using numerical optimization algorithms. Applied to forecasting incremental maintenance adapts the forecast model to the changing characteristics of an evolving time series typically by considering the forecast error or changes in observable, exogenous factors. One common example for incremental maintenance is the self-learning technique of artificial neural networks called back propagation. In this section, we use this technique to discuss incremental maintenance.

The basic idea of the back propagation algorithm is to adjust the weights ω of the edges E in an artificial neural network by considering the network output and the network error ε with the goal to minimize the error of the neural network [27, 124, 149]. One of the most commonly employed back propagation variant is the gradient descent approach. The gradient descent approach is based on the fact that the output error of an ANN can be interpreted as a function of the weights assigned to the edges. Accordingly, one tries to minimize the output error of the ANN by adapting the weights in the direction of the negative gradient [124]. Back propagation is an efficient method for finding parameters by feeding in the output error that is produced by the neural network and calculating the direction of weight changes directly from these numbers. However, while back propagation is an incremental maintenance approach, it is still using the process of the gradient descent technique that is a local numerical optimization algorithm. By saying that the initial learning of the network still requires a large number of iterations and also involves to determine beneficial values for the parameters of the back propagation algorithm itself (e.g., the learning constant). During runtime back propagation is highly efficient, but since the approach still represents a local optimization, it also exhibits similar drawbacks in the sense that it might get stuck in a local sub optima and thus, missing possible better solutions outside this sub optima.

There has also been some work done for other forecast models in particular simple regression models. An approach similar to back propagation used in ANN was introduced by Balakrishnan, where he propose an incremental adaptation for speech recognition systems. For this purpose, he improves the typical maximum likelihood regression with a gradient descent adaptation, which significantly reduces the computational complexity of the adaptation to a new speaker or environment [12]. Similarly, Jerome Klotz describes a mathematical approach of incrementally maintaining simple linear regressions by just considering arriving current data and prior estimates. Besides the goal of reducing the estimation times, Klotz also aims at avoiding to store previous individual observations [146]. For streaming time series Palpanas et al. propose a framework to allow for an online approximation of such time series streams [186]. The basic idea of their approach is to use amnesic functions adapted to the needs of the specific domains. Thus, they typically accept a less accurate representation for older time series values in comparison to the most recent ones. The amnesic functions are incrementally maintained when new data points arrive, which means for them that the approximation is updated in sub linear time.

While incremental maintenance is an efficient approach for maintaining forecast models and adapting them to the most recent developments, it also poses very specific requirements to the models and involved components (error calculation, optimizer, etc.). When referring to the back propagation algorithm, the error calculations as well as the calculations of the weights are required to be derivable. In addition, a strict and direct relationship between the multiple layers is required. Thus, only a limited number of forecast models do support incremental maintenance. This is especially an issue in the energy domain where a large variety of situation-specific and customer-specific forecast models exist. In addition, the most commonly used forecast models—namely exponential smoothing and box-jenkins models—are not or only to a very limited extend incrementally maintainable (for box-jenkins models we found in our research group that only AR(1) models are incrementally maintainable). Furthermore, in most cases incremental maintenance only provides solutions in a local environment. Thus, it exhibits the same disadvantage as local search algorithms, meaning that it might get stuck in a local sub optima. As a result, incremental maintenance is a very valid option for maintaining forecast models as long as all involved components support it. For the majority of all forecast models other solutions are required where we propose options that are both efficient and accurate at the same time.

3.4.4 Local and Global Forecasting Algorithms Used in this book

In the following we present some commonly used local and global optimization algorithms. The description focuses on the algorithms that we exemplarily use throughout this book.

Local - Arbitrary: Nelder Mead Downhill-Simplex

The Nelder-Mead Downhill Simplex algorithms is a local directed approach developed by John Nelder and Roger Mead [177]. It does not need any derivatives and thus, can be used with arbitrary functions. The algorithm is based on a simplex that contains $n + 1$ vertices in an n-dimensional optimization space. Thus, n in the context of forecast model parameter estimation represents the number of forecast model parameters. In each iteration the algorithm moves the simplex through the optimization space by substituting the currently worst point in the simplex. For this purpose, it employs five different simplex transformations illustrated in Figure 3.10.

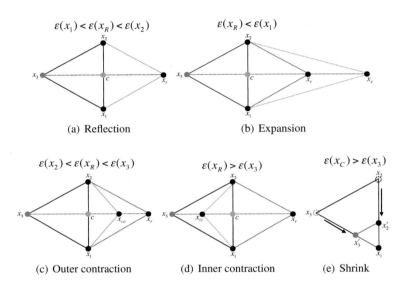

(a) Reflection   (b) Expansion

(c) Outer contraction   (d) Inner contraction   (e) Shrink

Fig. 3.10 Nelder mead transformation moves.

Among these transformations two are used to expand the simplex and three to reduce it. In general a single iteration of the Nelder Mead Downhill Simplex algorithm works as follows:

1. **Order:** Order the points in the simplex with respect to their quality, i.e., for forecast model with respect to their forecast error. Thus, we arrive at $x_1, x_2, ..., x_{n-1}, x_n$ with $\varepsilon(x_1) < \varepsilon(x_2) < ... < \varepsilon(x_{n-1}) < \varepsilon(x_n)$. In this context ε is the quality or error function and $<$ means better. The most important points are the best x_1, second worst x_{n-1} and the worst point x_n.
2. **Centroid:** Calculate the centroid c of the simplex using all points but the worst as the arithmetic mean of all points: $\frac{1}{n-1}\sum_{j=1}^{n-1} x_j$.
3. **Transformation:** Start transformations with special weighting factors for each transformation: Reflection $\alpha = 1$, Expansion $\gamma = 2$, Contraction $\beta = \frac{1}{2}$, Shrink $\delta = \frac{1}{2}$. The given values for the weights are commonly accepted as standard weights [177]. However, it is also possible to determine the weights in accordance to the dimensionality of the optimization problem, which typically yields

better results [106]. The parameters are then defined as: Reflection $\alpha = 1$, Expansion $\gamma = 1 + \left(\frac{2}{dim}\right)$, Contraction $\beta = \frac{3}{4} - \left(\frac{1}{(2 \cdot dim)}\right)$, Shrink $\delta = 1 - \left(\frac{1}{dim}\right)$. The first transformation in each iteration is to reflect the worst point x_n on the calculated centroid c using $x_r = (1 + \alpha) \cdot c - \alpha \cdot x_n$. Depending on the quality of the resulting reflected point $\varepsilon(x_r)$ the further steps are chosen.

4. **Accept Transformation:** If $\varepsilon(x_1) < \varepsilon(x_r) < \varepsilon(x_{n-1})$ accept the reflected point and start a new iteration.

5. **Expand:** If $\varepsilon(x_r) < \varepsilon(x_1)$ expand the reflected point as $x_e = (1 + \gamma) \cdot x_r - \gamma \cdot c$. If $\varepsilon(x_e) < \varepsilon(x_1)$ replace the worst point x_n with x_e, otherwise accept x_r. Start a new iteration. This means that the point x_e is accepted regardless of a quality comparison with x_r, which means that x_e is accepted even if $\varepsilon(x_e) > \varepsilon(x_r)$. The reason is that the simplex should be as large as possible to avoid premature convergence.

6. **Outer Contraction:** If $\varepsilon(x_{n-1}) < \varepsilon(x_r) < \varepsilon(x_n)$ an outer contraction is performed with $x_{co} = (1 + \beta) \cdot x_r - \beta \cdot c$. Replace the worst point x_n when $\varepsilon(x_{co}) < \varepsilon(x_r)$ and start a new iteration or otherwise perform a shrink transformation.

7. **Inner Contraction:** If $\varepsilon(x_n) < \varepsilon(x_r)$ an inner contraction is performed with $x_{ci} = (1 + \beta) \cdot x_n - \beta \cdot c$. Replace the worst point x_n when $\varepsilon(x_{co}) < \varepsilon x_n$ and start a new iteration or otherwise perform a shrink transformation.

8. **Shrink:** If the contraction fails a last emergency transformation is to calculate a smaller simplex around the currently best point using $x_n' = x_1 + \delta \cdot (x_n - x_1)$ with $n \neq 1$ and start a new iteration.

The Nelder Mead Downhill Simplex algorithm repeats the iterations until a termination criterion is met. Possible termination criterions are a minimum quality improvement, a minimum difference between the worst and the best point, and a time budget / number of iterations (non-convergence coverage).

Local - Derivable: Broyden–Fletcher–Goldfarb–Shanno ((L-)BFGS)

The BFGS optimization algorithm is a quasi-Newton optimization approach developed by Broyden, Fletcher, Goldfarb and Shanno [31, 99, 118, 210]. While the classical Newton's method optimizes a function using gradients and a calculated Hessian matrix of the second derivatives, quasi-newton approaches like BFGS avoid the complicated and computationally expensive calculation of the Hessian matrix H. Instead, they approximate the Hessian matrix using gradient vector analysis [32, 181]. A single iteration of the BFGS algorithms is represented by the following equation [43, 158, 180]:

$$x_{k+1} = x_k - \lambda_k H_k g_k \ k = 0, 1, 2, \ldots \tag{3.14}$$

where λ_k is the define step length at step k, g_k is the gradient of the function at point x_k and H_k is the approximation of the inverse Hessian matrix at point in time k. Thus, the next point x_{k+1} is determined as a step of length λ_k following the direction of the steepest descent given by the current gradient g_k towards the point given by the second order derivatives represented by the Hessian approximation. The Hessian matrix is updated in each iteration using vectors defined by the current movement s_k and the development of the gradient y_k, which results in the following update equation [43, 158, 180]:

$$H_{k+1} = V_k^T H_k V_k + p_k s_k s_k^T, \tag{3.15}$$

where

$$p_k = 1/y_k^T s_k, \qquad V_k = I - p_k y_k s_k \tag{3.16}$$

and

$$s_k = x_{k+1} - x_k, \qquad y_k = g_{k+1} - g_k \tag{3.17}$$

The L-BFGS algorithm or limited-memory BFGS is an enhancement over the original BFGS algorithm with less memory consumption [43, 158, 180]. Instead of storing a dense approximation of the Hessian like the original BFGS, the L-BFGS just stores an implicit Hessian approximation using a small number of representative vectors. In particular, the implicit representation means to just store a number m of last update vectors, meaning the last s_k and x_k vectors. The product $H_k g_k$ is then calculated using the gradient g_k and replacing H_k by recursively applying the m most recent update vectors [43, 158, 180]. Nocedal developed an efficient two loop recursion algorithm for performing this task [158, 180]. Due to not storing the entire Hessian approximation, the L-BFGS algorithm is especially suited for large optimization problems involving a large number of parameters. A further variation of the BFGS algorithm is the L-BFGS with support for bound constraints L-BFGS-B [42].

Global - Arbitrary: Simulated Annealing

Simulated annealing is a global optimization algorithm that is inspired by the natural thermodynamic process observed when cooling down different materials from a heated state. There, molecules randomly move around at high temperatures, but loose mobility with decreasing temperature and eventually take a stable state when the temperature is approaching zero degrees. Similarly simulated annealing conducts random moves similar to Monte Carlo algorithms in the beginning, but with progressing time converges to a final solution. Simulated annealing was developed by Scott Kirkpatrick et al. in 1983 [145] and is based on the metropolis algorithm developed by Nicolas Metropolis [167]. The basis for the simulated annealing algorithm are system states s including their energy configuration $f_e(s)$. The energy configuration in this sense can be seen as a quality function for a solution. The goal of the algorithm is to find a system state with minimal energy analogous to the cooling of heated material. To do so the current state is replaced by other states in the neighborhood defined by a given step length. States with a lower energy are directly accepted as a better solution. States with a higher energy can still be accepted as a regular move with a certain probability that is given by the metropolis criterion from the metropolis algorithm [167]. The associated probability function $P(f_e(s_n), f_e(s_{n+1})), T_n$ considers the energy of the current state $f_e(s_n)$, the energy of the possible next state $f_e(s_{n+1})$ and a temperature constant T_n. Using this function the probability that a state is accepted can be determined as:

$$P_{accept} = min\left(1, \exp\left(-\frac{f_e(s_{n+1}) - f_e(s_n)}{T}\right)\right) > r, \quad \text{with} \quad r = rand[0..1]$$

(3.18)

Here, r is a random number between 0 and 1 and thus, a state with an inferior energy is still accepted as long as r is smaller than the acceptance probability P_{accept}. Thus, with decreasing temperature values the affinity to accept worse states also decreases, meaning that the global simulated annealing algorithm becomes more and more similar to a local greedy algorithm over time. The temperature decreases following a user-defined annealing schedule, which should start with an initially high temperature and is required to end with $T = 0$. A typical execution schedule is for example to measure the time needed for one iteration and using this input to estimate the number of iterations within the given time budget. With that, the simulated annealing algorithm is expected to be close to its final result, when it is stopped by the given time budget. The complete progression of the simulated annealing algorithm is illustrated in Algorithm 3.4.1.

Algorithm 3.4.1: Simulated annealing algorithm.

---

input : initial state s, initial temperature T, step width s

$s_{best} \longleftarrow$ max();
$e_{best} \longleftarrow$ max();

repeat
    $s_{curr} \longleftarrow$ randNeighbor(s);
    $r \longleftarrow$ rand(0..1);
    if $P(f_e(s), f_e(s_{curr}), T) > r$ **then**
        $s \longleftarrow s_{curr}$;
        if $f_e(s_{curr}) < e_{best}$ **then**
            $s_{best} \longleftarrow s_{curr}$;
            $e_{best} \longleftarrow f_e(s_{curr})$;
    $T \longleftarrow$ schedule(T);
until *termination()*;
return s_{best};

3.5 Challenges for Forecasting in the Energy Domain

Based on our analysis of the current electricity market developments in Chapter 2 and our discussion of forecast models and optimization algorithms in this chapter, we identified the following fundamental challenges for forecasting in the energy domain:

3.5.1 Exponentially Increasing Search Space

To enable accurate forecasting it is necessary to specifically adapt the employed forecast models to the characteristics and development of the time series at hand. This is typically done by estimating the forecast model parameters on a training dataset with the goal of minimizing the forecast error. The optimization task is complex, because the parameter search space increases exponentially with the number of parameters. The energy-domain-specific EGRV forecast model [197] for example exhibits up to 30 parameters per sub-model, which means that for each sub-model we have to deal with a 30-dimensional search space . As a result, it is generally not possible to use the naïve approach of evaluating all possible parameter combinations in an arbitrary granularity, which is the only way of guaranteeing to find the global optimal solution. Instead, numerical optimization algorithms are employed that use heuristic approaches to evaluate different parameter combinations. This means following a directed progression when using local algorithms or a more general selection when using global algorithms. Even with using heuristic approaches, the optimization task involves a large number of iterations, where each iteration scans the entire time series provided as training data. The reason is that for each parameter combination the optimization algorithms simulates a rolling forecast and calculates the forecast error for each point in time over the entire training dataset. As a result, the parameter estimation renders the entire forecasting process very expensive and time consuming. Thus, the parameter estimation should be target of further improvements to allow a forecasting process that complies to the requirements of an efficient forecasting in the energy domain. These improvements mean for example, to provide suitable start points for allowing a better progression of the optimization algorithms, leading to fewer parameter combinations that are evaluated and improving the chance for the algorithm to converge. Furthermore, we can exploit specifics of the forecast models to increase the calculation efficiency and allow parallelization.

3.5.2 *Multi-Optima Search Space*

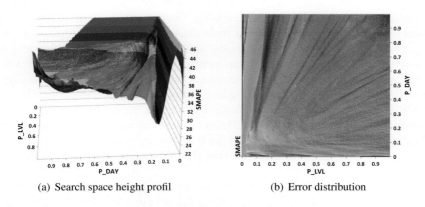

(a) Search space height profil   (b) Error distribution

Fig. 3.11 Example search space illustration (dataset D2, MSESM).

Besides the fact that the parameter search space increases exponentially with the number of parameters, it also exhibits a rather uneven surface with multiple local minima and maxima. This is illustrated in Figure 3.11, where we present the height profile and error distribution of an example stationary search space. The example was created using the MSESM model in conjunction with the MeRegio dataset D2 (compare Table 3.1 in Section 3.1) and the SMAPE error metric. We can see a very rough surface of the search space with a large number of local optima. This makes it hard especially for local optimization algorithms to not get stuck in these local sub-optima and to converge to the single global optima. In addition, due to the high-dimensionality of the search space, global optimization algorithms need a lot more time. This means that always using global search algorithms as the main optimizer class is not a feasible alternative in an environment that requires a rapid provisioning of accurate forecasts as for example when calculating short-term forecasts for the day-to-day grid operations. As a result, we concentrate on solutions that identify and provide beneficial starting points for the local optimization algorithms independently and asynchronously to the actual parameter estimation. However, it is important to note that it is not possible to guarantee that a solution is the global optimum, without trying out all possible solutions. Nevertheless, with a suitable heuristic and the usage of sophisticated local search algorithms, we can increase the chances for finding the global optimum.

3.5.3 Continuous Evaluation and Estimation

As already discussed in Section 3.1 the temporal development of time series in the energy domain is driven by time series context. Changes in this time series context can cause significant changes in the future time series development, for what reason it is necessary to detect these changes and adapt the forecast model accordingly. The reason is that changing time series characteristics often lead to changing optimal forecast model parameters. This is illustrated in Figure 3.12, where we evaluated the optimal forecast model parameters over time for one equation of the EGRV forecast model (Figure 3.12(a)) and the MSESM model (Figure 3.12(b)). For the EGRV model we can see strong fluctuation of all presented parameters for the entire time. The MSESM model exhibits strong fluctuations and large peaks at the beginning, but later on the parameters change more gradually. However, in both cases the forecast model should be adapted to allow for the best possible forecasting accuracy.

As a result, the constantly changing time series context leads to changing time series behavior, which in turn causes changes in the optimal values of the forecast model parameters. To address these challenges the forecast process should support a continuous evaluation of the forecast model accuracy and a constant forecast model maintenance to adapt the forecast models with respect to the most recent changes of the time series characteristics. This is especially a challenge in the view of the fact that in the energy domain accurate forecast are required at any point in time and many applications require rapid forecasting calculations upon request providing individual requirements to the forecasting process.

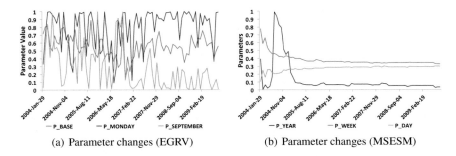

(a) Parameter changes (EGRV)   (b) Parameter changes (MSESM)

Fig. 3.12 Optimal forecast model parameters changing over time (dataset D1).

3.5.4 Further Challenges

In addition to the three specific challenges, there are also several additional challenges that are created by the process of balancing energy demand and supply within the electricity market.

Short-Term and Long-Term Forecasts: The separate processes of one-day-ahead planning and intra-day re-scheduling require forecast models that allows for very accurate very-short- and short-term forecasts and accurate long-term forecasts. In this book we explicitly focus on the very-short term and short-term horizon, meaning an intra-hour horizon up to some days ahead. The reason is that these horizons are most important for the day-to-day balancing and grid management in the changing electricity markets [153, 239, 251]. Also it is common sense in the research domain dealing with energy-related forecasting, that the short-term horizon is the most important horizon and the most interesting field of research [128, 251].

High Update Rates: Time series in the energy domain exhibit high update rate because one can measure the actual energy consumption and production at arbitrary granularity (with regard to all aggregation dimensions), where all these measurements exhibit an append-only characteristic. The advantage for forecasting is that the updates offer continuous feedback. A challenge results from the high update rate, because it poses high efficiency challenges and flexibility requirements. Thus, forecast models are required to pick-up these changes and adapt with respect to changing time series characteristics [11, 128, 165]. These adaptations typically involve the re-estimation of all forecast model parameters and are thus, almost as expensive as the initial estimation. As a result, these dynamics should be taken into account for defining efficient forecast calculation processes.

Hierarchical Data Warehouse: Due to the regionally distributed actors of the energy demand and supply balancing process, the data management architecture exhibit the character of a hierarchical or multi-tier data warehouse that is physically distributed in order to allow for high scalability (compare Sections 2.1.1 and 2.2.2 for the hierarchical organization of the European electricity market). This characteristic requires the distributed maintenance of forecast models and their synchronization in order to guarantee the convergence of forecasts. In contrast to existing systems where forecasting has been independent, now the need of synchronizing distributed models arises.

Chapter 4
The Online Forecasting Process: Efficiently Providing Accurate Predictions

Based on the new developments of the electricity markets and the resulting changing requirements for the forecasting calculation (compare Section 2) as well as the identified general challenges for forecasting in the energy domain (compare Section 3.5), we now introduce a novel online forecasting process that tackles these challenges and requirements. The online forecasting process uses forecast model materialization in conjunction with flexible, iterative parameter estimation to rapidly provide accurate forecasts in an application-aware manner.

Before defining the online forecasting process, we present the most important general requirements we have identified. Afterwards we discuss the currently used conventional process for calculating and maintaining forecasts and discuss the applicability by comparing them to the defined requirements. Following the detailed introduction of our novel online forecasting process, we introduce our design proposal of a tightly integrated forecasting component that directly works as part of an energy data management system. All components discussed in this chapter—the online forecasting process as well as the tightly integrated forecasting component—require further optimizations to fully comply to the defined requirements. These optimizations are introduced in the subsequent Chapters 5 and 6.

The content of this chapter was published in [55], [95] and [59].

4.1 Requirements for Designing a Novel Forecasting Process

The new developments in the European electricity market and an increasing amount of renewable energy sources pose new challenges and requirements on the forecasting calculation process. The energy production of renewables is very hard to predict due to their intermittency and suddenly occurring fluctuations. This is especially true for the most important short-term forecast horizon exhibiting lead times of not more than just a couple of minutes to hours. As a result, balance responsible parties and transmission system operators are required to react more flexible on changing load and supply situations. Furthermore, we can observe a strong push towards energy trading close to real-time, which is also motivated by the increasing share of renewable energy sources and the need for more frequent load and supply changes. The fundamental challenges as defined in Chapter 2 as well as the challenges identified in Section 3.5 lead to specific requirements for establishing a forecasting process in the current electricity market setting and its assumed future development. In the following, we describe the most important requirements:

Application-Awareness: Different application areas and responsibilities of entities in the electricity market, lead to application-specific requirements about the runtime and the accuracy of the forecasting calculation process. For this purpose, the forecasting process should be very flexible to adapt to the specific needs of an application. Additionally, applications should have the option to actively influence the progression of the forecasting calculation process.

Efficient Maintenance (Efficient Parameter Re-Estimation): Many applications in the energy domain require accurate forecasts at any point in time. To achieve this goal in the face of a continuous stream of time series updates it is necessary to adapt the forecast models prior to calculating a forecast or in regular intervals to consider the latest time series developments. Since the adaptation is typically very time consuming, more efficient model maintenance strategies have to be developed with the goal of providing a faster calculation of forecasts and thus, a rapid provisioning of forecast results.

Parameterfree Forecasting: Several systems used in the energy domain target to tightly integrate forecasting capabilities that should provide accurate predictions autonomously and without human-interaction. Likewise, the forecasting process should work parameterfree in the sense that no parameters, thresholds, and influencing factors must be specified by the user during runtime. As a result, a forecasting process should provide high accuracy and efficiency without the need of human intervention by trying to compute optimal or near-optimal parameters with regard to the given data.

Agnostic Against Models and Optimizers: In the energy domain a large number of different forecast models and forecast model variations are employed to address the specific requirements of different regions, countries, and companies. The same is true for numerical optimization algorithms. The forecasting calculation process should work with all kinds of forecast models and optimizers. For this purpose, the forecasting component of the EDM interface should define a dedicated interface that can be used to integrate further specific forecast models.

Efficient Integration of External Information: The development of time series is in most cases driven by background processes and influencing factors that we refer to as time series context. However, the incorporation of external information leads to an increasing number of forecast model parameters and thus, to an increase of the search space dimensionality. Thus, it is necessary to develop strategies for incorporating external information that at the same time limited the additional runtime as much as possible.

Hierarchical Forecasting: The electricity market is hierarchically organized as presented in Section 2.1. The forecasting calculation process in these environments is especially complex as it involves data and entities across hierarchical levels. In such environments, special forecasting approaches that allow an efficient forecasting calculation are required.

4.2 The Current Forecasting Calculation Process

In the face of the challenges (presented in Section 3.5) and requirements (defined in Section 4.1) the current forecasting calculation process used in today's energy data management systems (EDMS) exhibits several issues and drawbacks that we are discussing in this section. Figure 4.1 depicts an enhanced illustration of the standard forecasting process.

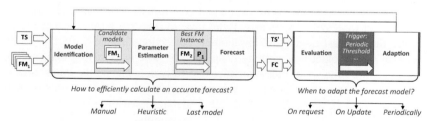

Fig. 4.1 The forecasting calculation process.

We start our discussion with the first phase of the forecasting process namely the calculation phase. This phase starts with identifying the most suitable forecast model for the current time series. Unfortunately, no analytical method is available to determine the best model solely by analyzing a time series. Only some advisor techniques exist, such as the (partial) auto correlation function ((P)ACF) that can limit the number of model candidates, but cannot provide a final choice. As a result, typically human experts or empirical evaluations are used to identify the most accurate forecast model. Both options involve a separate parameter estimation and forecasting calculation for each forecast model considered. This considerably increases the time required for the subsequent overall parameter estimation process.

The goal of this parameter estimation process is to identify parameter combinations that minimize the forecast error of a forecast model. The forecast error represents the deviation of the predicted values from the real values and is measured in terms of an error metric such as the well-known Mean Square Error (MSE) [25]. For this purpose, numerical optimization algorithms are used to empirically evaluate multiple parameter combinations on a training dataset that typically comprises the most recently known observations of the time series. The parameter estimation is computationally very expensive consuming the bulk part of the forecast calculation process. The reason for the computational complexity is that the parameter search space increases exponentially with the number of forecast model parameters. Thus a large number of simulations are required to explore this search space. Once an estimated forecast model is in place, the actual forecast calculation is rather cheap. Overall, the forecasting calculation phase raises the question: "How to efficiently calculate accurate forecasts?", which boils down to an efficient identification of a suitable forecast model and an efficient estimation of the forecast model parameters. Currently, the following three strategies are typically employed when calculating a forecast:

- Manual: A human expert manually selects the most appropriate forecast models and optimization algorithms based on his experience and the observed characteristics of the data. He either manually determines the parameters or triggers an automatic parameter estimation for the selected models. Afterwards he uses the forecast model resulting from his manual determination or from the parameter estimation to calculate forecasts. From time to time the human expert reevaluates the forecast model and implements corrections if necessary. Due to the human involvement this strategy is apparently slow in detecting and reacting on changing time series characteristics and fully depends on the knowledge of the expert. However, even when employing an automated system, this strategy would mean to empirically evaluate all available forecast models and selecting the best result, which is anyway very time consuming.

- Heuristic: Heuristic techniques are used to automatically identify a set of promising forecast models for the data at hand. Examples for these techniques are the (partial) auto-correlation function and the empirical approach of Hyndman et al. [133] that is based on the Akaike information criterion (AIC) [7]. All models identified in this way are estimated using numerical optimization algorithms, where the used algorithms are still selected manually during design time or runtime. Typically this strategy combines local and global optimization algorithms, to ensure the best possible accuracy. However, this strategy restarts the entire forecasting process for each forecasting calculation, meaning that the model identification as well as the parameter estimation of the identified models is repeated. As a result, each forecasting calculation is time consuming, which results in the fact that this strategy is not applicable for environments requiring a rapid provisioning of forecasting results.

- Last model: With respect to the heuristic strategy, we propose an enhancement that optimizes upon the model identification and the starting point determination [55]. After an initialization using the heuristic strategy, the last model strategy always starts from the last used forecast model and its parameter combination. With that, we avoid the costly repeating model identification and provide a good heuristic for determining a suitable starting point for local optimization algorithms. This approach is valid as the parameters of a forecast model typically change rather gradually. Accordingly, the last valid parameter combination usually is a good approximation of a starting point close to the new parameter combination. However, the last model strategy only focuses on a single forecast model. Results of other forecast models, which might be superior, are not covered in the process. Thus, the process is tantamount to starving in local optima.

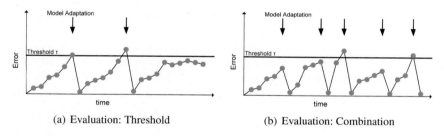

(a) Evaluation: Threshold   (b) Evaluation: Combination

Fig. 4.2 Threshold-based evaluation strategies.

The second phase in the forecasting process is the maintenance of the forecast models. The maintenance phase continuously monitors the accuracy of forecast models and adapts the models with respect to possible changing time series behavior and characteristics. The adaptation itself can be conducted by re-estimating the forecast model parameters or using one of the above mentioned forecasting calculation strategies. As a result, the forecast model adaptation, even when only re-estimating the forecast model parameters, is almost as time consuming as the initial forecasting calculation. Thus, it is important to limit the amount of adaptations to a reasonable amount. In this context, several maintenance strategies exist:

- On-request: The forecast model is adapted to the new time series characteristics every time a forecast is requested. This strategy is very common and for example used in the approach of Ge et al. [108]. The strategy does not require any system resources between requested forecasts. In addition it is very accurate, because it considers the most recent time series developments for the forecasting calculation. However, it also needs the most time to finally provide a forecast to the requesting application.

- On update: The on update strategy adapts the forecast model to each new value that is appended to the time series. As a result, the forecast model is always up-to-date and requests can be answered without any delay. However, this strategy exhibits the drawback of constantly requiring system resources, due to constantly adapting the forecast model. Additionally, not all time series updates change the time series behavior, meaning that in many cases the adaptation might not reveal a better forecast model. Thus, most of the adaptations are meaningless and just create unnecessary system load.
- Periodic: Here, the forecast models are update after a defined interval i.e., after a certain time or a specific number of updates (thus, the on update strategy is a special case of the periodic strategy). While this strategy allows to balance between system load and forecast model accuracy, it poses the challenge of choosing the most appropriate interval. Less frequent adaptations might lead to delays in picking up critical changes in the time series development and thus, causes inaccurate forecast models. In contrast, choosing a very high adaptation frequency, might cause a large number of unnecessary adaptations and thus, unnecessary system load.
- Threshold-based: When using the threshold-based adaptation strategy, the user defines a maximal allowed forecast error. As soon as this error is violated a forecast model adaptation is triggered. For this purpose, recently added values are used to calculate the forecast error with respect to a given error metric. Figure 4.2(a) illustrates this strategy. The threshold-based adaptation allows to adapt the maintenance process with respect to the needs of applications. They can define their maximal acceptable forecast error and the system tries to maintain the forecast error accordingly. However, this strategy also poses the issue of finding a suitable error threshold and thus, exhibits similar drawbacks like the periodic strategy. Additionally, it is not possible to guarantee a certain forecast error beforehand. This in turn results in the fact that one cannot guarantee the existence of a more accurate forecast model, leading to unsuccessful model adaptations in the sense of not reducing the forecast error below the given error threshold. In contrast it is even possible that the forecast error might continuously violate the forecast threshold, leading to further unnecessary forecast model adaptations. Furthermore, the produced forecast error might also change over time. Given an energy demand time series for example, the produced forecast error is typically lower during summer months and higher during winter months. The reason is that summer months exhibit a shape that is easier to describe using a forecast model (compare Section 3.1).

None of the above presented maintenance strategies is suitable for a forecasting system that works in the face of the new requirements posed by the current developments of the European electricity market. The reason is that they do not allow for providing the best possible accuracy, while at the same time limiting the necessary provisioning times and required system load. A first optimization that we published in [55] is a combination of the periodic and threshold-based strategy, which is illustrated in Figure 4.2(b). Thus, re-estimating a forecast model either after a certain amount of time (a certain amount of updates were added) or in between periods as soon as the forecast error violates a certain given threshold. The combination weakens the disadvantage of the single strategies, by eliminating the dependence on a single adaptation criterion. Thus it decreases the effort for defining and maintaining suitable thresholds and the effect of slightly false values is mitigated. However, even using the combination it is not possible to fully prevent the issues of both strategies, meaning that more sophisticated strategies are needed.

	Manual	Heuristic	Last Model	Request	Update	Periodic	Threshold
Application-Awareness	-	-	-	-	-	-	-
Efficient Maintenance	-	-	+	-	-	o	o
Parameterfree	-	+	+	+	+	o	o
External Information	-	-	-	-	-	-	-
Hierarchical Forecasting	-	-	-	-	-	-	-
Accuracy	o	+	o	+	+	o	o
System Load	+	-	+	+	-	o	o

Table 4.1 Applicability of current forecasting approaches.
Legend: + efficiently supported, o partly supported, - not efficiently supported

The typical strategies of calculating forecasts and for maintaining accurate forecast models, exhibit substantial drawbacks when used in conjunction with the new requirements posed by the changing electricity market. We compared the calculation and maintenance strategies with respect to the requirements stated in Section 4.1. In Table 4.1 we can clearly see that there is only very limited support with respect to application-awareness, efficient maintenance, efficient integration of external information and hierarchical forecasting. No strategy allows applications to control and influence the progression of the forecasting process. Even for the periodic and threshold strategy, the intervals or error thresholds are determined during design time and are not controllable by the application during runtime. However, assuming an appropriate interval or error threshold, both strategies have the potential to efficiently maintain forecast models. In contrast, all other strategies either need too much time (manual, heuristic, request), cause high system loads (on-update) or solely focus on a single forecast model (last model). The integration of external information is a good way to increase forecasting accuracy, but none of the above mentioned calculation and maintenance strategies offer an efficient way to incorporate them. The same is true for hierarchical forecasting.

While most techniques can in general be used in a hierarchical forecasting environment, they typically treat each hierarchical layer separately. Thus, they do not increase the forecasting efficiency in such environments. In contrast to the negative points, most strategies provide a sufficient accuracy. Besides the manual calculation strategy that involves human experts, all other strategies calculate forecasts fully automatically and thus, no human involvement during runtime is required. The system load as the last comparison criterion exhibits mixed results. While the manual and last model calculation strategies as well as the on-request maintenance strategy are very modest with respect to system resources, the heuristic strategy and the on-update strategy are computationally rather expensive. Regarding the periodic and the threshold-based strategy the system load depends on the concrete implementation. As a result, a more sophisticated forecasting calculation strategy especially with respect to the adaptation process (often following the forecast calculation strategies) is required to guarantee the constant availability of accurate forecasts.

4.3 The Online Forecasting Process

Our novel online forecasting process optimizes upon the aforementioned challenges by combining and enhancing some of the introduced traditional forecasting calculation and maintenance strategies. This approach addresses the drawbacks of the conventional strategies and creates a forecasting process that is suitable for the requirements of the modern European electricity market. For the forecasting calculation and execution of the adaptation, we combine our last model strategy [55] with the heuristic strategy. The last model strategy allows a relatively efficient adaptation of the forecast model, by reusing the most recently used forecast model instance. By additionally considering the heuristic strategy, we also add the continuous consideration of multiple forecast models and the usage of several local and global optimization algorithms to avoid getting stuck in local optima. As a result, we store a number of different previously used forecast model instances in a forecast model repository. We reuse those instances to calculate an initial forecast that is subsequently improved iteratively by a flexible, automatic optimization process involving several different estimators. With respect to the maintenance strategy our online forecasting process starts on-request. The reason is that with the help of our repository the initial forecast is provided almost instantly (below 1 ms throughout all our experiments). Furthermore, applications can leverage the improvements found during the optimization using a publish/subscribe communication offered by the online forecasting process. We combine the on-request maintenance strategy with a periodic global coverage that searches for further solutions. With that, we avoid the starvation in local optima with respect to forecast models and starting points considered in the forecast model repository.

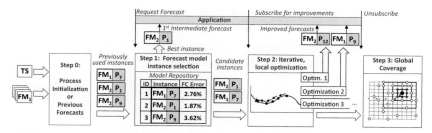

Fig. 4.3 Iterative process for online forecasting.

Figure 4.3 illustrates the online forecasting process in detail. The process starts from a one-time initialization (step 0), which is necessary to fill the forecast model repository with an initial set of forecast model instances. The initialization is required only once when adding a new time series and is executed using the heuristic strategy (compare Section 4.2). Afterwards each time a forecast is requested, we identify the most appropriate forecast model instances (Step 1) from our forecast model repository and use these instances to calculate the first initial solution. The first instance picked is the one used in the last iteration of the online forecasting process, which can be used to almost instantly provide a first forecast. Afterwards, we search the repository for the most accurate instance with respect to the current development of the time series and employ it to produce the first improvement that is provided to the requesting application. Subsequently, we refine all found candidate model instances by re-estimating their parameters using our flexible local optimization process (Step 2). During the optimization we execute pairs of candidate forecast model instances and local optimization algorithms in an order that reflects their potential of finding further improvements. The potential is estimated using statistics about the accuracy improvements over time an optimization algorithm achieved on a respective forecast model in the past. Applications may define runtime constraints or accuracy targets to influence the progression of the estimation process. More accurate forecast model instances found during the optimization are used to calculate improved forecasts that are iteratively provided to the requesting application. Applications can terminate the subscription at any time, in which case the online forecasting process delivers the most accurate forecast found so far. After we successfully processed the request and as soon as free system resources are available, we execute our global coverage process (Step 3). This means that the parameters of randomly selected forecast models are estimated using global optimization algorithms. Potential candidates found during the global coverage, replace less accurate forecast models in the forecast model repository.

They are further optimized when they are selected as forecast model instance candidates during the instance selection (Step 1). Figure 4.4 summarizes the online forecasting process by illustrating the interaction with an application during the execution of the steps 1 and 2.

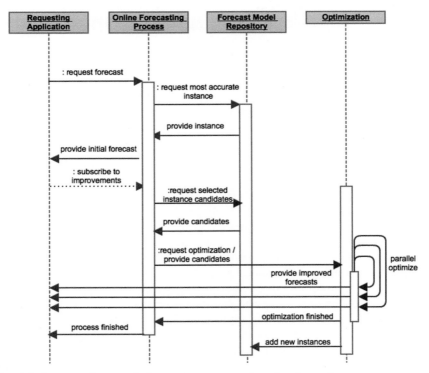

Fig. 4.4 Sequence diagram of a forecasting request to the online forecasting process.

In the following we explain all steps of the online forecasting process in detail.

4.3.1 The Forecast Model Repository

The basis for our online forecasting process is a collection of previously used forecast model instances stored in our forecast model repository. With that, we follow a case-based reasoning approach, where new solutions for a problem are found under consideration of previous solutions. During our experiments we found that forecast model parameters are constantly changing, but the changes are typically rather gradual (compare Section 3.5.3). Therefore, previously used instances are good initial solutions as well as good starting points for optimization algorithms with the goal of finding the most accurate forecast model for the current state of the time series. Accordingly, the most recently used instance contained in the repository is used to calculate the initial solution. Afterwards, we search the repository for instances with a high accuracy on the current state of the time series. The most accurate instance contained in the repository is used to calculate the first improvement that is communicated to the requesting entity. Furthermore, all identified candidate instances serve as the starting point for the subsequent local optimization. As we will show in Section 5.1.2 containing the details about our specific forecast model repository approach, evaluating the applicability and finding instances from the repository is very fast and accurate. As a result this case-based reasoning approach solves two very important issues of the forecasting process: (1) It provides accurate forecast model instances that can be used to calculate very good initial solutions as well as first improvements using only a very short amount of time. (2) It identifies suitable starting points (i.e., a number of very accurate forecast model instances) for the subsequent optimization. In the following we define general requirements that a repository is required to fulfill when used as part of our online forecasting algorithms. In addition, we provide information about the initialization that is necessary for our repository to work.

Requirements for Implementing a Forecast Model Repository

There are multiple options how to implement a forecast model repository that can work with our online forecasting process. Examples are a schema of relational tables or custom implementation-specific containers. However, all implementations of a repository have to comply to the requirements defined in the following:

- **Assess and order forecast model instances:** The repository has to be able to assess and order the forecast model instances by their applicability for the most recent developments of the time series. Thus, the forecast model repository has to provide metrics for evaluating the models (e.g., the metrics defined above). Also, it should allow the external definition of further evaluation metrics.
- **Agnostic against models and optimization algorithms:** The repository should work with all kinds of forecast models and optimization algorithms as long as their implementation complies to a provided interface and further definitions.
- **Tightly integrated into the forecasting system:** The repository should be tightly integrated into the forecasting system, rather than an external component. With that, we allow for an efficient communication between all components.

- **Provide results efficiently:** As the first intermediate forecast as well as the first improvement has to be provided as quickly as possible, the process for selecting the most appropriate forecast model instances has to work very efficiently.
- **Work without human intervention:** Besides basic configuration and design decisions during setup, no further human interaction with the forecast model repository should be necessary during runtime of the online forecasting process.
- **Support time budgets:** The selection process has to support the definition of time constraints and has to be interruptible at any time. When interrupted the selection process provides the currently found forecast model instances to the subsequent parts of the process.

For our implementation we tightly integrate the forecast model repository into the forecasting component of our EDM system. The instances are stored comprising: their forecast model, parameter combination, the start and duration of the model's validity phase, the accuracy they achieved during their last consideration as well as values with respect to the decision criteria.

Initializing the Repository

Before we can start our online forecasting process on a new time series, we have to fill the forecast model repository with an initial set of model instances. Our initialization starts with conducting a forecasting calculation using the heuristic strategy on the first half of the time series. In contrast to the original heuristic strategy, we do not identify the forecast models beforehand, but consider all forecast models available in the system. The resulting instances are added to the forecast model repository. Afterwards we use the periodically maintenance strategy and combine a threshold-based and periodic re-estimation. Thus, we incrementally append the remaining time series values and continuously monitor the forecasting accuracy. As soon as the forecast model violates the configured threshold (threshold-based), but at least once per day (periodic) the online forecasting process is triggered and executed. The simulation ensures a large variety of model instances contained in the repository as well as the consideration of the most recent time series values.

As an alternative it is also possible to avoid the initialization by recording statistics of an already running forecasting system. Forecast model instances created and used during runtime of the system are recorded and stored in the forecast model repository. This initialization option is used in most cases when a live forecasting system exists.

After the initialization the online forecasting process can be used with respect to its typical progression. A further re-initialization is not necessary since the local optimization process and the global coverage, provide sufficient maintenance for the forecast model repository. Typically, an initialization is a required step for any application calculating forecasts. In most cases, the initialization involves an initial global optimization and a subsequent local optimization for all considered forecast models similar to the heuristic strategy. However, due to the additional simulation of our online forecasting process to increase the variety of provided instances our initialization will take more time. Nevertheless, the significantly reduced query response times during runtime compensate for the small disadvantage of a longer initialization. In addition, during the initialization we can still provides forecasting results using either the heuristic approach or forecast model instances from the partially filled repository.

4.3.2 A Flexible and Iterative Optimization for Forecast Models

The flexible, iterative optimization process is the core part of our online forecasting system. In this process we estimate the forecast model instances provided by the forecast model repository using different local optimization algorithms. With that, we aim to increase the probability of finding improved forecast model instances. By starting the optimization from multiple starting points (i.e., forecast model instances) we cover multiple areas of the search space and also avoid getting stuck in a single local optimum. Furthermore, with using different optimization algorithms we avoid a manual choice of a single algorithm that might not find the best possible solution. Our optimization also allows applications to subscribe to the improvements found during the instance refinement. Applications can flexibly control their subscription to the optimization process by defining runtime constraints or accuracy targets. They can also terminate the subscription at any time. For this reason, we execute the combinations of forecast model instances and optimization algorithms called *optimization runs* in an order that reflects their potential to find improvements. We determine the potential by ranking the optimization runs using their expected runtime and accuracy, where we favor optimization runs that are expected to deliver the best improvements in the shortest runtime. In the following we describe the ranking of optimization runs and the handling of constraints in more detail.

Ranking of Optimization Runs

To rapidly provide significant improvements, we determine the most beneficial execution order of the optimization runs by ranking them based on their expected runtime and accuracy. The goal is to first execute optimization runs that are expected to deliver the highest improvements in the shortest runtime. To calculate the ranking we combine the accuracy of the candidate forecast model instance with the expected runtime and accuracy of the assigned optimization algorithm.

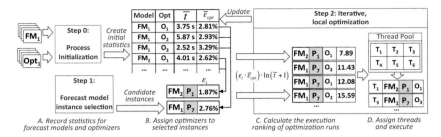

Fig. 4.5 Determining the ranking of optimization runs.

The ranking process is illustrated in Figure 4.5, where in the following we explain each step (A-D) presented in the Figure in more detail.

A: Record model-specific statistics

The basis for estimating the expected runtime and accuracy of the employed optimization algorithms, are statistics recorded during the initialization of our online forecasting process (compare Section 4.3.1). Since both runtime and accuracy of an optimizer highly depends on the forecast model and the starting point, we record individual statistics for each combination of available forecast models (FM_i) and local optimizers (O_j). Fortunately, during the initialization we use the heuristic forecasting calculation strategy considering all supported forecast models. Additionally, the initialization involves multiple starting points, which are all used for calculating the initial statistics. The expected accuracy of an optimizer in conjunction with one forecast model is the median of all resulting forecast errors $\bar{\varepsilon}_{opt}$ for the different starting points P_p. We chose the median over the average, due to its robustness against outliers. For estimating the expected runtime we use the more pessimistic 3rd quartile of the recorded runtimes $\bar{t}$. The reason is that violating runtime constraints is more critical. Thus, we chose a value closer to the worst case, while still ignoring single outliers. In the presence of runtime constraints, we only include optimizers into the optimization process that are expected to finish in the given limits.

B: Assign optimizers to instances

From the forecast model selection step of our online forecasting process we receive the instance candidates that are subject for further refinement. Those instances are already ordered by their accuracy (i.e., their forecast errors), which means that we can directly use these measurements as input for calculating our ranking. We then assign the optimizers to the provided instances. This assignment also involves to allocate the matching statistics with respect to the forecast model of the respective instance. Thus, for the later calculation of the ranking, the instances involving for example forecast model FM_1 (i.e., $FM_1 P_p$) consider the statistics of all optimizers that were recorded for this forecast model.

C: Calculate the execution ranking

In the third step we calculate the execution order of the optimization runs. All three components—the measured accuracy ε_i of the candidate instances as well as the runtime $\bar{t}$ and accuracy $\bar{\varepsilon}_{opt}$ of the optimization algorithms—are combined to compute the ranks of the optimization runs. The rank reflects the expected evolution of the forecast error over the runtime of an optimization run. There are multiple options for calculating the ranking. A first option is to directly use the expected accuracy of the instances or the runtime of the optimization algorithms. However, this would violate the ultimate goal of favoring optimization runs with the highest potential of finding the largest improvements in the shortest runtime. Executing the runs only by their runtime would mean that all fast running optimization runs would be executed first, regardless of their expected potential for finding improvements. Likewise, when ordering the optimization runs by their accuracy, we would execute them without considering their runtime, potentially leading to long execution times. An alternative would be to assume a dependency between the forecasting accuracy and the runtime and use this dependency to determine a calculation rule. A linear dependency for example would result in a simple multiplication of the forecast error and the average runtime $\varepsilon_i \cdot \bar{t}$. However, a linear dependency equally weights runtime and accuracy, meaning that it is hard for very accurate algorithms to compensate for a potentially long runtime. This contradicts to the fact that the ultimate goal is to provide a forecast with the best possible accuracy and not in the shortest possible runtime. Additionally, in our experiments we observed that the runtime $\bar{t}$ of an optimization run asymptotically scales as $t = \mathcal{O}(\exp(C/\varepsilon))$ with decreasing forecast error ε, where C is a parameter characteristic for the algorithm at hand. Accordingly, we assume

$$t = A\exp(C/\varepsilon) + f(\varepsilon) \tag{4.1}$$

where A and C are parameters to be determined and f is a correction to the leading exponential behavior that can be neglected in the limit $\varepsilon \to 0$.

Figure 4.6 presents a plot of $\ln t$ vs. $1/\varepsilon$ for the Nelder Mead algorithm optimizing the triple seasonal exponential smoothing model (compare Section 3.3) on the NationalGrid dataset (compare Section 3.1). We observe the expected linear behavior for small values of ε; the parameters C and A are easily extracted from the slope and intercept of the straight line (red color) fitting $\ln t$ for $1/\varepsilon \to \infty$. We

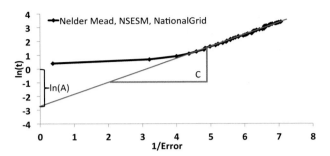

Fig. 4.6 Scaling of the logarithmic runtime $\ln(t)$ with $1/\varepsilon$.

repeated the experiment for other forecast models and optimization algorithms, leading to similar results. Asymptotically, for small forecast errors, runtime and accuracy thus depend on the two parameters A and C, which are characteristic for the forecast model and optimization algorithm of an optimization run. The slope C describes the pace by which an algorithm reduces the forecast error. The smaller the slope, the faster converges the optimization. The offset describes the minimal runtime to find a first result. For our ranking the pace of an algorithm turns out to be the only relevant parameter, as the minimal runtime changed only slightly across algorithms. Thus, omitting the constant offset we compute the rank of an optimization run as $C \leftarrow \varepsilon \cdot \ln(t)$. It is important to note that the expected accuracy of an optimization run is characterized by two forecast errors—the forecast error of the candidate instance ε_i and the expected forecast error of the optimization algorithm $\bar{\varepsilon}_{opt}$. To include both errors, we substitute ε in $C \leftarrow \varepsilon \cdot \ln(t)$ by the product of both forecast errors $\varepsilon_i \cdot \bar{\varepsilon}_{opt}$. We further replace t by $t+1$ preventing negative values arising from the natural logarithm. As a result, the final ranking takes the form

$$C = (\varepsilon_i \cdot \bar{\varepsilon}_{opt}) \cdot \ln(\bar{t}+1). \tag{4.2}$$

Using Eq. 4.2 we calculate a rank for all optimization runs and order them accordingly. The lowest rank represents the optimization run expected to find the largest improvement in the shortest time.

D: Executing the Optimization Runs

For eventually executing the optimization runs, we enqueue all optimization runs in the order of the ranking in a task queue. The system then assigns a number of threads that process the queue in parallel by always picking the optimization run currently on the top of the queue. As soon as an optimization run found an improvement the refined instance is transmitted to the system. If the refined instance is an improvement over the currently best instance, the system calculates an improved forecast that is afterwards provided to the application. Similarly, when an application terminates the subscription, the system immediately stops all optimization runs. We then collect the best instances found so far from all optimization runs and use the best one to calculate a refined forecast that is then delivered to the application as the final result. In addition to the forecasts, we always transmit the achieved forecast error, which can be used to evaluate the quality of the forecast and to create confidence intervals around the prediction. After all optimization runs have converged the flexible local optimization is finished and the subscription is terminated from the system side. In addition to the provisioning of the final forecast, we add the most accurate forecast model instance to our model repository.

Handling of Application Requirements

With the option to define runtime constraints and accuracy targets, we acknowledge the fact that some applications might need a final result after a specific time, while other target a certain accuracy independent of the runtime. Runtime limits provided by applications are handled as hard constraints, meaning that the optimization is canceled with the best results found so far as soon as the runtime limit is reached. Thus, defining a runtime constraint is especially useful when the receipt of a forecasting result is time critical, but the best possible accuracy is not required. Our pEDM ensures the compliance to given runtime constraints two-fold. First, our flexible local optimization ensures that we only execute optimization runs that are expected to finish in the given runtime limits. Second, during the optimization, we execute the optimization runs in the order given by their ranking, but also consider the remaining time that is available. This means that as soon as the next optimization run in line is not expected to finish in the remaining time, we choose other optimization runs with an expected runtime that complies to the rest of the time limit. If non of the remaining optimization runs matches the rest of the runtime, than the next optimization run in the order is chosen and is executed until the runtime limit is reached. It then finishes with the best instance found so far. For this purpose, all optimization algorithms are implemented in a way that they can provide the currently best result at any time.

Figure 4.7 illustrates the scheduling and assignment of optimization runs to multiple threads. There, we can see in field 1 that the first four optimization runs (OR_1 – OR_4) can be assigned under the consideration of the given runtime limit (12 s). However, the subsequent optimization runs OR_5 and OR_6 would violate the remaining time budget and thus, are not assigned at this point in time (field 2). Instead, we search for the next optimization that fits the remaining time. In this example the only remaining optimization run fitting the remaining budget is OR_7, which is assigned to the first thread accordingly. Since no remaining optimization

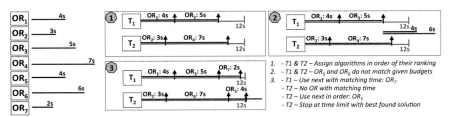

Fig. 4.7 Scheduling of optimization runs using multiple threads.

runs match the left runtime, we assign the next optimization run in order (OR_5) to thread 2 and allow its execution until the runtime limit is reached. If OR_5 is finding an improvement within the reduced runtime, it is likewise provided to the requesting application.

Besides defining runtime constraints it is also possible for application to set accuracy targets. We do not allow the definition of accuracy constraints, since is not possible to guarantee a certain forecasting accuracy. We interpret an accuracy target as a premature convergence criterion, meaning that we finish the optimization as soon as we reached the defined accuracy. This is especially useful for applications that can accept a certain forecast error for executing their tasks. As soon as we reached the target accuracy, we calculate the final forecast and provide it to the application. If the accuracy target cannot be reached, the optimization finishes after all optimization runs converged or when the application terminates the subscription. In this case we provide the best accuracy found during the optimization. Applications may also combine runtime constraints and accuracy targets.

Handling Multiple Requests

Besides the local scheduling of our optimization runs, we also have to deal with a global scheduling when handling multiple requests in parallel. The reason is that the system typically only has a limited number of system resources available (i.e., hardware threads) for executing the online forecasting process. However, we still aim at providing forecasting results as fast as possible for all requests that are issued to our system. In addition, we target to provide an efficient utilization of the available threads. For this purpose, we do not realize a global scheduling by using a fixed assignment of threads to requests, but instead utilize the flexibility of our online forecasting process and the ranking of the optimization runs. This means that each thread processes optimization runs independently of the source request in the order of a global priority. This global priority is determined using two criteria: (1) the original position of the optimization run in the local task queue of the request and (2) the order the requests arrived. From both criteria the local positioning is given precedence over the request arrival order. Thus, only when the positions in the local task queues are the same for all optimization runs, the priority is given to the optimization run from the first issued request. Overall, the proposed strategy is a variation of Tanenbaum's *priority scheduling* combined with his *fair-share scheduling* strategy [225]. With the fair-share part of our adapted priority scheduling approach we aim at executing at least the optimization run with the highest priority from each arriving forecasting request.

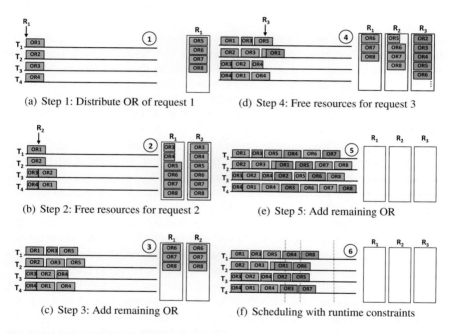

(a) Step 1: Distribute OR of request 1

(d) Step 4: Free resources for request 3

(b) Step 2: Free resources for request 2

(e) Step 5: Add remaining OR

(c) Step 3: Add remaining OR

(f) Scheduling with runtime constraints

Fig. 4.8 Global scheduling of optimization runs.

Figure 4.8 illustrates a task scheduling using our priority scheduling approach. As long as there is only a single request present in the system, all four hardware threads that we assume in this example are used to process the optimization runs (in the figure denoted by OR) of this request in parallel (Step 1: Figure 4.8(a)). Upon arrival of a second request, we pause the optimization runs from request 1 that have a lower global priority than optimization runs of the new request 2. This means in this case that we stop OR3 and OR4 of request 1 to execute OR1 and OR2 of request 2 (Step 2: Figure 4.8(b)). Thus, we still process the most important optimization runs of request 1, but additionally also process the two most important optimization runs of request 2. Afterwards we resume OR3 of request 1 and add

OR3 of request 2. We follow the same strategy for scheduling OR4 and OR5 of both requests (Step 3: Figure 4.8(c)). As soon as request 3 arrives, the candidates for pausing are OR5 of both requests 1 and 2. For this situation we use the second priority criterion that is the order of request arrival, which means that OR5 of request 1 has a higher priority. Thus, we pause OR5 of request 2 and use the thread to execute OR1 of request 3 (Step 4: Figure 4.8(d)). The remaining optimization runs are scheduled accordingly (Step 5: 4.8(e)). Using the scheduling strategy in conjunction with runtime constraints means that optimization runs not expected to finish before the deadline are not executed at all. The same is true for paused optimization runs that cannot be resumed before the runtime limit (Step 6: 4.8(f)).

In general the presented strategy of preferring the local queue position of an optimization over the arrival time of a request works well for most cases. The reason is that the optimization runs with the best position in the local queues, have the highest potential of finding the best improvements in a reasonable amount of time. With that, we ensure that for each request at least the most promising optimization runs are always executed and thus, we can quickly provide accurate forecasting results for all arriving requests. However, priority based strategies exhibit the major drawback that lower priority tasks might starve in the presence of a large amount of high priority tasks. As a consequence, requests might not finish at all and only provide the results of the optimization runs with the highest priority. In general, we may accept this drawback since optimization runs with a lower priority are only executed as a safeguard to ensure that no better solution is missed. Thus, it is reasonable to not sacrifice the execution of high priority optimization runs, for finishing a remaining request with only lower priority optimization runs in the queue. In addition, applications are still able to work with the results provided by high priority optimization runs and terminate the request if it takes too long.

Nevertheless, to still mitigate the issue of starving low priority tasks we propose an enhancement using dynamic priorities. This means that instead of assigning fixed global priorities, we increase the priority of optimization runs over time using some mathematical function e.g., a linear function or an exponential function. The priority increase can be done using a separate time schedule or between processing optimization runs. Thus, after some time low priority tasks receive a rating that allows their execution, even though higher priority tasks might arrive. This strategy avoids the risk that some tasks starve and are never finished. In contrast, it marginally increases the risk that high priority optimization runs are delayed. This can happen when a large number of requests is processed in parallel and thus, at some point a large number of low priority optimization runs is preferred over high priority optimization runs. Still, the proposed enhancement provides a reasonable balancing between accuracy and request execution time.

Besides priority-based scheduling, Tanenbaum proposed further scheduling techniques such as *first-come first-served*, *round robin* or strategies based on execution time. However, with these approaches it is not possible to distinguish optimization runs by their potential of finding improvements equally involving accuracy and execution time. Thus, optimization runs with a high potential could be delayed in favor of optimization runs with a lower potential but earlier arrival time. As a result, the alternative strategies would increase the initial response time of our local optimization for later arriving requests. This especially means that we could not comply to our goal of providing a first improvement as quickly as possible for each arriving request. Besides the approaches from Tanenbaum one could also use more sophisticated scheduling algorithms that try to find the most appropriate schedule in the sense of fair resource allocation and process finishing time. However, the problem of fair resource allocation is *NP-hard*, meaning that it is not possible to find the optimal solution in polynomial time [225, 240]. Thus, in most cases heuristic approaches such as simulated annealing [142] or particle swarm optimization [240] are used that however typically still need a large amount of time to propose a schedule and still cannot guarantee its optimality [184]. Since we target to create an interactive system that provides forecasting results as fast and accurate as possible, we do not want to waste execution time on re-executing the optimization algorithms each time a request is issued. In contrast, our goal is to use the time for executing as many optimization runs as possible. In addition, dynamic task scheduling is not the main focus of this thesis. For this reason, we exclude the consideration of sophisticated scheduling algorithms for handling multiple requests in parallel.

Covering the Global Search Space

We complete our online forecasting process with a global coverage step that aims at reducing the risk of missing better solutions in areas of the search space not covered by the local optimization. This concerns both forecast models supported by the system, but that are currently not considered by the forecast model repository as well as parameter combinations in other regions of the parameter search space. For this purpose the global coverage process executes multiple standard global search algorithms such as simulated annealing or generic algorithms on different forecast models with the goal of finding new promising forecast model instances. Promising instances in this sense mean forecast model instances that at least exhibit a better accuracy than the currently worst model included in the forecast model repository.

The global coverage process is illustrated in Figure 4.9. We start with assigning each global optimization algorithm randomly to one supported forecast model. Due to the random assignment, over time we eventually cover the complete space of possible combinations of forecast models and global optimization algorithms. Since global optimization algorithms typically consider the entire search space, it is not necessary to provide any starting points. We execute the global coverage pro-

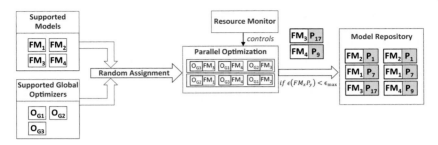

Fig. 4.9 Global coverage process.

cess asynchronously to forecasting requests as some kind of a background process and only if free resources are available. Accordingly, we manage the global coverage using a resource monitor that can pause and resume the process at any time. Models found during the global optimization are directly stored in the forecast model repository without further refinement. They are considered in future executions of the online forecasting process, where they are then refined during the flexible local optimization. Thus, the global coverage serves as the maintenance for our forecast model repository.

4.3.3 Evaluation

In our evaluation we show that our online forecasting process efficiently provides accurate results and iteratively delivers improvements as part of our process subscription. For this purpose, we use the multi-equation EGRV forecast model as well as the two and three seasonal version of Taylor's single-equation exponential smoothing model (ESM) (compare Section 3.3). For the optimization we use the local algorithms LBFGS and Nelder Mead Downhill Simplex as well as the global algorithm simulated annealing (compare Section 3.4). To allow a meaningful and fair evaluation as well as readable results, we limited the number of forecast models and optimization algorithms used in our online forecasting process. However, our prototype system supports a much broader variety of models and algorithms. The evaluation is based on the datasets D1 and D2 (compare Section 3.1).

The evaluation was conducted on a 4-Core Intel Core i7-870 (2.93 GHz, Hyper-Threading), 16GB RAM, 320GB HDD, Windows 7 SP1. Our prototype is written in C++ (GCC 4.6.1) and uses Intel TBB (4.1 U2) for the parallelization (8 threads).

Online Forecasting: Comparison of Estimation Strategies

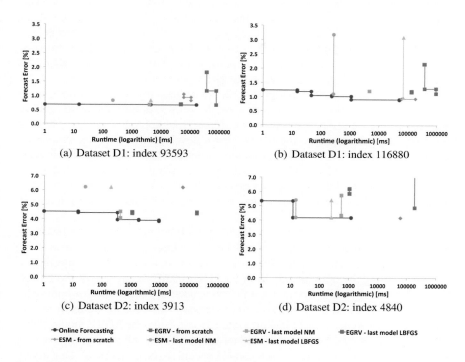

(a) Dataset D1: index 93593

(b) Dataset D1: index 116880

(c) Dataset D2: index 3913

(d) Dataset D2: index 4840

Online Forecasting • EGRV - from scratch • EGRV - last model NM • EGRV - last model LBFGS
ESM - from scratch • ESM - last model NM • ESM - last model LBFGS • ESM - last model LBFGS

Fig. 4.10 Comparing the online forecasting process to other strategies.

In our experiment we compare our online forecasting process with the last model strategy and an estimation from scratch that is typically part of the heuristic strategy (compare Section 4.2). The last model strategy separately evaluates both models and both local optimizers, starting the forecast model optimization from its last used instance. The estimation from scratch individually evaluates both forecast models, but executes all optimizers successively, starting with the global optimization. We empirically determined the best runtime for the simulated annealing and eventually used 60 s per equation for the D1 dataset and 10 s per equation for the D2 dataset. It is important to note that neither the last model strategy nor the estimation from scratch are iterative processes, meaning that no forecast is calculated from the last used model instance (last model) or from intermediate results (from scratch). Forecasts are only calculated from the final instance. However, to still present the error development, we added markers for the forecast error of the last used instance and the intermediate results. From the D1 dataset we used the years

2002 to 2005 for the initialization and the time frame 2006 to 30.04.2007 to simulate the strategies. Afterwards, we executed all strategies at distinct evaluation points and recorded the error development over the runtime respectively. The evaluation points we selected for presentation are (1) May 5th 2007, 21:30 and (2) September 1st 2008, 0:30. For the D2 dataset we used November 2009 to February 2010 for the initialization and simulated the approaches from March to April 2010. As evaluation points we used (1) April 13th 2010, 1:00 and (2) May 21st 2010, 16:00h. All not presented evaluation points showed similar results.

The results are illustrated in Figure 4.10. We decided to use a logarithmic scale for the runtime, to allow a detailed view on the results, despite the large runtime differences. On both datasets, our online forecasting approach showed the best performance with respect to the forecast error development over time compared to all other strategies. The first forecast model instance was always available after around 1 ms and provided in all cases a better or on par accuracy compared to the last model strategy. This means that with the help of the forecast model repository we can almost instantly provide a first very accurate forecast to the requesting application.

The results for the D1 dataset are illustrated in Figures 4.10(a) and 4.10(b). At the first evaluation point (Figure 4.10(a)) the online forecasting process selects the most accurate forecast model instance right at the beginning, which is only slightly improved during the optimization from 0.683 % to 0.677 %. Similarly, the EGRV last model strategy starts from almost the same accuracy (0.695 %) for both optimizers, which likewise did not find an improvement. However, the online forecasting process almost instantly (1 ms) provides a result, while the EGRV model needs 3,947 ms using Nelder Mead and 48,518 ms using LBFGS. All strategies involving the ESM model did not reach a comparable accuracy (best: 0.838 %). Regarding the from scratch strategy, only the EGRV model reaches an accuracy comparable to the online forecasting process (EGRV: 0.680 %, ESM: 0.835 %). However, the from scratch strategy needs much more time to provide the first and the final result (EGRV: 791,527 ms, ESM: 108,139 ms). This is a clear disadvantage of this strategy especially in the face of the current electricity market requirements. At the second evaluation point (Figure 4.10(b)), we can observe the advantageous error development of the online forecasting process. The process starts from a forecast error of 1.230 %, which is iteratively improved to a final forecast error of 0.885 %. None of the competing strategies provide a better accuracy at any point in time. With respect to the last model strategy, the EGRV forecast model provided a better result than the ESM model at the first evaluation point. This changed for the second evaluation point, where for both optimizers the ESM model instances exhibit a lower forecast error (ESM-LBFG: 0.971 %; EGRV-LBFGS: 1.167 %). This result clearly shows that focusing on a single forecast model does not lead to the most accurate forecast result. Thus, involving multiple forecast models as in our online forecasting process is clearly advantageous with respect to the probability of finding the most accurate instance. The results for the from scratch estimation are similar to the first evaluation point. The ESM model exhibits a final accuracy similar to the online forecasting process (0.959 %), but needs much more time to converge (Online first: 1 ms; Online last: 51,041 ms From scratch first: 180,726 ms).

For the D2 dataset we observed similar results, which are illustrated in Figures 4.10(c) and 4.10(d). At the first evaluation point (Figure 4.10(c)), our online forecasting process again exhibited a final accuracy similar to the EGRV last model strategy (Online: 3.843 %, EGRV-Nelder Mead: 4.07 %). However, the EGRV model needed 424 ms to provide a first result, while our online forecasting process iteratively improves the almost instantly found first result. Both ESM last model strategies exhibited a worse forecast error compared to both EGRV last model configurations (both: 6.2 %). The from scratch strategies reached a similar accuracy, but needed much longer to provide results. At the second evaluation point (Figure 4.10(d)) the final results of the last model strategy using the ESM model were close to the online forecasting process (online: 4.175 %, ESM: 4.189 %). The online forecasting process again, quickly finds a first improvement from the repository after only 12 ms (5.354 % → 4.184 %), which is slightly improved to the final result after 1,201 ms (4.184 % → 4.175 %). The last model strategy with the ESM model required 15 ms for the Nelder Mead and 249 ms for the LBFGS to find a first improvement. Additionally, we observed that large accuracy deviations between optimizers might occur. While the EGRV last model strategy with the Nelder Mead algorithm provided a forecast error of 4.329 %, the EGRV model with the LBFGS algorithm arrived only at 5.869 %. Thus, focusing on a single optimizer only, might lead to inferior forecasting results. This clearly motivates to consider multiple combinations of optimization algorithms and model instances as we do in our online forecasting process. The from scratch strategies again needed much more time (61,072 ms and 181,555 ms) to converge, but only the ESM model reachs a comparable accuracy (ESM: 4.176 %).

During our experiments the selection process even with a large number of forecast model instances took always below one second; using an extreme example with 20,000 EGRV instances the time for the entire selection process took around 1.1 seconds and for 300 models of different types the result from the repository was delivered in below 10 milliseconds. As we can see for all presented experiments the first improvement, which resulted from search the repository was always provided after far below 1 second (on average after around 15 ms). Thus the selection of forecast model instances from the repository is rather uncritical from a time perspective, however, we still recommend to define a maximum number of instances contained in the repository with respect to the system resources and the time budget that is available for the instance selection process. The same is true for the maximum allowed number of results for the selection process, where the concrete number of resulting instances is configuration specific. Thus it is even more important to support a termination of the selection process at any point in time.

Upon termination the resulting instances are provided in an order determined by the last completed decision criterion. In the following section, we show the impact of different number of selected model instances.

Overall, our online forecasting process provides a very efficient and flexible way to calculate accurate forecasts. The first intermediate result is already very accurate and delivered in around one millisecond. In contrast to the other forecasting calculation strategies, the optimization of the online forecasting process involves multiple forecast models in parallel. With that, we substantially increase the probability of finding the most accurate forecast model instance.

Number of Parallel Instances Selected from the Forecast Model Repository

We also evaluated the most important scaling factor of the online forecasting process—the number of instances selected from the forecast model repository. During the evaluation we always selected the N most accurate forecast model instances, which were later on optimized. This scaling factor is configuration specific and can be set by the user. The evaluation was conducted on the D1 dataset and we used May 3rd, 0:30 as evaluation point. The results are illustrated in Table 4.2.

No. of instances	3	5	10	20
Runtime [ms]	386,400	1,542,650	3,070,226	4,748,425
Error [%]	0.382	0.371	0.357	0.357
# Improvements	7	9	11	11

Table 4.2 Accuracy results for different number of instances selected from the repository.

We observed that an increasing number of instances causes only a slight decrease in the forecast error. The reason is that three selected instances, exhibiting the best accuracy on the current state of the time series, already provide very accurate forecasts. However, increasing the number of instances causes a substantial increase of the process runtime. Especially when increasing from three to five instances the runtime increases by factor 4, because we can fully parallelize 3 instances (3 instances, 2 optimizer = 6 threads), but not five instances (5 instances, 2 optimizers = 10 threads). It is important to note that the numbers in this evaluation highly depend on the used hardware as well as the number of forecast models and optimizers. However, we can still state that increasing the number of parallel instances does not necessarily mean an increase in the forecasting accuracy, but significantly increases the process runtime.

4.4 Designing a Forecasting System for the New Electricity Market

The online forecasting process provides a very efficient way for calculating forecasts in an iterative fashion. It is part of our energy data management system (EDMS) prototype called *predictive EDM* or short pEDM. The pEDM system is a special-purpose EDMS specifically designed for working in the face of the new requirements posed by the current electricity market developments. The basis of the pEDM system is an in-memory data store with tightly integrated time series analysis algorithms. With this tight integration we aim at bringing the algorithms close to the data and allowing their direct execution on the data persisted in the data storage layer. Thus, we avoid the expensive copying of data between the database and the application and hence, allow an increased efficiency when calculating forecasts. A tight integration of analysis algorithms in data management systems (DMS) follows a recent trend in research and industry motivated by an increasing amount of data and the requirement for ad-hoc analytics [49, 245]. Both requirements are equally important for the energy domain, where real-time balancing of energy consumption and production requires an efficient calculation of accurate forecasts at any point in time. Currently, a wide variety of statistical tools exists, providing enhanced statistical methods and functionality. However, they typically lack in scalability and efficiency, since data is copied between the database layer and the application. As opposed to this, the data management system persisting the data already provides powerful mechanisms for aggregating, partitioning, filtering, and indexing data, which is especially true for emerging in-memory databases such as SAP HANA [89]. Thus, combining both worlds by integrating statistical methods directly into data management system promises great performance benefits when executing time series analysis.

In this section we present a high-level integration approach for forecasting into data management system, where we specifically focus on EDMSs. We start the discussion with a short discussion of related work about integrating forecasting into data management systems. Since currently there is no reference architecture for EDMSs, we define a set of typical components that belong to an EDMS and create a high-level proposal for a common architecture. Afterwards we introduce an approach for tightly integrating forecasting into data management system (DMS) that we are pursuing in our pEDM system. In particular, we describe the design of the forecasting component used within the pEDM system. This forecasting component is responsible for executing the online forecasting process as well as the advanced techniques discussed in the subsequent Chapters 5 and 6.

4.4.1 Integrating Forecasting into Data Management Systems

The increasing amount of data and the requirement for ad-hoc advanced analytics lead to an increasing interest in research and industry to integrate statistical methods and forecasting into data management systems [49]. Recent developments include approaches that intent to tighten the coupling of specialized external tools such as R, which is typically done by improving the interaction with the database. Examples for this kind of approaches target the integration of the statistical tool R in database system. Grosse et al. describe a shared memory approach for integrating R into an in-memory database [120]. Similarly, Das et al. propose an approach called Ricardo that improves the handling of R in clustered storage environments (specifically on the example of Apache Hadoop) [64]. Since such approaches reuse existing tools, they can utilize well-tested efficient implementations and are thus, typically easier to realize. However, they still require to specifically condition and transfer the data to the application. Thus, improving the storage and data processing capabilities of the database systems, do not automatically improve the calculation efficiency of the external tools.

The second research direction concerns specialized data management systems and database systems that offer integrated support for statistical calculations. The first general approach that describes the integration of forecasting queries within traditional database system is the research prototype Fa developed by Duan and Babu [70]. In addition, to a general integration concept they optimized the model identification by proposing an incremental approach to build models for multi-dimensional time series. Aside such research prototypes, forecasting has also been integrated into commercial DBMS. Examples are the Oracle OLAP DML [183] and the Microsoft SQL Server data mining extension [168, 169]. In general, built-in and custom forecast algorithms can be integrated as user-defined functions or using other extension points such as the Microsoft integration services. However, the available research approaches and commercial products typically do not provide optimized data storages and forecasting calculation processes specifically suited for efficient forecasting in real-time environments such as the European electricity market.

In the energy domain EDMSs are specialized systems that are specifically suited for working in different areas of the electricity markets. Such systems typically provide extensive support for (smart) grid operations, data analysis and reporting as well as forecasting. The EMS/EDM Prophet systems is an EDMS developed by the Fraunhofer ITB in conjunction with Siemens that offers a wide range of forecasting capabilities [19, 28]. Similarly SAP is offering its SAP IS-U-EDM solution [201, 204] as well as its smart meter and smart grid analytics [202, 203]. The focus of the SAP solutions is more on the financial reporting, billing, and real-time pricing site, but it also offers support for calculating forecasts. A last representation is Oracle Utilities Solutions that are based on the EDMS build by the acquired company Loadstar [182].

For our pEDM system we specifically use a direct and tight integration that extends all layers of the employed data management system (DMS). With that, we target to ensure consistency between data and models, to increase efficiency by reducing data transfer and exploiting database related optimization techniques. Thus, in contrast to other approaches our pEDM system includes optimizations on the logical as well as on the physical level. In particular, we are optimizing the process of calculating forecast among others with our online forecasting approach (compare Section 4.3 and Chapter 5) and complement these logical optimization with enhancements to the time series storage (compare Chapter 6).

4.4.2 Creating a Common Architecture for EDMSs

Since many countries and even companies have specific requirements with respect to the specification and functionality of an EDMS there is no single or dominating EDMS solution. The reason is that although a single European electricity market is planned for the near future, different regions in Europe still pose different regional rules and requirements to electricity market participants. In addition, there is no joint business target between market players, which means that different companies exhibit different business needs and with that, expect different functionalities from their EDMSs. As a result, there is no single reference architecture or common sense about the necessary and implemented components. However, since the pEDM system is targeted to work in the joint European electricity market, we created a high-level overview of a common EDMS architecture blueprint. For this purpose, we tried to identify similar design concepts of existing EDMSs and combine them with the general EDMS architectural design proposal defined by Ulbricht et al. [237]. Figure 4.11 illustrates an overview of our resulting common architecture proposal for EDMSs in the European electricity market.

Our proposal architecture comprises a database and four major components responsible for a specific area of the EDMS. The database is the core component, storing all data that is available throughout the system. This includes the storage of consumption and production time series in multiple aggregation levels, customer data necessary for managing the various consumers and producers, the storage of the plain meter data that exists on multiple levels of the hierarchy (customer, utility, grid,...) and general master data. Multiple implementation options for this data storage component are possible including a simple database exchanging information with the other components using standard database interfaces (SQL, MDX, etc.) or a tightly integrated solution that we describe in the following Section 4.4.1. To allow reporting and data analysis on top of the data stored in the database an

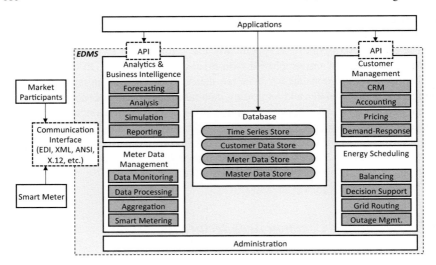

Fig. 4.11 A proposal for a common EDMS architecture (inspired by [237] and commercial EDMSs).

Analytics & Business Intelligence component is available, which comprises algorithms, models, functionality etc. for data analysis, forecasting, simulation, and reporting. This thesis specifically focuses on the *Analytics & Business Intelligence* component and especially the forecasting module. A further component is responsible for the customer management (in this context customers can mean producers and consumers) and with that, provides CRM and accounting capabilities. Furthermore in many systems a component for calculating the optimal prices in real-time is contained. We also added a module that is responsible for controlling consumer appliances as part of a smart grid demand response system, which will become very important in the future European electricity market. The eventual scheduling and balancing of energy consumption and production is provided by the scheduling module. Besides the basic balancing tasks, it also contains a module for outage management providing specific functionality in case of power outages. We also included a decision support module that allows autonomous reactions or at least quick reactions depending on the changing grid situation. Similar to the demand-response module, a decision support module will be very important in the new electricity market. The last module is responsible for the actual management of the incoming meter data. In this context meter data does not necessarily means the data recorded at the customer-side, but also data that is measured in different granularity on the energy grid. The module supports automatic data processing and aggregation and allows the control of smart meters. In addition, a module for monitoring the current measurements is available, which provides specific input for analytical modules and decision support functionality. Each component provides specific APIs to allow applications utilizing the functionalities and query the data. This API is especially important for the *Analytics & Business Intelligence* component and the *Customer Management* component. Besides the functional components, each EDMS should provide a specific communication interface supporting a wide range of data exchange standards such as EDIFACT, XML, or X.12. The interface is responsible for accepting meter data and other requests as well as providing the data to the responsible components within the EDMS.

4.4.3 Architecture of an Integrated Forecasting Component

With *predictiveEDM* (pEDM) we propose an EDM system with the components described in Section 4.4.2 above. The most important part of the pEDM system is a special forecasting component that allows for the calculation of forecasts using the online forecasting process. The component tightly integrates the time series storage with the forecasting algorithms. The main reason for this tight coupling is to enable the forecasting algorithms to directly access and process the time series data. In addition, the integration allows to apply special optimizations to the data storage that improve the data handling with respect to the needs of the employed forecasting models. Examples for such optimizations could be special indexes, specifically adapted compression techniques or data storage layouts that acknowledge the data access characteristics of the used algorithms.

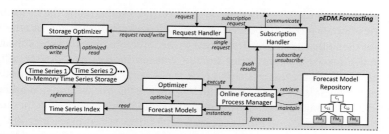

Fig. 4.12 Architecture of the pEDM forecasting component.

In the following we describe the architecture of the forecasting components as a blueprint for a tight coupling of a data storage with an improved forecasting process. The component diagram presented in Figure 4.12 serves as the basis for our explanations. The core parts of the forecasting component are the *Online Forecasting Process Manager* (OFP-Manager) and the *forecast model repository*. The OFP-Manager is responsible for the execution of the online forecasting and thus, for the iterative provisioning of forecasting results and the refinement of forecast models. For this purpose, the OFP-Manager instantiates forecast models and assigns optimizers to them for executing the parallel local optimization. Improved forecast models found during the optimization process are used to calculate new forecasts that are provided back to the OFP-Manager and are then pushed to the requesting application. To materialize previously used forecast model instances the OFP-Manager is using a forecast model repository as introduced in Section 4.3.1. When starting a new forecasting calculation the OFP-Manager retrieves the most accurate forecast model instances from the repository. Following this, the forecast model repository is responsible for storing forecast model instances in an efficient way and to assess their accuracy with respect to the current developments of the time series. In Section 5.1 we discuss a more advanced approach of a forecast model repository that has a very efficient way of storing and retrieving forecast model instances.

The pEDM forecasting system utilizes an *in-memory data storage approach* for storing time series data. Storing and processing the data in the main memory, avoids reading from the hard disk and thus, significantly reduces the data processing time. Currently, the availability of large amounts of main memory and increasing parallelization capabilities facilitate the broad use of in-memory databases and allow us to store all time series data within the main memory. Disk space is only used for logging and backup. We propose to enhance the in-memory time series storage with special storage layouts that are specifically suited for forecasting time series data. These layouts organize the time series in the main memory in a way that they comply to the memory access-pattern of the employed forecast models. With that, we are able to significantly speed up the forecasting calculations. The storage layouts are discussed in detail in Section 6.2. Furthermore, the in-memory time series storage provides special *Time Series Indexes* to further improve the data access for the forecast models. Thus, next to the option to directly access the time series in the in-memory time series storage, forecast models may use the offered time series indexes for faster access to the series data. The time series storage is managed by the *Storage Optimizer*, which is responsible for ensuring compliance to the selected storage layouts during read and write operations.

For handling requests to the forecasting component, we leverage a central *Request Handler*, which is responsible for forwarding the request to the right parts. For directly reading and writing time series the request is forwarded to the storage optimizer. Single forecasting requests without subscription to the online forecasting process are handled by the online forecasting process manager directly. In this case if a forecast model instance is available that matches the forecasting query, this instance is directly used to produce a forecast. Otherwise, we execute the heuristic forecasting process (compare Section 5.1) to produce a forecasting result. Requests containing a subscription to the online forecasting process are handled by the *Subscription Handler*. Upon arrival of a new request the subscription manager registers this request at the online forecasting process manager and afterwards directly handles the entire communication with the requesting applications. This includes forwarding calculated forecasts as well as processing control requests such as process terminations. The independent handling of subscription-based requests allows us to use more efficient communication protocols specifically suited for providing forecasts in a publish/subscribe way. In particular, we propose to use a protocol similar to the one introduced by Fischer et al. [93]. There they propose the concept of continuous forecasting queries that provide new forecasts as soon as the underlying forecast model changed significantly. Besides this basic concept, they specifically optimize the processing costs for the subscriber by determining an optimal notification interval based on the significance of the change and the remaining forecasting horizon that is available at the requesting application. While our approach and use-case significantly differs from theirs (we transmit improvements as a result of our iterative forecast model refinement, while they create new forecast model instances, whenever the current one became inaccurate), we still have similar requirements with respect to transmitting forecasts. Especially, since we likewise target to only transmit significant improvements to avoid an extensive number of transmissions.

Chapter 5
Optimizations on the Logical Layer: Context-Aware Forecasting

Our online forecasting process serves as the basis for an efficient calculation of forecasts. However, further optimizations on the logical and on the physical layer are necessary to fully realize the efficiency improvements. In this chapter, we discuss approaches on the logical layer. In the energy domain we can observe a strong dependence of the time series development on external factors and background processes (compare Section 3.1.3). The energy domain is unique in the fact that we can observe most of this time series context. We propose to exploit this information to further improve the online forecasting process.

Our first approach describes an improvement to the forecast model repository introduced in Section 4.3.1. The basic idea is to enrich the forecast model instances stored in the repository with information about the time series context that was present during the instance usage. We can then use this information to search the repository for instances that were valid in a context similar to the current one and thus, potentially produce accurate forecasts again. Those instances serve as good starting points for the local parameter estimation. A major advantage of using context similarity as a selection criterion is the fact that it allows to quickly reduce the number of considered instances. Thus, it enables a less time consuming search process in the forecast model repository as well as a better identification of good starting points for the subsequent optimization.

Our second approach deals with the direct incorporation of external information, as they are required when forecasting the energy production of renewable energy sources. For renewables we can calculate meaningful forecasts only when considering the most important environmental factors; e.g., wind speed for wind power or cloud coverage for solar panels. However, also energy demand forecasts profit from an increased accuracy when considering external information. The issue with including this information into forecast models is that they substantially increase the number of forecast model parameters and with that, the parameter search space. In this chapter, we introduce a framework for integrating external information into any kind of forecast model, while at the same time limiting the number of additional parameters. With that approach, we enable very accurate forecasts for energy supply of renewable energy sources and energy demand and still ensure a very efficient calculation of forecasts.

Our third approach exploits a different kind of context information. The European electricity market is hierarchically organized with multiple entities and time series on different hierarchical levels. While in such environments forecasting is relatively complex, we can exploit information in the hierarchy to increase the forecasting efficiency. In particular, we can reuse forecast models on lower levels to determine the parameters of forecast models on higher levels by our forecast model aggregation concept. This forecast model aggregation consumes several orders of magnitudes less time than a conventional parameter estimation, while still providing a very high forecasting accuracy.

The content of this chapter was published in [60], [61], [159], [58] and [59].

5.1 Context-Aware Forecast Model Materialization

One of the major components of our online forecasting process is the forecast model repository, where we provided a general description as well as requirements and a description of the initialization in Section 4.3.1. With respect to the defined requirements we created a very efficient specific implementation of the forecast model repository that we are describing in this section. The core idea underlying our approach is to store previously used forecast model instances in conjunction with information about the time series context state that was in place during the time the instance was valid (i.e., produced accurate forecasts). The instances are preserved in a novel repository type called *Context-Aware Forecast Model Repository* (CFMR). Upon receiving a forecasting request, we use the current time series context to search the CFMR for the most appropriate instances and use them as the basis for further optimizations. This procedure follows the paradigm of a problem solving approach called *case-based reasoning*.

5.1.1 Case-based Reasoning and Context-Awareness in General

Case-based reasoning (CBR) is a paradigm that solves new problems by considering and refining stored previous solutions for similar problems. In general, case-based reasoning is inspired by a typical human-reasoning behavior. In particular, humans learn from previous encounters of a problem or challenge and build up experience that they can exploit for solving similar problems in the future. Accordingly, case-based reasoning has been investigated in both computer science and more specifically in machine learning [1, 206] and in psychology [129, 214, 236, 247]. The foundation for case-based reasoning in computer science was laid out by the works of Schank ([206]) and Porter et al. ([194, 195]), who developed different memory and reasoning models for problem solving. Schank introduced his concept of dynamic memory, which fundamentally relies on solving problems using earlier situations and situation patterns [1, 206]. Porter et al. designed a system for solving classification tasks called PROTOS. Since then a lot of CBR systems such as GREBE [26], CASEY [148] and HYPO [9] were developed that also evolved and enhanced the CBR paradigm.

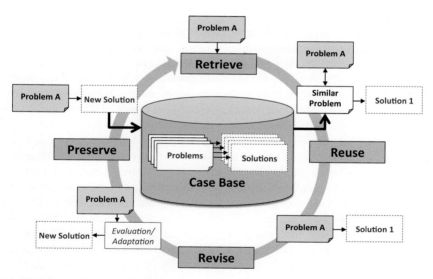

Fig. 5.1 Case-based reasoning cycle (adapted from [1]).

Due to the large number of different systems there is no general process for solving problems with the help of CBR. However, Aamodt et al. defined a generalized CBR cycle as part of their generic CBR framework [1] that we are using as the basis for our CFMR. In Figure 5.1 we present an adapted version of this CBR cycle. The basic component of this cycle is the case-base that contains previously encountered problems connected to their respective solutions. The problems are described using case attributes that can be used to identify the characteristics of a problem. (1) The cycle starts with the *retrieve* phase as soon as a new problem "Problem A" is received. In this phase the case-base is searched for previous problems that are similar to the received "Problem A". (2) The most similar case is chosen from the case base and in the *reuse* phase we can use the solution ("Solution 1") of the identified most similar problem as the solution for the new "Problem A". (3) In the *revise* phase we first evaluate how well "Solution 1" solves "Problem A" and afterwards adapt the solution to the specifics of "Problem A" forming a new solution. (4) Finally we *preserve* the new case in our case-base by storing the new solution determined in the revise phase in conjunction to the description of the received "Problem A". Upon retrieval of another problem the CBR cycle starts again with an updated case-base containing the case created in the last iteration.

5.1.2 The Context-Aware Forecast Model Repository

The case-based reasoning approach of the online forecasting process is based on the assumption that similar time series contexts (compare Section 3.1.3) lead to similar model parameters. In general, this assumption holds, since the time series context directly influences the further development of a time series. A specialty of the energy domain is that most of the time series context is observable. Calendar effects such as holidays and vacation seasons are typically known far beforehand, meteorological data is available throughout Europe in a very fine granularity and economic factors such as energy saving campaigns and sport events typically comply to long-term plans. Thus, the amount of unobservable context is relatively small. Accordingly, we employ the CFMR as our case-base containing previous cases (i.e., forecast model instances) that serve as potential candidates for future iterations of the online forecasting process. We then use the time series context as a decision criterion for selecting beneficial forecast models from the CFMR. The instances identified with this criterion are supposed to already have a high potential of providing very accurate forecasts with respect to the current developments of the time series. Furthermore, they are potentially very beneficial starting points for the subsequent local optimization.

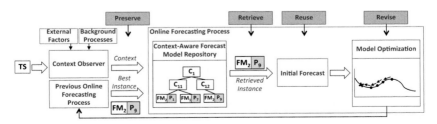

Fig. 5.2 Context-Aware forecast model maintenance process.

Figure 5.2 illustrates the online forecasting process when using our context-aware forecast model repository. First, instances added to the repository are enhanced with information about external factors and background processes provided by a *context observer*. This step complies to the *preserve step* of the original case-based reasoning approach. Second, we *retrieve* appropriate instances by searching the repository using multiple decision criteria (described in the following Section 5.1.3). The most appropriate instance with respect to the decision criterion is *reused* to potentially provide a first improvement over the instance from the last iteration of the online forecasting process. Third, all candidate instances identified from the repository are *revised* in the subsequent local optimization of the online forecasting process.

This approach is not limited to the energy domain, CBR-based techniques can be applied to arbitrary forecasting applications where similar models are periodically reused. However, there might be different selection criteria in different domains. For this reason, before we discuss the details of the CFMR in Sections 5.1.4 to 5.1.5, we provide detailed information about possible selection criteria we are using in the CFMR.

5.1.3 Decision Criteria

When searching the context-aware forecast model repository (CFMR) for the most appropriate instances, we are using several decision criteria. Some of them are specific for the energy domain, while others can be applied for multiple domains. Below we discuss a selection of decision criteria that we found for our implementation most suitable. However, further criteria that might increase the applicability of the approach for some other domains or use-cases are highly imaginable.

- **Context similarity** As discussed in Section 3.1.3, the development of a time series is influenced by background processes and influences that we refer to as *time series context*. The core idea of this decision criterion is to find forecast model instances that produced accurate forecasts in a time series context that is most similar to the current time series context. This decision criterion is the basis for our context-aware forecast model repository. Using the context similarity as a decision attribute, enables the CFMR to use an optimized retrieval algorithm, where we do not need to touch all instances contained in the repository, but only the ones that are potentially close to the current time series context (compare Section 5.1.5). While this approach works very reliable in most cases, using only the time series context is somewhat vague, because some non-observable processes might additionally influence the current development of the time series. Additionally, the current context state might appear for the first time and thus, the similarity between the contexts available in the repository and the current context is rather low. Thus, adding additional criterions improves the accuracy of this selection process.

- **Subsequence shape similarity** This decision criterion assess the suitability of forecast model instances by evaluating the similarity of the time series shape at the current point in time to the shape at the point in time the respective instance was most recently used. The similarity can be evaluated using time series distance measure such as the Pearson cross correlation coefficient or more advanced techniques such as dynamic time warping [15]. While this approach reliably identifies forecast model instances describing a similar shape as the current time series, it is computationally expensive to assess all forecast model instances stored in the repository with respect to this criterion. As a result, it is necessary to pre-select the most promising candidates before applying the subsequence shape similarity.
- **Accuracy** The accuracy of all stored forecast model instances is assessed on the current time series or a part of the time series involving the current point in time. The best instances can then directly be used to calculate the forecast and to serve as starting points for the subsequent parameter estimation. While this approach involves an evaluation of the suitability of the forecast model instances for the current time series development, it is considered as the computationally most expensive criterion due to potentially involving a large number of forecast models in the evaluation.
- **Elapsed time** This criterion orders the instances by the time that elapsed since their last usage. The most recently used instances, similar to the last model strategy, are used to calculate a first forecast and serve as input for the subsequent optimization. While this is the criterion that requires the least runtime, it also does not provide an assessment about the applicability of an instance to the current time series behavior.

All of the decision criteria introduced above can be used separately or combined in an arbitrary way. However, for our implementation we decided to combine all four criteria, since it yields better results, due to avoiding the disadvantages of the single techniques. We first start from the most accurate forecast model instances found during the last iteration of the process (criterion: elapsed time), similar to the last model strategy. Using this forecast model we can almost instantly (around one millisecond) calculate and provide a first forecasting result. Afterwards, we chain the remaining criteria in multiple selection steps, where each step only selects the most reasonable candidates. This selection process orders the selection criteria by their computational complexity, starting from the criterion with the least expenses and lowest complexity (context similarity; average complexity $O(\log n)$) and progressing to the more expensive ones with linear complexity (subsequence shape similarity, accuracy). Accordingly, after using the best instance from the last iteration of the process, we continue with the *context similarity* selection criterion. This criterion supports a very efficient selection, where we are required to only include instance candidates with a high potential of being close to the current context. This selection already prunes a large number of model instances not being closely associated with the current context and thus, reduces the number of model instances considered in the further computational more expensive selection steps. Afterwards, we compare the subsequence shape similarity of the remaining instances to the shape of the most recent time series values. Only the instances describing a very similar shape are selected for the final selection step, which evaluates the accuracy of the remaining forecast model instances on the current development of the time series. Combining all criteria to the described multiple step selection process increases the probability that only the most reasonable instances, describing the most similar context and subsequence shape as well as providing the best accuracy for the recent time series development are considered for the subsequent optimization. Thus, instead of simply relying on our major selection criterion—the context similarity—we prune forecast models that were admittedly valid in a similar context, but are not the best forecast model for the current time series development.

The output of the selection process is a list of the most suitable forecast model instances ordered by their accuracy. From this list we use the most accurate forecast model instance and calculate a first improved forecast and all instances resulting from the selection process are used as starting points for the optimization step of the online forecasting process.

5.1.4 Preserving Forecast Models Using Time Series Context

The CFMR allows to store and retrieve previous model instances using their time series context information as the major selection criteria. When we start a new online forecasting process, in a first step we search the CFMR for forecast model instances that produced accurate forecasts in similar past contexts. Consider for example a cloudy and rainy day. The meteorological state influences the energy consumption and production and hence the shape of the respective time series. Provided the weather conditions change to a similar state on a later occasion, we can search the CFMR for forecast model instances that were valid during such weather conditions. The weather is just one example and the time series context is typically composed of multiple influences or characteristic factors that we refer to as context attributes.

Notation 5.1 (Context Attribute). A context attribute A is a background process, characteristic, or external factor influencing the development of a time series (compare Section 3.1.3) such as for example the weather. The value of a context attribute is denoted as a.

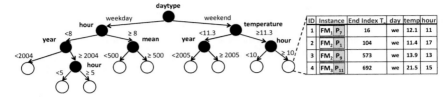

Fig. 5.3 Example model history tree.

Notation 5.2 (Time Series Context). The time series context C_x of a time series $x(t_i)$ in the sense of our context-aware forecast model repository is a collection of all observed context attributes $C_x = \{A_1, A_2, ..., A_n\}$ that influence the development of the time series $x(t_i)$.

The CFMR stores the previously used instances in a binary search tree named *Model History Tree* were the instances are stored in the leaf nodes of the trees and decision nodes divide the instances by their assigned time series context:

Notation 5.3 (Model History Tree). A model history tree (*MHT*), defined over the context attributes $A_1, ..., A_n$, a maximum leaf node capacity cap_{max} and a forecast model instance description (containing a forecast model FM_m and a parameter combination P_p), is a binary search tree, whose nodes are either decision nodes or leaf nodes.

- *Decision nodes* contain a splitting attribute $\dot{A}_i \in \{A_1, ..., A_n\}$ which exhibits a splitting value $\dot{a}_i$. It further includes references to the left and right successor nodes. Splitting attributes are context attributes chosen for splitting the stored forecast models into several classes.
- *Leaf nodes* contain a list $[A_i]$ of context attributes including their values a_i, at most $cap \leq cap_{max}$ forecast model instances $FM_m P_p$, and for each instance an end index T_e representing the last time the instances were used.

Figure 5.3 shows an exemplary model history tree, built over the context attributes *daytype, temperature, hour, year* and *mean*. The highlighted leaf node stores four forecast model instances, each of which refers to a specific forecast model (FM_1 to FM_3) as well as a specific parameter combination (P_n). The tree essentially forms a recursive partitioning of the instance search space (comprising forecast models and parameters combination) into a set of disjoint subspaces whereas splitting attributes can be thought of as $(n-1)$-dimensional axially parallel hyperplanes (n in this case refers to the number of context attributes). At each decision node, the tree branches the instance search space into instances with splitting attribute values smaller than the reference splitting value and those with splitting attribute values greater or equal than the reference splitting value. Leaf nodes store the actual instances along with the values of all assigned context attributes a_i and the corresponding end indices T_e.

Context Attributes

Our model history tree generally supports two types of context attribute values, namely numerical and nominal attribute values a_i, which can take values within a domain $[a_i^{min}, a_i^{max}]$ (the max and min values in table 5.1 are examples). Numerical attributes can directly be compared using the explicit mathematical ordering of real numbers. In contrast, nominal attributes describe a discrete set of values or states that do not exhibit an explicit order. Fortunately, some nominal attributes such as the year or the month provide an implicit ordering based on explicit definitions. This means that for the attribute year it is defined that 2005 < 2006. For other nominal attributes such as special days (special day = true —— false) or weather seasons (winter ¡ ? ¿ summer) we define a special internal ordering for our MHT. Furthermore, numerical as well s nominal attributes may be defined as cyclical attributes, whose values repeat every n instances $a_i \in (a_1, ..., a_n)$ with $a_1 = a_n$.

		Numerical	Nominal	Cyclic	a_i^{min}	a_i^{max}	Example
	Year		✓		2000	2020	2005
Temporal	Month		✓	✓	1	12	Apr (4)
	Day		✓	✓	1	7	Tue (2)
	Special Day		✓		0	1	False (0)
	Temperature	✓			-30	40	27.7° C
Exogenous	Wind Speed	✓			0	30	15 m/s
	Electricity Price	✓			0	100	70.38 Eur/MWh
Statistical	Mean $\bar{z}$	✓			0	40000	12435.5 MW
	Variance σ^2	✓			0	10000	1719.6 MW²

Table 5.1 Context attributes for electricity demand and supply.

In Table 5.1 we provide a list of example context attributes including their affiliation to the above described attribute value types. Selecting the most appropriate attributes as splitting attributes for guiding the search in the MHT is highly dependent on the time series at hand and the applicability of an attribute to split the stored instances as evenly as possible. Such an even split is of utmost importance to keep the tree in balance and thus, to avoid increased search efforts due to a tree degeneration.

It is important to know that in our MHT we normalize the values of all attributes to a range of $a_i \in [0, 1]$. Numerical attributes are scaled as follows:

$$a_i' = \frac{a_i - a_i^{min}}{a_i^{max} - a_i^{min}}.$$

For nominal attributes we do the normalization based on the ranking values of the attributes. This results in a scaling that is given by:

$$a_i' = \frac{rk(a_i) - rk(a_i^{min})}{rk(a_i^{max}) - rk(a_i^{min})},$$

where $rk(\cdot)$ denotes the rank of an attribute value.

Inserting Models into the Model History Tree

When inserting models into the MHT we follow the typical divide and conquer strategy that is used in most binary search trees. Thus, we first traverse from the root node to the leaf node that represents the most similar context by comparing the context attributes. Afterwards, the new instance is added to the leaf node. If the number of stored instances cap exceeds the maximum node capacity cap_{max}, the leaf node is split into two leaf nodes and is subsequently converted into a decision node with references to the new successors. The new splitting attribute $\dot{A}_i$ and splitting value (cut-point) $\dot{a}_i$ is determined from the context information of the model instances stored in the node. As the splitting value $\dot{a}_i$ we use the median of all values the respective model instances exhibit for the splitting attribute $\dot{A}_i$. The median typically provides appropriate splitting results on numerical as well as on nominal and cyclical attributes, since it chooses a central value that partitions the available values in even halves. Thus, by using the median we ensure an equal number of models in both successors of a decision node. A prerequisite for the median is to first sort the attribute values in ascending order, which is trivial for numerical values. For nominal attributes we use a ranking based on the number of occurrences in all available instances. For cyclical attributes we define the start of the cycle as the minimum and the value before the cycle restart as the maximum value.

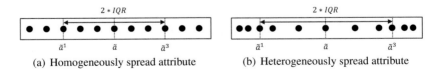

(a) Homogeneously spread attribute   (b) Heterogeneously spread attribute

Fig. 5.4 Illustration of example attribute spreads.

While the medium is well suited to split a node in even halves, it does not distinguish homogeneously and heterogeneously spread attributes (compare Figure 5.4). Thus, while it provides a beneficially splitting value, it does not provide beneficial results when used to choose an appropriate splitting attribute. We can assume that attributes with higher density towards the ends constitute better splitting attributes, as the median value separates both halves more clearly. For this reason, we additionally apply the *(Percental) Inter-quartile Range* ((P)IQR) as a measure of dispersion within attributes values and therefore as a measure for the suitability of an attribute as splitting attribute.

Notation 5.4 (Inter-quartile Range / Percental Inter-quartile Range). The **inter-quartile range** (IQR), defined over the list of attribute values $[a_i \mid i = 1,\dots,N]$, denotes the average of the first and third quartiles:

$$IQR = \frac{\tilde{a}^3 - \tilde{a}^1}{2}$$

with $\tilde{a}^1 = \tilde{l}$ and $l = \{a_i \leq \tilde{a}\}$ 1st quartile (median of left half)

with $\tilde{a}^3 = \tilde{r}$ and $r = \{a_i \geq \tilde{a}\}$ 3rd quartile (median of right half)

To ensures that attributes with a homogenous distribution, but large total range and thus large IQR, are not preferred over those with a heterogeneous distribution and a small range the IQR is normalized by the total range of attribute values leading to: $PIQR = \frac{IQR}{2(a_N - a_1)}$.

The attribute with the highest PIQR value, i.e., the one with the lowest dispersion, is chosen as splitting attribute. The following example and Figure 5.5 illustrate a sample PIQR calculation.

Fig. 5.5 Example for the PIQR calculation.

Example 5.1.

$$PIQR = \frac{0.7 - 0.4}{2(0.9 - 0.2)} = \frac{0.3}{1.4} = 0.214 \qquad PIQR = \frac{0.4 - 0.15}{2(0.5 - 0.1)} = \frac{0.25}{0.8} = 0.312.$$

To determine the concrete splitting attribute, we compute first the median, the 1st quartile and the 3rd quartile over all context attributes within the current node (two in the example). The first attribute has a larger total range and hence a larger IQR than the second attribute. Still, normalizing the IQR by the range leads to the selection of the first attribute as splitting attribute as its PIQR is larger.

Although the median and PIQR guarantee an equal distribution of forecast model instances for single nodes, model history trees can still degenerate to imbalanced, list-like trees. The reason is that both measures make local decisions only, for what reason it might happen that new instances are always added to one side of the tree. In order to keep the tree globally balanced, we continuously measure the heights of the subtrees as follows:

Notation 5.5 (Node Height / Balanced Node).
The **height** $h(n)$ of a node n is defined as

$$h(n) = \begin{cases} 0 & \text{, if } n \text{ is a leaf node} \\ 1 + \max(h(n.left, n.right))) & \text{, if } n \text{ is a decision node.} \end{cases}$$

We account an MHT to be balanced as long as the heights of the left and right subtrees of each node differ at most by a predefined maximal balance factor Δ_{max}: $|h(n_i.left) - h(n_i.right)| \leq \Delta_{max}$. In case we detect an imbalance in the model history tree, we re-build it from scratch. When the tree is regenerated, the splitting decisions made at upper nodes are based on all models below that node. Thus, since the tree is recreated from the top the resulting tree is balanced again. Given the typical number of nodes (decision and leaf nodes) being below 1000 in most cases, the rebuilding is computationally relatively inexpensive. In addition, it is done asynchronously to any other task by creating a copy that is exchanged with the used tree as soon as the copy is fully balanced. With that, we reduce the perceptible effect to a minimum. There are alternative balancing strategies such as AVL-tree-like rotation [209], which however, do not bare a large optimization potential for relatively small trees like the MHT.

5.1.5 Forecast Model Retrieval and Assessment

After introducing and defining the model history tree of the CFMR to preserve forecast model instances, we now show how to use the CFMR to quickly retrieve promising instances based on the stored context information. Afterwards the resulting candidates are again assessed by their subsequence similarity followed by an accuracy evaluation (compare Section 5.1.3).

Retrieving Forecast Models

When searching the model history tree we target to receive all instances that are assigned to a context most similar to the one provided to the CFMR as the search criterion. Our search algorithm is an adapted *k-nearest neighbor search* and based on the principle of backtracking, which means that it first descents to a leaf node and gradually adds solutions on its way back to the root. For computing the similarity between the given context C_x and the contexts stored with the forecast model instances C_k we are determining the euclidean distance over all context attributes a. The smaller the euclidean distance between the contexts the more both contexts coincide in important context attributes a_i and thus, the more both contexts are similar to each other.

Algorithm 5.1.1: mhtRetrieve().

input : *currContext*, *currNode*, *best*, *k* (number of results)

if *isLeafNode(currNode)* **then**
    foreach *(context, forecast model instance($FM_m P_p$), endIndex) in currNode* **do**
        dist $\longleftarrow$ *getEuclidDist(currContext, context)*
        if *dist* < *getMaximumDist(best)* **then**
            best.update(context, paramComb, endIndex, dist)
            distanceComputation(paramComb, endIndex)
else
    if *currNode.à_i* < *currContext[i]* **then**
        best, maxDist $\leftarrow$ *mhtRetrieve(currContext, currNode.left, best)*
        if *bobTest(currContext, currNode, maxDist)* **then**
            best, maxDist $\leftarrow$ *mhtRetrieve(currContext, currNode.right, best)*
    else
        best, maxDist $\leftarrow$ *mhtRetrieve(currContext, currNode.right, best)*
        if *bobTest(currContext, currNode, maxDist)* **then**
            best, maxDist $\leftarrow$ *mhtRetrieve(currContext, currNode.left, best)*
return *best*

Algorithm 5.1.1 describes in detail how we retrieve forecast model instances from the model history tree. For finding the k most similar instances with respect to the given context (currContext) the algorithm works as follows:

1. We first traverse from the root to the leaf node that corresponds best to the provided context, which is done by recursively executing mhtRetrieve() on the left or right branch of a decision node (top-level else branch).
2. At the leaf node we compute the euclidian distance between the provided context $currContext(v)$ and contexts (w) stored together with the respective instances in the leaf node. The identifiers of the k most similar instances are stored in the list *best* and *maxDist* is set to the euclidean distance of the most distant solution ($Eu(C_{max}) = \max(Eu(C_x, C_k))$) contained in *best*.
3. We start ascending back to the root node as provided by the backtracking principal. At each intermediate decision node, we evaluate the potential existence of additional solution in the opposite branch by using a *bounds-overlap-ball* (bob) test [104, 200]. For this purpose, the bob test assumes an n-dimensional virtual

ball centred around the context provided as the search criterion C_x with a radius r_{C_x} corresponding to *maxDist*. In this case n represents the number of splitting attributes used throughout the decision tree. We now check if this virtual ball stays within the boundaries of the current solution, i.e., within the borders given by the splitting attributes $\dot{a}_i$ and respective splitting values of the current path of the decision tree. This is the case as long as for each node on our way back to the root Equation 5.1 holds:

$$maxDist \leq |a_i^x - node.\dot{a}_i|. \tag{5.1}$$

If Equation 5.1 is violated the ball intersects with the hyperplane of the opposite branch and thus, potentially better solutions might exist in this branch. As a result, a positive bob test means that we need to descent into the opposite branch and evaluate the applicability of the solutions stored in it. Better (closer) solutions we are finding among the additionally evaluated model instances are added to *best* until the maximum number of solutions k is reached. Afterwards further better solutions replace worse solutions in *best*. In all cases we update *maxDist* to the most recent changes. If the splitting attribute is cyclic, we also need to specifically check the cycle borders. The reason is that the bob-ball may range over the end of the cycle and thus, into the beginning of the cycle again.

4. As soon as we reached the root node again and as long as no further subtrees have to be evaluated the algorithm terminates and provides the model instances belonging to a context closest to the context given as the search criteria.

Overall, the bob test significantly increases the efficiency of the search, since it checks for potential solutions without actually traversing a branch or touching the contained instances. Thus, in most cases the number of evaluated models is considerably reduced during the search process. However, in the worst case, the search process evaluates all nodes in the tree. This might be for example the case when the given context C_x is far away from all previously observed contexts. However, this degeneration is very seldom and never occurred in our evaluation.

In the following example 5.2 and Figure 5.6, we illustrate the execution of Algorithm 5.1.1:

Example 5.2. Attribute A_1 is non-cyclic and attribute A_2 is cyclic. The given context C_x exhibits the context attribute values $a_1 = 0.85$ and $a_2 = 0.1$. The goal is to find the $k = 1$ nearest neighbors. For this purpose, we perform the following steps and calculations:

1. Descent to leaf node corresponding best to provided context and compute the Euclidean distance to all models in the node (O and P).

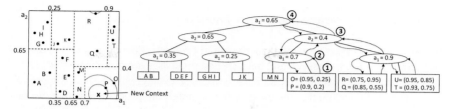

Fig. 5.6 Example model retrieval in a 2-dimensional model history tree.

$$dist(C_x, O) = \sqrt{(0.85 - 0.95)^2 + (0.1 - 0.25)^2} = 0.18$$

$$dist(C_x, P) = \sqrt{(0.85 - 0.9)^2 + (0.1 - 0.2)^2} = 0.12$$

Save P as the best candidate to *best* and update *maxDist* to 0.12.

2. Ascent to the predecessor decision node and perform the bob test. The splitting attribute and value for this decision node is $a_1 = 0.7$.

$$maxDist = 0.12 \leq |a_1^x - node.\mathring{a}_1| = |0.85 - 0.7| = 0.15 \checkmark$$

The equation holds, which means that there is no better solution in the opposite branch of this decision node (M and N are not evaluated).

3. Ascent to the next decision node and perform bob test. The cyclic splitting attribute a_2 yields the value $a_2 = 0.4$. Since a_2 is a cyclic attribute, we need to additionally involve the range borders 0.0 and 1.0 in the bob test evaluation.

$$0.12 \leq |a_2^x - 0.4| = |0.1 - 0.4| = 0.3 \checkmark$$
$$\vee\ 0.12 \leq |a_2^x - 1.0| = |0.1 - 1.0| = 0.9 \checkmark$$
$$\vee\ 0.12 \leq |a_2^x - 0.0| = |0.1 - 0.0| = 0.1 \times$$

The last condition of the equation does not hold, meaning that there is a potential solution in the opposite branch of this decision node. Descend to this branch and find R as the new nearest neighbor. Update *best* to R and *maxDist* to 0.11. Please note that for a cyclic attribute it is necessary to calculate the euclidean distance with respect to the minimum value (in this example 0.0) as well as to the maximum value (in this example 1.0).

4. Ascent to the root and perform bob test. There are no further solutions in the opposite branch of the root note. Provide R as the nearest neighbor to the given context.

Comparing Time Series Subsequence Similarity

While similar contexts typically lead to similar time series behavior, even in the energy domain some influences and background processes are not observable. Thus, the final progression of the time series might differ, even given the same time series context. Thus, to ensure that the most suitable models are processed further, we additional reduce the number of instance candidates by executing our subsequence similarity evaluation. This evaluation is based on the fact that a forecast model is describing the underlying time series and its development. As a result, a forecast model that produced accurate results for a specific shape of a time series, is very likely to produce again accurate forecasts for another time series subsequence with a similar shape. For the purpose of this evaluation we store for each instance information about the time series segment it was used in. This comprises time series indexes marking the usage start K_s and end K_e of an instance. Based on these indexes we measure the distances between previous time series subsequences described by the instances stored in the CFMR to the time series subsequence of the current situation. The distance between recent and past subsequences is calculated using the well-known Pearson cross-correlation coefficient $R_{zz'}(\tau)$:

$$R_{zz'}(\tau) = \frac{\sum_{i=1}^{N-\tau}(z_i - \bar{z})(z'_{i+\tau} - \bar{z'})}{\sqrt{\sigma_z^2 \sigma_{z'}^2}}. \tag{5.2}$$

High values of the pearson coefficient provide strong evidence that the involved subsequences are very similar. Thus the instances with the highest coefficient values are chosen for the next steps of the selection process. Using the pearson correlation coefficient as a similarity measure poses the major conditions that: (1) the subsequences are required to have equal length and (2) that they are not phase-shifted. To ensure the first requirement, we always start the calculation from a fixed point (i.e., the current point and the end index of the instance usage K_e) and use the validity length from the retrieved instance $N = K_e - K_s$. In addition, we define a maximum subsequence length of two days (i.e., 96 values given half-hourly values) to avoid temporal degeneration of this comparison step.

To address the second requirement we align both subsequences with respect to a common reference point. For this purpose, we exploit the repeating pattern behavior of the seasonal cycles and define a lag τ over the period of a seasonal cycle s with respect to the time series index marking the end of the instance usage K_e and the current time series period K_c as follows:

$$\tau = |K \bmod s - N \bmod s|.$$

Accordingly, with the help of the lag τ we crop the endings of the subsequences with respect to the period of the chosen seasonal cycle s. We already included τ in the presented pearson cross correlation coefficient definition in Equation 5.2. It is important to note that the presented alignment technique limits the applicability of our subsequence similarity comparison to time series that do not change the length of their seasonal cycles. While this is the case for almost all time series in the energy domain (especially for energy demand time series), it might be different for time series in other domains. However, in the case of unstable seasonal cycles, one can use other similarity comparison techniques such as Dynamic Time Warping [15], which makes the general approach applicable to a much broader application area.

Evaluating the Accuracy

As a last step in the selection process we evaluate the accuracy of the resulting instances provided from the subsequence similarity comparison. The evaluation is conducted on the time series values of the last day. This length was specifically chosen, since for the energy domain considering the accuracy of the instances on the most recent day, provides a good indicator for accurate predictions of values for the following day. For other application domains another number of considered past values might be more appropriate. In principal, the history length typically should be chosen with respect to the forecast horizon. Thus, for one day ahead forecasts, one should accordingly choose a one day history length, while for a monthly forecast horizon one should consider a past month. As a result, we finally provide a number of instances, ordered by their accuracy on the most recent past. These instances comply with a time series context most similar to the current one, exhibit a shape most similar to the most recent subsequence and are the most accurate instances on the current development of the time series. Thus, it is safe to assume that they provide accurate forecast and serve as good starting points for the subsequent optimization process.

5.1.6 Evaluation

In this evaluation we proof the claims of our approach and show that with the help of the CFMR we can increase the parameter estimation efficiency by means of delivering more accurate forecasts in a shorter time frame compared to other approaches. Our evaluation compares the accuracy and the time necessary to gain the accuracy and is based on the two forecast models TSESM and EGRV (compare Section 3.3). The evaluation was conducted on the national grid dataset D1, the customers 7 and 40 from the MeRegio dataset D2 and the CRES solar dataset S1. As the test system we used an AMD Athlon 4850e with 4 GB RAM, Microsoft Windows 7 64bit and Microsoft Visual Studio C++ 2010.

We compare our approach to the following four common local and global parameter estimation approaches:

- *Monte-Carlo*: Iteratively evaluate random solutions.
- *Simulated annealing*: Global search without starting values.
- *Random-Restart Nelder-Mead*: Iterated local searching with starting values obtained by random search.
- *Single Nelder-Mead*: Local search with current parameters as starting values

Dataset	Error threshold	Window size
D1: National Grid	6%	12
D2: MeRegio	20% (Customer 7) 30% (Customer 40)	3
S1: CRES Solar	30%	2

Table 5.2 Error thresholds and window size per dataset.

The forecast models were optimized for one-step ahead forecasts and using the SMAPE error metric. We traced the lowest SMAPE obtained during optimization every two seconds and averaged over four runs per approach. For EGRV, the random-restart Nelder-Mead strategy was budgeted at five minutes, because unsuitable starting points lead to a very slow convergence. The presented results illustrate a single point in time only and are based on threshold-based model adaptations. In detail, we used data-set specific error thresholds/sliding windows sizes as defined in Table 5.2. These configurations lead to about 100 models stored into the tree at the time the model was re-estimated. We repeated our evaluation at other points in time and achieved similar results.

Figure 5.7 illustrates the results for the Triple Seasonal Exponential Smoothing model. We observe that our approach in general quickly reaches good accuracies on all datasets. For the datasets D1 and D2 (Customer 40) our approach achieved the best results regarding accuracy and time for the entire test period. There, the single simulated annealing approach achieved the worst results for dataset D1 and the Monte-Carlo approach performed worse for dataset D2 (Customer 40). For dataset D2 (Customer 7) and S1 our approach also achieved good results but performed not as well as other approaches. Regarding dataset D2 (Customer 7) our approach had a good start, but both local search approaches that involve the Nelder-Mead algorithm achieved better results at the start. Simulated annealing and the Monte-Carlo approach performed worse at the start. With further progression all approaches achieved similar results and differ by less than 0.5% SMAPE. For

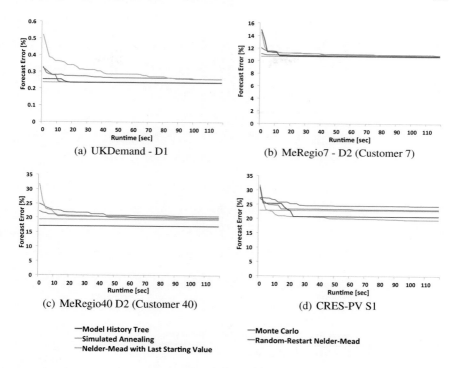

Fig. 5.7 Time vs. Accuracy - Triple Seasonal Exponential Smoothing.

dataset S1, our approach converged slower than all approaches except the Monte-Carlo sampling, but at the end it achieved the second best result. Only simulated annealing performed better by less than a half percent. We blame the results to the sequential execution of the local searches which are occasionally supplied unfavorable starting values in the beginning and the best starting values in the end. All other approaches differ by a more significant amount of two or more percent. Overall we can state that for the triple seasonal exponential smoothing our approach achieved good results on all datasets. In two cases it performed worse than other approaches, but however the other approaches have a larger divergence concerning their results, e.g. simulated annealing performed worse for dataset D1 and best for dataset S1. In contrast, our approach constantly achieved very good results, which leads to the assumption that it is useable for all datasets from the energy domain without prior evaluation. We furthermore observed only small overhead from using the tree. Depending on the dataset, the context computation, model insertion, and model retrieval took together always less than 4 msec. We also tested scalability of these operations for trees with up to 20,000 models and obtained a joint worst case

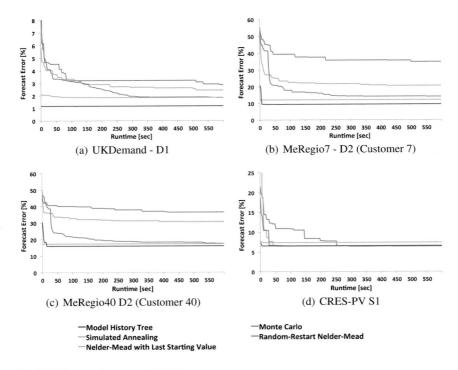

Fig. 5.8 Time vs. Accuracy - EGRV.

insertion and access time of less than 0.6 sec, which is negligible in comparison to the overall re-estimation time.

Figure 5.8 illustrates the results for the EGRV forecast model. In general, due to a much higher number of parameters, these models are more challenging to update than the previously discussed seasonal exponential smoothing models. In addition, we can observe that the differences in the reached maximal accuracy between the best and worst strategy are larger than for the TSESM, which means that the choice of a good re-estimation strategy is hence more critical. Our approach achieved the best results for all evaluated datasets by means of both accuracy and time. All strategies obtained improvements particularly quickly within the first minute of execution, but with further progression they were not able to reach the accuracy of our approach. For dataset D1 and D2 (Customer 7) the accuracy gap between our approach and its competitors is comparatively large. For dataset D2 (Customer 40) the local search strategies at the end achieved similar but slightly worse results. In contrast, the produced accuracies of the global search strategies were far off. Regarding the supply dataset S1 four out of five approaches converged to a similar result and except for Nelder-Mead with Last Starting Value the difference in accuracy is rather small. In addition the random-restart Nelder-Mead strategy shows only slow convergence in average, but it often finds good results after some minutes. This demonstrates the need to start optimization from suitable starting parameters. Again, the runtime overhead for inserting and retrieving models from the CFMR depends on the dataset, but was less than 5 msec in the worst case. Further experiments with 20,000 EGRV models in the tree still show access times of less than 1.1 sec which suggests that the tree scales also for large history bases. Overall, our approach achieved better results when used in conjunction with a more complex forecast model. For all datasets the CFMR outperformed all other estimation approaches, which makes it the most suitable approach for models that involve a large number of parameters. An interesting effect we observed during evaluation was the steadily improving capability of the tree to provide instances that were already optimal without further optimization. For later stages of the demand datasets, optimization was fully redundant and improved the result only on special days such as Christmas. However, to ensure the best possible result, the parallel optimization should still be conducted.

5.2 A Framework for Efficiently Integrating External Information

Besides using external information as a decision criterion for the online forecasting process it is also important for some use cases to directly consider this additional information in the forecast model. A very prominent example illustrating a crucial need for adding external information is the forecasting of renewable energy sources. In Section 3.1.3 we have shown that the development of production time series from renewable energy sources strongly depends on environmental influences such as the weather; meaningful predictions of wind energy for example are only possible when among other influences considering the wind speed. While time series describing the production of renewable energy source profit most from including external information, it is also beneficial to include such information when forecasting energy demand. Abnormal heat in the summer months for example, leads to an increased usage and energy consumption of air conditioning systems. Thus, including the weather information might allow to take such changing energy consumption into account when calculating respective energy demand forecasts.

The inclusion of external information is typically realized by adding the external time series as an additional component into the forecast model. This naïve approach in principal allows to consider the correlation between the time series and draw conclusions for the future development of the main time series. As a result, in most cases considering external information increases the forecasting accuracy. However, the integration also adds additional parameters to the model and thus, adds additional dimensions to the parameter search space. Thus, highly accurate forecast models that consider external information might significantly increase the time necessary for calculating forecasts, potentially rendering them unusable in real-time environments.

In the following we introduce an integration framework that greatly reduces the additional efforts when adding external information. Our approach optimizes the handling for external information and reduces the number of additional parameters added to the forecast model.

5.2.1 Separating the Forecast Model

The core idea underlying our approach is to separate the modeling of external information from the actual forecast model. The idea is reasoned by the fact that the relationships between the dependent variable and the external information as well as between the external information only change very slightly. This holds especially true for external information forming a stable physical system (because physical systems typically do not change rapidly) and external information with a high correlation to the main dependent variable (rapid changes would lead to a rather low correlation). The weather information typically used as external information in the energy domain, form such a stable physical system and thus, exhibit a stable relationship to energy demand and supply. The stability of the relationships leads to the assumption that a separate model for the external information is also more stable than the forecasting model. Thus, for the forecast model adaptation in most cases it is sufficient to just re-estimate the base model's parameters and exclude the separate external information model. This means that with the help of the separate model no additional time for adapting the forecast model is needed when considering external information. Furthermore, when dealing with multi-equation models, only a single external information model is necessary that can be reused for all involved sub-models.

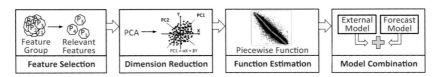

Fig. 5.9 Process for integrating external information.

In addition, we apply multiple techniques to the separate external information model to reduce the parameters in this model as much as possible. With that, we target to avoid a degeneration of the external model, allowing a more efficient parameter estimation even when both models—the main time series model and the external information model—are re-estimated. Overall, we use the process illustrated in Figure 5.9 to create the separate model describing the external information: First, we use feature selection techniques to select only the most relevant external information. Second, we apply dimension reduction techniques to reduce the number of parameters involved in the external information model. Afterwards, we estimate a function that describes the output of the dimension reduction best. Finally, we combine the base forecast model with the external information model. In the following, we describe the steps of our framework in more detail.

5.2.2 Reducing the Dimensionality of the External Information Model

The first two steps of the process target to reduce dimensionality of the separate external information model. For this purpose, we first conduct a selection step identifying the external time series that drive the development of the main time series most. Afterwards we apply Principal Component Analysis (PCA) to condense the information of the separate model into a reduced number of dimensions.

Feature Selection

In a first step to optimize the external information model, we determine the most relevant external information. With this step, we avoid the inclusion of less relevant factors that most probably are not substantially driving the development of the main time series, but in turn might have negative implications when used in conjunction with dimension reduction techniques. For this purpose, we create a correlation matrix, comprising the correlation between the dependent variable (i.e., the main time series) and the external factors as well as the correlation between external factors. The correlation is quantified using a correlation measure like the Pearson Correlation Coefficient (PCC) $r_{x,y}$ [25, 188, 190] or Spearman's Ro ρ [198, 221]. The choice of a suitable correlation measure depends on the type of the considered variables. The PCC for example does only support nominal variables and requires a linear dependency between them. In contrast Spearman's Ro does also allow non-linear dependencies and additionally support ordinal variables. In this book we focus on the PCC, since time series in the energy domain typically only contain continuous variables and ordinal variables are very rare. Figure 5.10

illustrates an example correlation matrix using the PCC. The PCC provides a correlation measure in the range of $-1 < r_{x,y} < 1$. We omit the notation of $\pm$, since both high positive as well as high negative correlations likewise refer to an important external factor. With the help of the correlation matrix, we now select the features as follows:

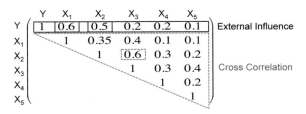

Fig. 5.10 Example correlation matrix.

1. We determine an inclusion threshold ε that is the median of the absolute correlations to the dependent variable Y. We chose the median for the inclusion threshold due to its robustness against outliers and its ability of being a good distinction between relevant and non-relevant influences independently of the absolute value. In our example $\varepsilon = 0.35$, thus the external influences X_1 and X_2 (black box in Figure 5.10) are selected as being relevant.
2. To avoid redundant external factors, we evaluate the correlation between the selected influences and prune one of two influences whenever the correlation r is larger (or smaller in case of a negative correlation) than our defined similarity threshold ω. In our example we define $\omega = \pm0.9$ and thus, no influences are pruned.
3. To also cover inter-relationships between the selected influences and all available external factors, we also evaluate the cross correlation between them. We then select all influences with a correlation factor $|r|$ larger than our defined cross-correlation threshold σ. In our example, $\sigma = 0.5$ and X_3 with a correlation of 0.6 to X_2 (grey dashed box in Figure 5.10) is selected.

As a result, from our example the influences X_1, X_2 and X_3 are candidates for the external information model. The values of the parameters ω and σ are configuration-specific and greatly depend on the use case. From multiple empirical evaluations on several energy demand and supply datasets we recommend to define $\omega = 0.9$ and $\sigma = 0.5$ for energy demand and supply time series. With these values we provided the most meaningful results from the feature selection step to the subsequent dimension reduction. A very high correlation between two external time series (i.e., when the correlation roughly corresponds to our similarity threshold $\omega = \pm0.9$) likewise influencing the development of the main time series, means that both time series are very similar and are highly describing a very similar fact. In addition, in this case both factors are driving the development of the dependent variable in the same way, meaning that including both factors in the following dimension reduction process step would overemphasis a specific development over other likewise important developments. With respect to the value of σ the value of 0.5 is generally acknowledged as an at least moderate correlation. This means that a currently not included external factor exhibiting a correlation factor of 0.5 and higher to an already selected influence is at least moderately describing the development of one or multiple already selected influences. As a result, such indirect influences bare the potential to increase the information content of the external information model by describing inner relationships and coherences between the external information. This is especially helpful to retrieve meaningful results from the subsequent dimension reduction step. It is important to note that ω and σ are design time parameters that are determined once during the configuration of the system and that do not change during runtime. Accordingly, these two parameters do not violate our *parameterfree forecasting* requirement. In particular, adding those two design time parameters avoids a human invention when selecting the most appropriate influencing factors.

Condensing Information using Dimension Reduction Techniques

In the feature selection step unnecessary influences are pruned form the external influence model to avoid negative side effects and an unnecessary high number of parameters. In a second step, we directly reduce the parameters involved in the external information model, using dimension reduction techniques. We decided to focus on the Principal Component Analysis (PCA) [139, 189]. The PCA removes redundancies in the data, but aims to preserve as much valuable information as possible. For this purpose, it uses an orthogonal linear transformation to project a dataset comprising multiple features into a new vector space with less or equal dimensions than the original space. In the new space, the original variables are represented by a set of linear combinations of them, where as part of the transformation the correlation between the linear combinations is minimized. The resulting combinations are called the principal components and can be seen as lines through the multi-dimensional space starting from the origin and minimizing the mean square error (MSE) to the data points. The principal component with the smallest MSE is called the first principal component and describes the greatest variance in the data. Each further principal component is orthogonal to the preceding one. Thus, in contrast to other dimension reduction techniques such as factor analysis, the PCA produces a result ordered by the significance of the influence on the dependent variable.

Figure 5.11 illustrates the steps of the PCA, which is applied to our external influence model as follows:

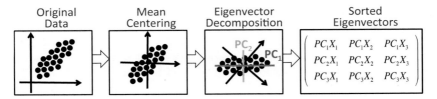

Fig. 5.11 Steps of the principal component analysis.

1. Subtract the mean from the influences to create a mean-centered matrix.
2. From the mean-centered matrix compute the $p \times p$ covariance matrix.
3. Conduct the eigenvalue decomposition to create the eigenvalues and corresponding eigenvectors.
4. Eigenvectors are principal components and can be sorted by their eigenvalues. The vector with the greatest eigenvalue is the first principal component.

From the resulting set of principal components we can in principal choose an arbitrary number of representatives to approximate the original dataset. The beneficial number of principal components substantially depends on the desired accuracy and performance. Typically, the first principal component provides sufficient accuracy and means the least number of involved parameters. However, for some use cases it is also possible to dynamically add additional principal components as long as they significantly increase the accuracy. The selected principal components represent the entirety of all external factors that mainly influence the development of the main time series.

While we focused our descriptions on the dimension reduction using PCA, it is also possible to employ alternative dimension reduction techniques. One important representative is Factor Analysis [152, 224] that provides a dimension reduction based on identifying latent factors. A comprehensive overview about dimension reduction is given in a study of Burges [41]. The final applicability of different dimension reduction techniques greatly depends on the use-case, where for the energy domain PCA provides very good results.

5.2.3 Determining the Final External Model

The principal components provided by the dimension reduction step could directly be used as linear combinations for our external model. However, from our experiments we found that relating the principal components to the dependent variable and estimating functions describing the relationship increases the final accuracy for most datasets. In particular, each function approximates the response values of the dependent variable for different values of the selected principal component.

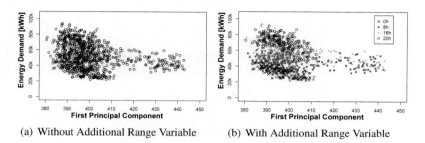

(a) Without Additional Range Variable   (b) With Additional Range Variable

Fig. 5.12 Range splitting using additional variable.

To estimate suitable functions, we combine linear regression with the concept of piecewise functions. Thus, we use different linear functions for different value ranges. For this purpose, we follow a two-step process, were we (1) determine suitable ranges and (2) then estimate a linear function for each range.

To divide the data into suitable ranges, we first estimate a function that describes the entire value range of the explanatory variable. We can then use the extreme points of this function as the borders for the value ranges. However, the most suitable degree of the function is unknown in advance. Thus, we apply non-linear regression and increase the power of the polynomial step-by-step, starting with a linear function. This process converges when the accuracy benefit of increasing the degree is smaller than the configurable significance parameter θ that is determined during design time (e.g., from our experiments: 0.5% for energy demand and 2% for energy supply). As soon as we found a suitable polynomial, we calculate its extreme points and use these points to divide our data. If the resulting polynomial is still linear, no extreme points exist and we directly use the resulting linear function.

However, for some data this method fails, because the principal components do not sufficiently describe the dependent variable, even though they are correlated. This is illustrated in Figure 5.12(a), where we see the first principal component and the energy response values for the MeRegio energy demand dataset. This data is hard to fit and thus, it is hard to find suitable ranges for the principal component. The issue mostly occurs when the external information are not significant enough. In the energy domain this might for example occur, when forecasting energy demand, where the influence on the weather is significantly lower compared to energy supply. However, some applications might require the best possible accuracy, meaning that it is still worth to consider the external information. To address these issues, instead of only dividing the data with respect to the principal component, we also employ an approach similar to multi-equation models. Thus, to ease the data that a single model is required to describe, we decompose the data of the principal component into several time slots. For each time slot we determine a separate sub model describing the data in the respective range Figure 5.12(b) illustrates the data divided per time range. We can see that the data for a time range is much easier to describe using a polynomial function. Thus, after dividing the data with respect to the most influencing factor, we calculate the extrema for all functions using the approach mentioned above.

In the second step, we apply linear regression for each identified range to calculate a linear function that describes this data portion best. The result of our external influence model creation step is a set of linear functions that forms in its entirety a multi-equation external influence model. As for other multi-equation models each sub-model is responsible for providing forecast for its specific time range. In the example described in Figure 5.12 our multi-equation external influence model consists of 4 sub-models, where each model is assigned to an eight hour time range.

5.2.4 Creating a Combined Forecast Model

In the next step we need to combine the external information model with the original forecast model. We suggest two options: First, the *Indirect Integration*, where both models are combined using a weighted linear combination. The efforts for this additional estimation are low, because the linear combination consists of only two parameters. Second, the *Hybrid Integration*, which is a variation of the indirect integration. There, in addition to the external information model, we include the most important external factor directly (and without using PCA) into the forecast model. Thus, we combine the efficiency of the indirect integration with the possible accuracy gain of directly integrating external information. This model is especially useful when the connection between the dependent and the explaining variables exhibits a rather low significance as it is the case for example when considering weather information for energy demand time series. The reason is that dimension reduction is always removing some information from the data, even though PCA tries to preserve as much information as possible. If the influence of the explaining variable is anyway relatively low, directly including the variable with the highest influence compensates for this loss of information that in this case has a more severe impact. In contrast, when considering time series with a strong relationship to the main time series, the dimension reduction even removes negative effects from opposing strong influences, overemphasis of a single component and overfitting. For these time series adding the most influencing value as a separate parameter in addition to the separate model means to unnecessarily amplify the influence of a single variable that also provides a large share of the information content contained in the principal components. Thus, the high influence of the selected explaining variable is considered twice, which typically does not increase the resulting accuracy, but in some cases even leads to an accuracy reduction.

Besides the advantages with respect to including external information with limiting the additionally required efforts, combining an external information model with a statistical model as described above, bares the potential that even models that do not support the consideration of external information can benefit from including them. The highly accurate multi-seasonal exponential smoothing for example, does not support the inclusion of external information, meaning that it falls behind other forecast models in cases where external information are considered or even required. With the help of our integration framework we can compensate for this disadvantage.

5.2.5 Integration with the Online Forecasting Process

The framework described above directly integrates with our online forecasting process in scenarios where external information is considered. As part of the process we can exploit the fact that for many external influences, especially the ones typically used in the energy domain (compare Section 3.1.3), a separate external information model remains relatively stable. This means that the relationships and interdependencies between the external factors as well as the influence on the dependent time series do not change frequently, but rather very gradually over a long time frame. The energy production of a wind mill for example, greatly depends on several physical variables and characteristics of the wind mill; important ones are among others wind speed, wind direction, air density, and the electrical efficiency of the wind mill. The physical coherences between those factors and especially between the given physical conditions remain constant throughout a long time frame and changes are only very slightly. The age of the wind mill for example reduces the electrical efficiency of the wind mill over time and thus, reduces the energy production. However, it typically takes years for the aging effect to show a measurable impact on the energy production and it is not fluctuation between multiple states.

The stability of the separate external information model provides the advantage that we neither need to create a new model for each forecasting request nor do we need to consider it in every parameter estimation. Thus, with respect to our online forecasting process, in most cases we can create and/or adapt the separate external information model asynchronously to forecasting requests. We may then use an already estimated external information model instance for several online forecasting process executions. Furthermore, we can reuse the estimated instance of the separate model for all forecast model instances considered during the local optimization. This also means in particular that multi-equation models do only require one external information model instance for all comprised sub-models. As a consequence, during the local optimization process, we only need to estimate the actual forecast models without additional parameters plus the very cheap linear combination of the actual forecast model instance and the external information model instance (linear combination with only two parameters). As a result, with the help of the separate external information model we are significantly reducing the efforts for calculating accurate forecasts when considering external information. Finally, for the rare case where we need to estimate the parameters of both the external information model and the actual forecast models at the same time, we can exploit the fact that the separate external information model is inherently independent and estimate it in parallel to the actual local optimization process. After this one time re-estimation we can then use the estimated instance for the entire remaining local optimization process.

To further foster the integration of our external information framework into the online forecasting process, we allow to adapt the creation and estimation process of the external information model with respect to the requirements of the requesting applications. The most important adjustments with respect to runtime and accuracy are provided by the selection of the involved principal components provided in the dimension reduction step. It is important to note that each selected principal component requires the step of determining its own piecewise function and thus, basically each principal component creates its own partial external information model. Thus in the step of determining the final external information model, we need to combine all sub-models created by the selected principal components. This is again done by calculating a linear combination of all the involved sub-models where the parameters of the linear combination are subject to an estimation process. As a result, adding additional principal components to the typically selected first principal component significantly increases the time needed for creating and estimating the external information model. The gain is in some cases an improved accuracy. As a result, we propose to create multiple versions of the external information model during the initialization phase of the online forecasting process and store them in an additional external information model repository. Such a repository contains a set of differently configured external information model instances for its specific time series. In particular, the contained instances include a different number or composition of the available principal components. In this context, the maximum number of principal components is equal to the number of external information selected in the *feature selection* step. Thus, the number of different instances in the repository is limited. In addition, only instances that significantly improve the accuracy over the base external model (containing only the first principal component) are eventually stored in the repository. Together with the instances we store information about the accuracy gain and the additional time that is required when using a specific instance in exchange for the base external model. As a result, during runtime we can very flexibly decide on the basis of the given

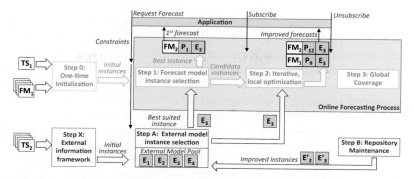

Fig. 5.13 External information framework integrated with Online Forecasting Process.

application constraints, which external information model we are using from the external information model repository. Hence, we are again able to likewise serve the needs of applications requiring short runtimes or the maximal possible accuracy. Between forecasting requests, in most cases together with the global coverage process, we maintain the external information model repository.

Figure 5.13 illustrates the integration of the external information model with the online forecasting process. There in the first one-time initialization step (step X) we see the creation and initial estimation of the external information models that are the initial part of the external information model repository. This is done during the initialization of the online forecasting process. During a forecasting request we execute step A. In this step we select from the repository the external information model that is considered to be best suited for the given application constraints. It is first combined with the most accurate forecast model instance from the forecast model repository to create the first intermediate forecast and then provided to the local optimization process for consideration during the parameter estimation. The maintenance step B is executed asynchronously to forecasting requests, similar and in most cases in parallel to the global coverage process. There, the instances are re-estimated and provided that an improvement was found, the improved instance is replacing its respective counterpart in the external information model repository.

5.2.6 *Experimental Evaluation*

In our evaluation, we substantiate the claims of our integration framework and discuss options for implementing it. The evaluation shows that our approach significantly reduces the additional efforts when integrating external information. For our experiments we used the EGRV model and the double seasonal exponential smoothing (DSESM) model (compare Section 3.3). The experiments were conducted on two single customer (in particular customer 7 and 40) time series from datasets D2 and S2 as introduced in Section 3.1. For the parameter estimation, we used the Nelder Mead Downhill Simplex algorithm (compare Section 3.4). The re-estimation process comprises the estimation of the forecast model, the estimation of the separate external information model (EGRV: one model for all sub-models) and the estimation of the final combination. Thus, we decided to present the extreme case, where the estimation of the external information model is part of the forecasting process. It is important to note that, as explained in Section 5.2.5, the (re-) estimation is typically conducted asynchronously to the estimation process. Only the linear combination joining the external information model with the actual forecast model instances is part of the local optimization. Thus, the actual additional runtimes in our pEDM system are typically neglectable or at least very small. For our experiments we assumed exact predictions for the external information, because uncertain time series are an orthogonal issue that are not subject of this work.

As test system we used an Intel Core i7 2635QM (2.0 GHz), 4GB RAM, Mac OSX 10.6.8, C++ (GCC 4.2.1). All results are the average of 100 subsequent runs.

Time vs. Accuracy

In the first experiment we evaluated the runtime and final accuracy (using the SMAPE error metric) of the parameter re-estimation. Overall, we compared our separate external information model with the indirect modeling approach (Framework(Indirect)) with the models when adding no external factors (Pure Model), a naïve direct integration of the external information without using a separate model (Direct Model) and the hybrid version of our framework (Framework(Hybrid)) (compare Section 5.2.4). Selected results are illustrated in Figure 5.14 (EGRV model) and Figure 5.15 (DSESM model). We observed very high forecast errors for the dataset S2 (Figures 5.14(a) and 5.15(a)) when not considering external information (Pure Model). Thus, only including external information enables accurate predictions for energy supply. For both forecast models and both datasets, the indirect version of our framework (Framework (Indirect)) showed the best runtime of all solutions considering external information. In addition, our approach even showed the best accuracy for the dataset S2, even though the dimension reduction using PCA condensed the included information. Focusing on the EGRV forecast model: Using the indirect model approach of our framework (Framework (Indirect)) we limited the additional efforts for adding external information to only 48.64 ms and increased the accuracy by 38.40 %. In contrast, using the naïve Direct Model the additional effort was 580.77 ms and the accuracy increase was only 34.24 %. The hybrid model approach of our framework (Framework (Hy-

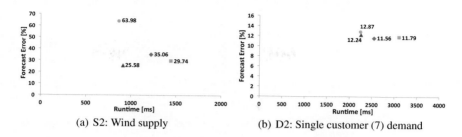

(a) S2: Wind supply   (b) D2: Single customer (7) demand

Fig. 5.14 EGRV model: Comparing different integration approaches for external information.

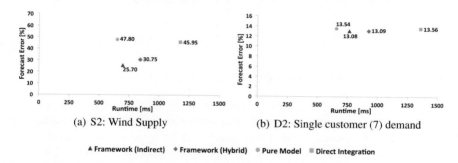

(a) S2: Wind Supply   (b) D2: Single customer (7) demand

▲ Framework (Indirect)   ◆ Framework (Hybrid)   ● Pure Model   ■ Direct Integration

Fig. 5.15 DSESM: Comparing different integration approaches for external information.

brid)) did not provide better results. We account the accuracy advantage of the indirect modeling approach (Framework (Indirect)) to a possible overfitting when directly including external information as done in the Direct Model and the hybrid version of our framework (Framework (Hybrid)). In addition, dimension reduction techniques also show the impact of removing negative effects from opposing strong influences and avoid overemphasizing a single component. The results for the DSESM model are similar. For the MeRegio single customer energy demand dataset (smaller dependency on external information) the results are more diverse (Figures 5.14(b) and 5.15(b)). Using the indirect modeling approach (Framework (Indirect)) we still increased the accuracy with small additional effort of only 12.40 ms, but as expected the accuracy gain was less significant (only 0.63 %). For the EGRV model the Direct Model approach provided a better final accuracy (increase of 1.07 %), however, the additional effort is much higher (857.24 ms). A suitable alternative in this case is the hybrid modeling (Framework (Hybrid)), providing a good balance between additional effort (305.78 ms) and accuracy gain (1.30 %). Overall, our framework provides an efficient way of integrating external information and increasing the forecasting accuracy using the indirect variant for supply and the hybrid variant for demand.

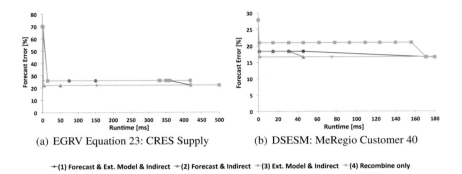

(a) EGRV Equation 23: CRES Supply   (b) DSESM: MeRegio Customer 40

-•(1) Forecast & Ext. Model & Indirect -•(2) Forecast & Indirect -•(3) Ext. Model & Indirect -•(4) Recombine only

Fig. 5.16 Comparison of re-estimation strategies.

Different Re-Estimation Strategies

In this experiment, we evaluated different re-estimation strategies with the goal of showcasing that the external information model is more stable and does not require to be part of every re-estimation. We compared (1) the re-estimation of all models, (2) the re-estimation of the forecast model and the combined model, (3) the re-estimation of the external influence model and the combined model and (4) the re-estimation of the combined model (Combination) only. Figure 5.16 illustrates the results. For the dataset S2 (Figure 5.16(a)) all estimation methods finally reached the same accuracy. However, the runtimes of strategies 1 and 3 were longer. When repeating the experiment at different points in time, we observed that strategy 4 did not always reach the best accuracy, while Strategy 2 produced the maximal accuracy at all times. The results are similar for the DSESM model. Using the dataset D2 (Figure 5.16(b)), still all strategies ultimately reach the same accuracy, but their speed is different. We observed the shortest runtime using strategy 4 followed by strategy 2. Strategy 1 and 3 are slower. Strategy 3 exhibits the longest runtime. However, strategy 4 again did not reach the maximal accuracy at all points in time, which finally renders method 2 as most appropriate for both datasets. This experiment confirms our assumption that the best possible accuracy in the least time is reached when re-estimating the forecast model and afterwards creating the combined model without estimating the external information model (strategy 2). Thus, integrating the external information model with the online forecasting process as described in Section 5.2.5 is reasonable and leads to the best performance while providing the best accuracy.

To substantiate the results, we simulated an evolving time series, repeating the experiment at several points in time. To do so, we only used $3/4$ of the CRES dataset (9 months) and added the remaining $1/4$ of the data (3 months) successively. After each added value we evaluated the accuracy. We triggered a re-

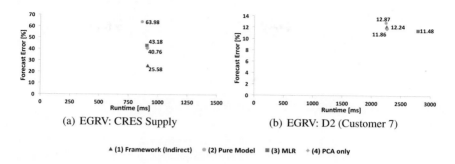

(a) EGRV: CRES Supply

(b) EGRV: D2 (Customer 7)

▲ (1) Framework (Indirect)   ● (2) Pure Model   ■ (3) MLR   ◆ (4) PCA only

Fig. 5.17 Comparison of different external model variants.

estimation, whenever the average error for the last 10 values was 10 % higher than the last estimation error. We observed similar results at all occasions. However, when only re-estimating the forecast model or the model combination the number of re-estimations increased to 887 compared to 607 when re-estimating all models. Thus, while in most cases it is sufficient to re-estimate the forecast model only, from time to time all models should be re-estimated. This is done by the periodic and asynchronous maintenance of the external information model repository.

Comparing Different Types of External Information Models

In this experiment, we evaluated design alternatives for the external influence model. We compared our approach (Framework(Indirect)) to alternatives that employ multiple linear regression (MLR) or that directly use the eigenvectors of the PCA without conducting a subsequent piecewise function determination. Figure 5.17 illustrates the results for the EGRV model. The results for the DSESM model are very similar and are thus we omit them here. For the CRES wind supply dataset (Figure 5.17(a)), all approaches need almost the same time to converge (~910 ms), but our framework provides the best final accuracy (improvement of 15 %). For the dataset D2 (Figure 5.17(b)) the pure PCA method and the MLR provide slightly better results (~0.75 %) compared to our approach. While the MLR in return needs more time, the pure PCA method finishes in similar time. We repeated the experiment for several points in time and observed similar results, but with changing final accuracies. Hence, the pure PCA method seems to be better suited for the dataset D2. We assume that the smaller dependence of the time series on the external influences is the reason for this observation. This results in the need for a less complex model, the calculation of a piecewise function is not required and might sometimes even lead to slightly inferior results. However, our approach provides more robust results on both demand and supply datasets. Furthermore, the difference on the demand dataset is rather small, while the advantage of our approach on the supply dataset is significant. Thus, our approach is more general and suits demand and supply datasets equally.

5.3 Exploiting Hierarchical Time Series Structures

In the previous two sections we presented how to utilize time series context information to improve the forecast model selection process as well as the integration of external information. However, besides the context information in the sense of external influences, there is also a further class of additional information provided for some time series. In particular, many application domains exhibit a hierarchical data organization, with time series and forecast models on multiple hierarchical levels. Here, the time series are typically aggregated along the hierarchy based on dimensional attributes such as location or product [96, 98, 132]. The forecasting calculation process in these environments is especially complex since it is necessary to involve data and entities across hierarchical levels and to ensure forecasting consistency among them. In the following, we introduce an approach that exploits knowledge from these hierarchies to increase the efficiency of forecasting in hierarchical environments.

The approach presented in this section is especially suited for the energy domain, since the European electricity market (similar to markets in other regions) is hierarchically organized as illustrated in Section 2.1.1 and especially Figure 2.1. Forecasting in such an environment typically means that higher level entities calculate forecasts based on the aggregated data of lower level entities. Thus, a balance responsible party (BRP) on the second hierarchy level for example, forecasts the energy consumption and production for the entire balance group, using the data provided by the corresponding entities (private and industrial consumers, producers, prosumers). Furthermore, the BRP also forecasts the individual energy consumption and production of large companies as well as of smaller consumers in a certain granularity for example private households on a street level. The measurements from the smart meters are transmitted to the BRP, which aggregates the data with respect to its needs and creates respective forecast models. The BRP is responsible for maintaining all forecast models and adapting them to the most recent measurements, which means large efforts, due to the time consuming parameter estimation. Thus, the BRP might face the issue of not being able to fulfill execution deadlines posed by real-time balancing, since similar to non-hierarchical time series, also for hierarchical time series it is very important to provide accurate forecasts at any point in time.

We tackle this challenge by introducing a novel hierarchical forecasting system that exploits the hierarchical organization of the electricity market to increase the forecasting efficiency. In particular, we propose to decentralize the forecasting calculation by deploying forecast models directly to the smart meters of customers. Companies on higher levels of the hierarchy (e.g., balance group, city, district), may then request the individual customer models to form a global forecast model representing the entire consumption and production of the included lower level entities. This merging process is several magnitudes less expensive than the (re-)estimation of the forecast model parameters. As a result, with the help of our hierarchical forecasting system balancing companies are able to rapidly calculate very accurate forecasts and hence to balance energy demand and supply in real-time. In addition, also the customers benefit from the additional forecasting capabilities available in their smart meters. The emerging trend of smart building and smart home systems can use these forecasting capabilities to offer enhanced functionalities.

5.3.1 Forecasting in Hierarchies

The topic of forecasting in hierarchical environments and especially increasing the forecasting efficiency in such environments is recently gaining more and more attention in research and industry. Some historic and recent studies analyze forecasting for hierarchically organized time series [71, 103, 252]. They typically examine the issue of the most beneficial aggregation type. In general two approaches exist. When using the bottom-up aggregation, forecast are calculated on the lowest hierarchy level and aggregated to determine higher level forecasts. In contrast, for the top-down approach the forecast calculation is conducted on the higher level and the results are disaggregated to determine the forecasts of the lower levels. The question about the most beneficial aggregation is not ultimately decidable. Additionally, all studies only consider the complete aggregation of forecast results and do not deal with the aggregation of forecast models.

Hyndman et al. introduced a hierarchical forecasting approach aiming to improve the hierarchical forecasting with the goal to provide a higher accuracy than either a complete top-down or bottom-up forecasting approach [132]. They do so by calculating independent predictions of all time series on all hierarchical layers. Afterwards, the use a regression model to combine forecasting results in accordance to the hierarchical structure. The general target of Hyndman et al. is to increase the forecasting accuracy at the expense of being computationally more expensive. The reason is that multiple forecast models are estimated on the aggregated levels using numerical optimization methods. This contradicts to the goal of the approach we are presenting in this section, where we clearly target to increase the forecasting efficiency while maintaining a high level of accuracy. At the end we could even combine both approaches allowing for a higher accuracy using the approach from Hyndman et al. while our approach would limit the necessary runtime increase their approach is causing.

Recently, Fischer et al. published an approach that uses only a sample of base forecast models to calculate the forecasts in a time series hierarchy [97]. Thus, a forecast on a specific hierarchy level may be based on forecasts produced by only a subset of optimized models on other hierarchy levels. With this approach Fischer et al. were able to achieve reliable forecast accuracy comparable to aggregating all predictions of the base models. If they base the forecast on only 21% of the base models, the precision is as high as if all the models were considered. Thus, they could significantly reduce the time required for calculating forecasts for hierarchically organized time series, while still maintaining a high level of accuracy. To identify the optimal levels and distribution of forecast models Fischer et al. also presented a model configuration advisor for forecast models in hierarchical environments such as data cubes [98]. The model configuration advisor iteratively creates model configurations by adding and removing forecast models throughout the hierarchy. After each iteration the improvement (forecast accuracy and costs) of the new model configuration is evaluated. The advisor task is stopped as soon as some pre-defined stopping criteria such as a specific accuracy or a cost limit is reached.

However, none of the above mentioned approaches specifically targets to reduce the costs of the expensive parameter estimation by exploiting information from the hierarchy. For this reason, in the following we introduce our hierarchical forecasting framework that allows an almost instant calculation of forecasting results, while at the same time ensuring a very high forecasting accuracy.

5.3.2 Approach Outline

The core idea of our approach is to specifically push the responsibility to build and maintain a forecast model to the base level of the hierarchical electricity market. This is motivated by the fact that smart meters are expected to be widely deployed and we may exploit their available computing capacity. Thus, next to their task of recording current measurements, smart meters gain the capability to express historical and future consumption and production behavior of a customer using the now included forecast model. Generally speaking we can see a forecast model as a compact representation of the customer data. In an ideal case the forecast model describes values that are identical to the time series of a customer. While, in the real-world forecast models always exhibit a certain error for describing the data, this error is typically reduced with an increasing aggregation level. The reason is that fluctuations of single customers are to a large extent neutralized by other entities in the aggregation group. Following these facts, the idea is to transmit the forecast models of the single customers and aggregate them to directly determine forecast models on different levels of the hierarchy describing the overall energy consumption and production of the respective entities. Forecast model aggregation means that each of the global forecast model components (i.e., the combination of a forecast model coefficient x and its parameter p) is calculated using a weighted linear combination of the respective single customer components.

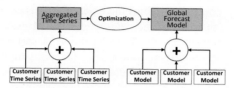

Fig. 5.18 Estimation vs. aggregation approach.

Figure 5.18 illustrates our forecast model aggregation on the right-hand side, while on the left side we see the conventional model construction using time series aggregation. In our evaluation (compare Section 5.3.7) we show that a forecast model aggregation is several orders of magnitudes less time consuming compared to the conventional parameter estimation using numerical optimization algorithms, while maintaining a comparable accuracy. As a result, we significantly reduce the time for calculating and providing accurate forecasts and thus, improve the capabilities of companies competing in the European electricity market to comply to the new real-time requirements.

In the following, we describe the mathematical details of the forecast model aggregation. Afterwards, we show how to apply our approach to two real-world forecast models commonly used in the energy domain—namely exponential smoothing in the variant introduced by Taylor et al. [229] and the multi-equation forecast model EGRV [197] (compare Section 3.3).

5.3.3 Classification of Forecast Model Coefficients and Parameters

A prerequisite for aggregating forecast models is to have a detailed look at forecast model coefficients and their corresponding parameters. Coefficients can be divided into endogenous and exogenous coefficients depending on their characteristics and their handling on the next hierarchy level. Endogenous coefficients describe the main time series that is aggregated through the hierarchical levels by summing the component values of the involved lower level entities. In the energy domain for example a typical endogenous coefficient is the energy consumption.

In contrast, exogenous coefficients are not directly connected to the main time series, but describe an external influence. They can be either entity-specific or valid for larger entity groups. Exogenous coefficients occur as additional time series or boolean variables, where boolean variables simply distinguish between existence or non-existence of a fact using the values 0 or 1 (e.g., current day is a holiday: yes (1), no (0)). When using an additional time series, the external influence is determined by the external time series value and the corresponding parameter. In contrast, when using boolean variables the external influence of the coefficient is reflected entirely by the value of the parameter. Typical examples for this coefficient group are the current day of the week (boolean variable, e.g., Monday=0 or 1) or the temperature (additional time series, e.g., temperature at customer k is 15 °C, parameter is 1.2, temperature increases forecasted value by 18). External influences are typically aggregated by using the average of all values. We classify typical coefficients from the energy domain as follows:

Exogenous

- Calendar information: day, week, month, year. This information is typically the same for all entities and is incorporated as boolean variables.
- Weather: wind speed, temperature, cloudiness. The weather situation is often the same for a large group of entities, depending on their local distribution. Mostly they are incorporated as additional time series.
- Special events: sport events, political decisions, holidays. Special events are mostly the same for a large number of entities, but their influence greatly varies between them. They are commonly represented as boolean variables.

Endogenous

- Consumption/production: This is typically the main time series when predicting energy demand and supply.
- Seasons: They consider historic time series values in a specific distance from the current point in time (e.g., one day).
- Past errors: The historic forecast error describes the deviation of the forecast from the real time series.

The reason for discussing exogenous and endogenous coefficients is their different consideration in the final aggregated forecast model. This means that separate aggregation rules apply for each coefficient group. In addition, the final influence of the coefficient groups is varying between forecasting points in time and is entity specific.

5.3.4 Aggregation in Detail

Creating aggregated global time series $x(t_i)$ on a higher level means to sum the time series of all lower level entities $x_k(t_i)$, with k referring to the k-th customer and t_i to the current point in time. Accordingly, following our assumption that a forecast model approximately describes its underlying time series, we create the next level global forecast model $M(t_i)$ by aggregating the forecast models of all lower level entities $M_k(t_i)$ as illustrated in Equation 5.3.

$$x(t_i) = \sum_{k=1}^{n} x_k(t_i) \approx \sum_{k=1}^{n} M_k(t_i) = M(t_i). \tag{5.3}$$

In the following, we omit the notation (t_i) for readability reasons.

A forecast model M can be divided into separate components $M(C_1,...,C_k)$, where we define a model component C_k as a specific forecast model coefficient x combined with its parameter p: $C = p \cdot x$. A linear model $a \cdot x + b$ for example consist of two model components $a \cdot x$ and b (where the coefficient is 1). To create the global forecast model M, we separately aggregate the components C_k of all corresponding lower level forecast models ($M_k, k \in K$), including their co-efficients x_k and parameters p_k. Accordingly, the calculation of the global forecast model component C, which likewise consists of a global parameter p and a global aggregated time series coefficient $x = \sum_{k=1}^{K} x_k$, is defined as:

$$C = p \cdot x = \sum_{k=1}^{K} p_k x_k. \tag{5.4}$$

Since the aggregated time series of the coefficient x is available to the upper level entity, the only missing factor for calculating a global forecast model component is the global parameter p. We adapt Equation 5.4, to define a general aggregation rule for determining the parameter of a global forecast model component as:

$$p = \sum_{k=1}^{K} \frac{p_k x_k}{x}. \tag{5.5}$$

Dividing the single entity time series value x_k by the global aggregated time series coefficient x, as done in Equation 5.4, is equivalent to determining the current share of a single entity value on the global value. Thus, the global forecast model parameter p is derived by creating a linear combination of the single entity parameters multiplied by their share on the global time series.

Equation 5.5 is already sufficient to determine the parameters and with that, the components of a global forecast model. However, it has the disadvantage of considering the coefficient values of the individual entities x_k and the values of the respective global coefficient x. Thus, we would have to request and process the current measurements of all lower level entities each time the global forecast model is adapted, instead of communicating only with entities that adapted their local model. This clearly contradicts to our target of establishing a more flexible communication between the hierarchical levels (compare Section 5.3.6), where values are only transmitted if they are really needed. To address this issue, we approximate the current share (x_k/x) of an individual entity by its average historic share (λ). The reason is that the average share of an entity is typically relatively stable over time and thus, it is not necessary to re-calculate it for every adaptation of the global forecast model. We define the historic share of an individual entity as:

$$\lambda_k = \frac{\bar{x}_k}{\sum_{k=1}^{K} \bar{x}_k}, \text{ where } \bar{x}_k = \frac{1}{N} \sum_{i=1}^{N} x_k(t_i). \tag{5.6}$$

Thus, the average historic share is the ratio of the arithmetic mean over a time series sample $(1...N)$ of an individual entity to the summed arithmetic mean of the time series sample of all entities. The size of the sample is configuration-specific. In our experiments for the energy domain, we found a sample size of one day as most beneficial. To create the historic average share for the lower level entities, we transmit the average values of the respective time series coefficients $\bar{x}_k$ in conjunction with the individual forecast models. Accordingly, the initial share is determined during the system initialization, when all entities transmit their initial forecast models (see Section 5.3.6). We sum up the averages of all entities $\sum_{k=1}^{K} \bar{x}_k$ to create the global average value, which we use to determine the shares for the single entities (λ_k). Afterwards, we adapt the share of an entity, whenever it submits new average time series values together with an adapted forecast model. In the energy domain the determination of the average historic shares is even simpler, because for billing purposes all lower level entities transmit their actual consumption and production values once per accounting period anyway. This transmission is done asynchronously to the forecasting process, which means a substantial reduction of the communication efforts compared to transmitting values for every model adaptation.

With the average historic share (λ_k) we adapt Equation 5.5 to calculate the forecast model parameters for the next level entity as a weighted linear combination:

$$p = \sum_{k=1}^{K} p_k \lambda_k. \tag{5.7}$$

The global forecast model is now created by applying the aggregation rule to all components of the model $M(C_1,...,C_n)$ and plugging in the parameters accordingly. Thus, for aggregating a single global forecast model component $C = p \cdot x$ we combine Equations 5.4 and 5.7 to finally arrive at:

$$C = \sum_{k=1}^{K} p_k \lambda_k x. \tag{5.8}$$

For exogenous coefficients we adapt Equation 5.5, since for such coefficients the global time series is formed by averaging the customer values instead of summing them. Thus, in this case $x = \bar{x} = \frac{1}{K} \sum_{k=1}^{K} x_k$ and the aggregation rule for exogenous parameters is:

$$p = \sum_{k=1}^{K} \frac{p_k x_k}{\bar{x}} = \sum_{k=1}^{K} p_k \sigma_k. \tag{5.9}$$

This means that we scale the parameters of exogenous coefficients by the ratio of the single entity value to the global average value σ. Like for endogenous parameters we approximate the current ratio by the historic ratio based on the entity values communicated during the last forecast model transmission. Thus, no additional communication efforts are necessary. For the special case of exogenous coefficients exhibiting the same value for all entities, which is the case for most boolean variables, we can further simplify the aggregation rule. For this kind of parameters $\bar{x} = x_k$, which means that the global parameters p can be calculated by simply summing the parameters of the corresponding lower level entities.

As a result, we now have aggregation rules for endogenous and exogenous coefficients, we can use to create higher level forecast models without conducting a time-intensive parameter estimation. All aggregation rules do not only work between consecutive hierarchical levels, but across all hierarchy levels. In addition, the maintenance of the higher level model is even cheaper, because we can incrementally adapt the global forecast model. The used linear combination for each parameter allows to simply subtract the old parameter values of lower level entities and add the most recent ones. Thus, we can incorporate adapted forecast models from lower level entities without recalculating the entire linear combination. This is computationally cheaper as long as less than 50% of the entities transmit changes simultaneously, because the incremental adaptation uses two operations (subtraction, addition) per entity instead of just one when re-calculating the linear combination. Thus, if more than 50% of the lower level entities adapt their forecast model, we simply recalculate the entire linear combination. Both is much cheaper compared to a parameter re-estimation.

While our introduced hierarchical forecasting approach works for forecast models involving either endogenous or exogenous coefficients, we found a lack in accuracy for forecast models combining both coefficient groups. The reason is the varying influence of each coefficient group that is entity specific. Using common forecasting approaches these variations are automatically addressed during the parameter estimation step, by increasing or decreasing all parameter values of the respective group. However, our hierarchical forecasting approach does not include a parameter (re-estimation) and thus, the parameter are not automatically adapted with respect to the varying group influence. Thus, we need to specifically address the aggregation of forecast models incorporating both coefficient groups. For this purpose, we enhance our approach accordingly by introducing an influence weight for each coefficient group that is estimated for the global forecast model. Thus, we adapt Equation 5.7 for all parameters of endogenous coefficients $p(end)$ and Equation 5.9 for all parameters of exogenous coefficients $p(exo)$ leading to:

$$p(end) = \theta_1 \sum_{k=1}^{K} p_k \lambda_k \text{ and } p(exo) = \theta_2 \sum_{k=1}^{K} p_k \sigma_k \qquad (5.10)$$

With this enhancement we address the varying influence of both coefficient groups on the global forecast model. While our enhancement involves to estimate the group weights θ_1 and θ_2 using optimization algorithms, the estimation of two parameters is computationally very cheap. This is especially true in comparison to the typically large number of parameters within the coefficient groups.

With our hierarchical forecasting approach it is possible to determine a forecast model at higher hierarchy levels by simply aggregating the forecast models of lower level entities. Besides the general advantage of increasing the forecasting efficiency in hierarchical environments, in the energy domain balance responsible parties (BRP) and transmission system operators (TSO) are enabled to rapidly provide accurate forecast as needed in the new real-time balancing environment. However, also customers might benefit from the availability of forecast models in their smart meters. They can use these models to analyze their consumption and production behavior and even predict their future demand and supply. Hence, they are for example enabled to use cheaper pre-paid consumption contracts due to knowing the possible demand in advance. In addition, the single customer forecast models can also be used to enhance the functionality of smart home or smart building systems by analyzing consumption patterns and determining saving potentials or more intelligently regulate the building or home environment. Even the usage of concepts such as the MIRABEL flex-offers or other demand-response systems [116] can be better implemented with the availability of local forecasts.

5.3.5 Applying the System to Real-World Forecast Models

In this section, we exemplarily present how to apply our approach to two forecast models typically used in the energy domain. First, we present the Double Seasonal Exponential Smoothing (DSESM) model as introduced by Taylor et al. Second, we discuss the application of our approach in conjunction with the EGRV model as introduced by Ramanathan et al. With both models in place we cover a large space of typically employed forecast models considering single and multi-equation models as well as exponential smoothing and autoregression.

Aggregation of Double Seasonal ESM

The double seasonal exponential smoothing model is a typical forecast model used in the energy domain. We introduced the model in Section 3.3, but present the calculation rule of the DSESM variant as a reminder below. DSESM takes two seasonal patterns into account—a daily and a weekly season. Overall the forecast model is denoted as:

$$
\begin{aligned}
\text{Forecast} \quad & \hat{x}_t(m) = S_t + D_{t-s_1+m} + W_{t-s_2+m} \\
& \quad + \phi^m(x_t - (S_{t-1} + D_{t-s_1} + W_{t-s_2})) \\
\text{Level} \quad & S_t = \alpha(x_t - D_{t-s_1} - W_{t-s_2}) + (1-\alpha)S_{t-1} \\
\text{Saison 1} \quad & D_t = \delta(x_t - S_{t-1} - W_{t-s_2}) + (1-\delta)D_{t-s1} \\
\text{Saison 2} \quad & W_t = \omega(x_t - S_{t-1} - D_{t-s_1}) + (1-\omega)W_{t-s2}
\end{aligned}
$$

The variables α, δ, ω and ϕ are the parameters of the components, that are aggregated when forming the global forecast model. The value of m reflects the forecast horizon. The DSESM model only contains endogenous coefficients and thus, we can apply the aggregation rule denoted in Equation 5.7 for all parameters. However, for ϕ we have to include the m-th root into the aggregation rule, resulting in:

$$
\phi = \sqrt[m]{\sum_{k=1}^{K} \phi_k^m \delta_k}
$$

Aggregation of EGRV

The EGRV model is an autoregressive model in a multi-equation form as introduced in Section 3.3. Please recall the notation for a single hour sub-model with coefficients grouped into several components:

$$
\begin{aligned}
HOUR_i = {} & BASELOAD + \alpha DETERMINISTIC \\
& + \beta TEMPERATURE \\
& + \gamma LOAD + \delta PASTERROR
\end{aligned}
$$

Each component has an assigned group of parameters (α, β, γ and δ), containing multiple parameter values for the individual variables of the components. The component DETERMINISTIC contains exogenous coefficients like the day of the week represented by boolean variables. The model also allows the inclusion of the TEMPERATURE, which is typically treated as exogenous. LOAD and PASTERROR are endogenous coefficients representing the actual auto correlated time series, respectively the last forecast errors.

To create the global forecast model, we separately aggregate all sub-models, following the rules of our hierarchical forecasting approach. The EGRV model contains both endogenous and exogenous parameters, which means that we have to deal with a varying influence of each coefficient group. Thus, the aggregation of the EGRV model requires the enhanced aggregation rule described in Equation 5.10. Overall, the EGRV model contains around 30 parameters and thus, is a good example for a forecast model exhibiting a computationally expensive parameter estimation. Thus, the benefit of our approach is even larger in conjunction with this model.

5.3.6 Hierarchical Communication

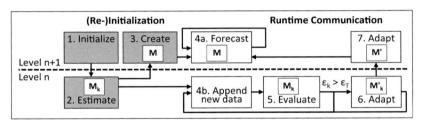

Fig. 5.19 The communication protocol of the hierarchical forecasting system.

In this Section we specify the communication protocol for transmitting information between the hierarchy levels. Previously the lower level entities provide measurements every time a forecast model on a higher level is adapted or in fixed intervals (e.g., every 5 minutes). With our protocol we establish a more flexible communication, where information is only transmitted when it is needed. The protocol is illustrated in Figure 5.19 and consists of an initialization and the actual hierarchical forecasting. The initialization is conducted when first using our hierarchical forecasting or when a re-initialization is necessary (e.g., large organizational changes). During the initialization the upper level entity requests the individual forecast models M_k of all corresponding lower level entities. The lower level entities estimate their forecast models and afterwards transmit them to the next level entity. Transmitting a forecast model in our hierarchical forecasting approach means to transmit a vector containing all forecast model parameters in a specified order. The higher level entity aggregates all transmitted forecast models of the lower level entities and with that, creates the initial global forecast model M.

After the initialization, the second part of the communication protocol starts. While the higher level entity uses the global forecast model M for calculating forecasts, the lower level entities append new measurements to their time series. The new values are used to evaluate the accuracy of the individual forecast models M_k. This continuous until the forecast error ε_k exceeds a specified error threshold ε_T. Afterwards, the forecast model of the specific entity is adapted and the adapted forecast model M_k' is then transmitted to the next level entity. The adapted model is used to incrementally adapt the global forecast model M.

For our approach to work we assume that higher level entities have the capabilities to record the most recent consumption or production for their entire group. This implies for BRPs for example that they have metering devices at the level of their balance group. This assumption holds, because previously there was only a limited deployment of smart meters at the lowest level of the hierarchy and balancing was mainly done using global measurement data. In addition, with an increasing employment of smart grids, TSOs have much finer monitoring capabilities and could additionally provide the necessary information to entities on other levels.

When using our communication protocol, we aim at only submitting the model parameters when a forecast model was adapted. However, for billing purposes it is still necessary for the lowest level entities to transmit their consumption and production data once per accounting period. Additionally, we use these measurements to verify and adapt the average historic share λ (Equation 5.6). Nevertheless, instead of transmitting the measurements live, they are communicated asynchronous to forecast model adaptations, when free resources are available. Thus, our communication protocol substantially increases the communication flexibility, while enabling the creation of higher level forecast models without estimating their parameters.

Our communication protocol also works between multiple hierarchy levels in a cascading way. The lowest level entities provide information to the second level, which adapts the global forecast model accordingly. Afterwards the entity on the third level of the hierarchy is informed by the respective second level entity and so on. To sum up, our hierarchical communication protocol provides an efficient way for exchanging information within a hierarchy. In most cases it is sufficient to just transmit data when changes occurred at the lower level entities. In addition, it is possible to limit the communication effort even further by defining the necessary significance of a change that leads to initiating a communication.

5.3.7 Experimental Evaluation

In our experimental evaluation we show that our hierarchical forecasting approach can rapidly calculate forecasting results, while still providing a high accuracy. In this evaluation we use the multi-equation EGRV forecast model [197] and the DSESM model as introduced in Section 3.3. The single-equation DSESM model exhibits four parameters for including the daily and the weekly season. The EGRV is configured to use a separate sub-model per hour and different models for working days and weekends. This results in a total number of 48 sub-models. For our evaluation we did not consider temperature data or any other external information. Altogether, our implementation of the EGRV model exhibits 28 parameters per sub-model in total. The parameter estimation was conducted using the local optimization algorithm Nelder Mead Downhill Simplex [177] and the global optimization algorithm simulated annealing [145]. For the global simulated annealing algorithm we empirically determined a time budget, where we found a steady state of the forecast after around 90 seconds for the EGRV model and 17 seconds for the DSESM model. Accordingly, we set the time budget to 100 seconds and 20 seconds respectively.

The basis for our evaluation is the real-world demand dataset D2 (compare Section 3.1) from the MeRegio project [166]. The dataset contains the hourly energy demand of 86 private customers from the 1st Novermber 2009 to the 22nd March 2010. For the lowest level in the hierarchy we directly used the 86 customers from the MeRegio dataset. To form the second level entity, we aggregated the time series of all 86 customers. While this dataset is rather small, it still shows the applicability and advantages of our approach on a real-world dataset.

The results are presented with respect to forecast error and efficiency. We measured the forecast error using the well-known SMAPE error metric [131]. The efficiency is represented by both the execution time as well as the number of iterations the respective optimization algorithms needs. With that, we abstract from solely using the runtime, but also show a reduced complexity of the optimization problem using the number of required iterations. All experiments were conducted on an Intel Core 2 Duo P8400 (2.26 GHz) processor, 8 GB DDR3 RAM, Mac OSX 10.7. The prototype was implemented in C++ using gcc 4.2.1. The experiments were repeated from multiple start points with 30 runs. The results represent the average of all runs.

Model Aggregation using DSESM

In this experiment we compare our hierarchical forecasting to the conventional forecasting method in conjunction with the DSESM model. We first estimated the parameters of all 86 individual customer forecast models, which were then aggregated to form the global forecast model on the second level. Due to the fact that all parameters are endogenous parameters, we used the aggregation rule described in Equation 5.7. In comparison to our approach, we started a regular parameter

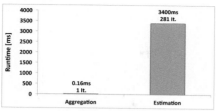

(a) Efficiency (Nelder Mead)

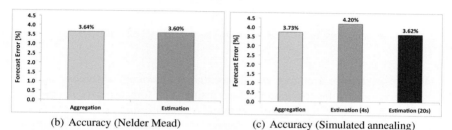

(b) Accuracy (Nelder Mead) (c) Accuracy (Simulated annealing)

Fig. 5.20 Results for the hierarchical forecasting with the DSESM model.

estimation using the local Nelder Mead as well as the global simulated annealing algorithm.

The results are illustrated in Figure 5.20, where Figures 5.20(b) and 5.20(c) compare the accuracy when using the Nelder Mead and the simulated annealing algorithms respectively and Figure 5.20(a) compares the runtime for the Nelder Mead algorithm. With respect to the efficiency measured as runtime and number of iterations, we can see that our approach substantially outperforms the conventional parameter estimation. The creation of the aggregated forecast model only takes 0.16 ms compared to 3,400 ms the Nelder Mead algorithm needs to converge. Thus, for our single-equation DSESM model the model aggregation is multiple orders of magnitudes faster than the conventional parameter estimation. Recall that we could only use a very small dataset. When forecasting on larger datasets containing a longer history (e.g., multiple years) the conventional parameter estimation will take even more time, due to numerous iterations over the dataset. In contrast, our model aggregation does not require to iterate over the dataset and thus, remains stable with an increasing number of time series values. Only the number of customers slightly increases the time for creating the global forecast model. Still, solving a weighted linear combination for the individual parameters remains computationally inexpensive, compared to a time-consuming parameter estimation using numerical optimization algorithms. As a result, with an increasing size of the dataset the advantage of our approach increases even further.

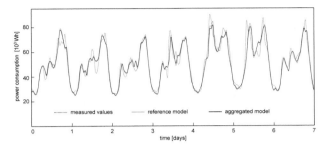

Fig. 5.21 Conventional vs. hierarchical forecasting curves 2010-03-02 – 2010-03-08.

With respect to the accuracy, we can see that our hierarchical forecasting is almost as accurate as the conventional forecasting. The forecast error is only very slightly higher with +0.04% compared to the regular estimation using the Nelder Mead algorithm. This means, that we provide almost the same accuracy, but in only a fraction of the runtime. Comparing the accuracy when using the simulated annealing optimization algorithms, we observe a similar picture. The accuracy again differed only marginally, with our hierarchical approach exhibiting a forecast error of 3.73% and the conventional estimation providing an error of 3.62%. Due to the fact that we manually set a time budget for the simulated annealing algorithm, we additional present the accuracy results, when significantly reducing the time budget from 20 s to 4 s. When using a runtime to 4 s, which is still much longer than the 0.16 seconds of our approach, we can see a clear decrease in accuracy. In this case the forecast error is 4.20%. Thus, reducing the time budget for the simulated annealing algorithms to bring the runtime closer to the runtime of our hierarchical forecasting approach comes with the trade-off of significantly reducing the forecasting accuracy.

As a result, for the single-equation DSESM model we can significantly reduce the runtime by several orders of magnitude, while still providing a very high accuracy. Figure 5.21 presents the aggregated model and the reference model in comparison to the measured values for the example days 2010-03-02 to 2010-08-03.

Results for the EGRV Parameter Adjustment

In this experiment we compare the efficiency and runtime of our hierarchical forecasting to the conventional parameter estimation for the EGRV forecast model. The EGRV forecast model contains both exogenous and endogenous coefficients. The setting of this experiment is the same as for the DSESM model, meaning that we first estimated the individual customer forecast models and then created the aggregated global forecast model by aggregating all comprised sub-models. How-

ever, in this experiment we additionally compared the accuracy when using our
enhanced aggregation rule for forecast models comprising both coefficient groups
as described in Equation 5.10. The enhanced forecast model aggregation is denoted
as *Weighted Aggregation*.

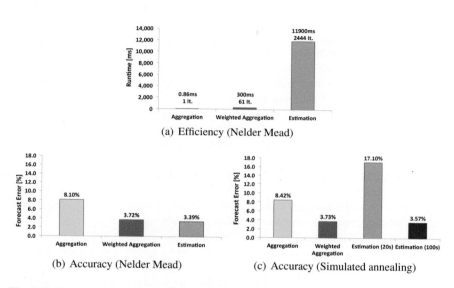

(a) Efficiency (Nelder Mead)

(b) Accuracy (Nelder Mead)

(c) Accuracy (Simulated annealing)

Fig. 5.22 Results for the hierarchical forecasting with the EGRV model.

The results are illustrated in Figure 5.22. Figures 5.22(b) and 5.22(c) present
the accuracy results for the Nelder Mead and the simulated annealing algorithms
respectively. Figure 5.22(a) compares the runtimes of the hierarchical forecasting approach and the conventional estimation approach using the Nelder Mead
algorithm. The hierarchical forecasting without weighting the different parameter groups exhibits the best runtime with only requiring 0.86 ms compared to the
Nelder Mead optimization runtime of 11,900 ms. However, the aggregation also
causes a substantial accuracy decrease, with a forecast error of 8.10% for the aggregated forecast model compared to 3.39% for the estimated reference model.
The same is true when using the simulated annealing algorithm, where our hierarchical forecast approach exhibits an forecast error of 8.42% compared to 3.57%.
However, when separately weighting the influences of the exogenous and endogenous parameter groups (Weighted Aggregation), the picture changes completely.
There, we admittedly have to estimate two weights for the two parameter groups,
but this is still substantially cheaper compared to estimating all forecast model parameters. Accordingly, our hierarchical forecasting using the weighted aggregation
needs a runtime of only 300 ms for 61 iterations compared to 11,900 ms and 2,444

iterations when using the conventional parameter estimation. With respect to the accuracy, the separate weighting of the parameter groups significantly increases the accuracy by reducing the forecast error to 3.72%. Thus, we are again very close to the accuracy of the conventional parameter estimation with 3.39%, especially when considering the substantial runtime decrease. Thus, the experiments clearly show the importance of weighting the concrete influence of the exogenous and endogenous parameter groups.

The results for the Nelder Mead algorithms are confirmed by the results for the simulated annealing algorithm. There, we also observe a clear benefit when separately weighting both parameter groups. The weighting reduces the forecast error from 8.42% for the simple aggregation to 3.73% when using the weighted aggregation. This is again an only slightly higher forecast error compared to the conventional parameter estimation exhibiting an error of 3.57%. We again also compared the possible accuracy when significantly reducing the time budget for the simulated annealing optimization, bringing the runtime closer to the runtime of our hierarchical approach. Thus, we allowed the algorithm to only run for 20 s, which resulted in 63,475 iterations compared to 326,983 iterations when running 100 s. With that, the forecast error was significantly increased to 17.10% which means that the forecast is unusable for most purposes.

To sum up, for the EGRV model our hierarchical forecasting again provides a significant runtime improvement, allowing an almost instant calculation of accurate forecasts. However, the separate weighting of both parameter groups, is very important to allow for a high accuracy. Overall, the accuracy difference is slightly higher than for the DSESM forecast model, but still well in range of the accuracy provided by the conventional parameter estimation process that however, is far more computationally expensive. Thus, with our hierarchical forecasting approach we can provide very accurate forecasts in a fraction of the time needed by the traditional parameter estimation using optimization algorithms.

5.4 Conclusion

In this chapter we demonstrated the usefulness of context information in conjunction with the forecasting process. As part of the online forecasting process, we store previously used forecast model instances in conjunction with information about the time series context that were valid during their usage in our novel context-aware forecast model repository. The time series context is used as one of our selection criteria to select the most appropriate forecast model instance from the repository with respect to the current state of a time series. The underlying assumption is that forecast model instances, which provided highly accurate forecasts for a certain time series context, are also providing highly accurate forecasts when a similar context occurs. Our evaluation on four datasets confirmed our assumption and showed that our solution provides an efficient way for estimating parameters, especially when dealing with complex forecast models. In most cases we were superior to all evaluated competitors in providing more accurate forecasts in less time.

Besides using the time series context as a selection criterion for previously used forecast model instances, it is also important to directly include this information into the forecast model to increase the forecasting accuracy. This is especially important for energy supply time series, where meaningful forecasts are only possible when considering external information such as the weather and characteristics of the used installations. Directly integrating these external time series into forecast models bare the disadvantage that we add additional parameters to the forecast model and thus, enlarge the parameter search spaces. Thus, we significantly add additional effort to the forecasting process. In addition, only forecast models with specific support for external information may directly integrate them and thus, profit from the additional information provided by them. To tackle this issue we present a framework for creating a separate external information model that is only combined with the forecast model at the end of the forecasting process. Since the external information model is more stable compared to the actual forecast model, in most cases it is sufficient to just estimate the actual forecast model without considering the additional parameters from the separate model. As a result and as showcased in our evaluation we were able to significantly increase the forecast model accuracy with only very limited additional efforts.

Another way of interpreting context is to use information from the hierarchy of hierarchical time series. Our forecasting approach for hierarchical time series allows to significantly speed up the forecasting process for such time series, without sacrificing accuracy. The core idea is to create forecast models on the lowest level of the hierarchy and aggregate the forecast models all the way up to the to of the hierarchy. With that, we can create forecast models on arbitrary hierarchical levels without conducting a time consuming parameter estimation. In our evaluation we showed that the accuracy loss is neglectable, but we enable a creation of forecast models on higher hierarchical levels that is orders of magnitudes faster compared to creating a forecast model from scratch.

All introduced approaches optimize the forecasting process on the logical level and contribute to providing an efficient forecasting calculation suitable for real-time environments such as the changing European electricity market. Altogether, we provide an approach that optimize towards the goals of calculating forecast with a similar accuracy in less time or more accurate forecasts in similar time.

Chapter 6
Optimizations on the Physical Layer: A Forecast-Model-Aware Time Series Storage

The logical optimizations introduced in Chapter 5 concentrate on optimizing the process of calculating forecasts. They are independent of the data organization and agnostic to the chosen forecast models. However, optimizations on the logical layer do not influence the way data is stored and handled within main memory and the way modern hardware can be utilized to improve the forecasting calculations. Thus, to further improve the forecasting efficiency and performance, the forecast process should also be optimized on the physical layer. This comprises enhancements for the data storage, the calculation rules of forecasting models, the estimators used in the parameter estimation and the platform on which the forecasting is being executed. In particular, the physical optimizations introduced in this chapter directly target to provide an efficient way for forecast models to access time series values to significantly improve the speed of the forecast model parameter estimation. One direction to achieve an increased forecasting calculation performance is to exploit modern trends in database technologies by utilizing the increasing data processing capabilities of modern in-memory database systems such as SAP HANA [89, 205]. For this reason, in our pEDM system we use an in-memory data store combined with tightly integrated forecasting capabilities as discussed in Section 4.4. Thus, we store all considered time series data in main memory, hence reading data from disc is not necessary any more.

While such systems bare the potential to substantially increase the calculation performance, they pose the issue that access times and bandwidth of the main memory do not increase as fast as the computational power. Thus, memory latency and bandwidth became new limiting factors for the achievable performance [22, 249]. To reduce the influence of memory latency we introduce a storage approach for time series data that substantially increases the spatial locality of the data within the main memory. Our storage exploits the time series access patterns of the used forecast models to layout the data for sequential access, which is much faster compared to random access. Our approach is strongly encouraged

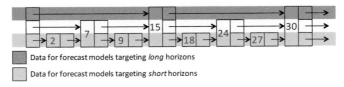

Fig. 6.1 Skip-list providing different data granularities for different forecasting horizons [108].

by previous research showcasing great performance benefits for algorithms and software with data storage and memory access specifically adapted to the underlying hardware characteristics [144]. In addition, multi-equation forecast models such as the EGRV forecast model bare massive parallelization potential with respect to estimating the respective number of sub-models. Thus, we can exploit the steadily increasing degree of parallelism offered by modern multi-core hardware systems. This is important since increasing the core frequency is limited by physical constrains such as an increasing heat loss and power consumption. All of the approaches present in this section substantially contribute to significantly increase the calculation speed of the forecast model parameter estimation.

The content of this chapter was published in [56] and will be published in [57].

6.1 Related Work

Some research for optimizing forecasting on the physical level has been done in the last couple of years. In the following we present the two main research directions that concern localized optimization techniques as well as database approaches natively integrating time series support.

6.1.1 Optimizing Time Series Management

In their work Ge and Zedonik deal with the task of determining which time series values to consider for a forecasting calculation [108]. In particular, they propose a skip-list approach, where they adapt the provided data granularity and history length with respect to the forecast purpose and the forecast horizon. For forecasts with a longer horizon they provide the data in a coarser granularity than for forecast models targeting a shorter forecasting horizon. This is illustrated in Figure 6.1, where we can see multiple levels of the skip list. Forecast models accessing the data over the skip-list, only consider the values that are designated for their respective level. The underlying assumption is that forecasting request targeting a long forecasting horizon profit from and need only data in a similarly large interval. Considering for example a store predicting the overall sales for the next year. In this case, the forecasting algorithm should consider the data in monthly granularity rather than in daily or even hourly granularity. However, when forecasting the energy consumption of a factory for the next day, one should use a much higher data resolution (e.g., hourly data). The history length and the ultimate number of data points is chosen using the statistical testing of hypothesis approach. This involves increasing the history length and the number of data points respectively as long as the accuracy of the result is increased.

Similarly, Agrawal et al. present an approach specifically targeting data in a high-dimensional attribute space [3]. There they merge the time series of similar attributes to subsets. For the most relevant attribute subsets they pre-compute and materialize the respective forecasts. In addition, they determine and store a correlation model for high-dimensional data. Forecasting queries are then answered by identifying a materialized time series for a subset of the query attributes and involving the remaining attributes by multiplying the identified time series with the correlation model.

While the presented approaches potentially increase the forecasting efficiency, they share the disadvantage of influencing the underlying data. In particular, they decrease the amount of considered data, which in most cases leads to a decrease in the forecasting accuracy. Thus, for applications requiring forecasts with the best possible accuracy, these approaches are not applicable. In contrast, our physical optimization approach does not influence the underlying time series and thus, preserves the forecasting accuracy. In addition, for time critical applications that need forecasts as quick as possible, one could combine several of the presented approaches with our improved time series storage.

6.1.2 Special Purpose DMS

A first system that specifically describes the processing of forecasting queries in a database system was proposed by Duan and Babu with their Fa system [70]. The authors propose to optimize the calculation of forecasts by specifically determining the composition of the employed forecasting techniques. They do so by analyzing the respective time series and deciding about attributes (in their sense values of a time series) they consider within a forecasting model. During this process they also identify the most promising model from the set of forecast models supported by their system. In particular, they search for the most beneficial forecasting plan similar to the standard database query plan. The forecasting plan search of their Fa system is illustrated in Figure 6.2. In a first step they use different statistical corre-

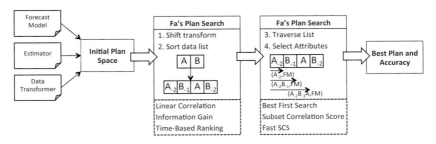

Fig. 6.2 The model creation process of the Fa system (according to [70]).

lation techniques to identify an initial set of attributes considered for the forecasting task. The output is a list of potential attributes ranked by their relevance for the forecasting output either determined correlation-based or time-based. Afterwards, the list is refined by adding attributes from the list to the forecasting models as long as the accuracy increases (i.e., best first search). Alternatively, the final attributes are selected using the (fast) subset correlation score approach. Unfortunately, their identification of the forecast model is done empirically since no analysis technique exists that reliably provides the most appropriate forecasting algorithms. However, they additionally propose to use statistics from previous requests as some kind of a heuristic.

In addition to the integration solutions mentioned above, there are also complete database systems adapted for handling statistical and time series data. Brown at al. introduced the SciDB database system that provide as special multi-dimensional array storage approach, which specifically targets application domains that involve very large array data such as scientific applications [30]. In addition, they provide native support for array operations and massive parallel processing. While in general time series data can be represented as arrays, the multi-dimensional arrays used in SciDB exhibit other query and access patterns (e.g., filter, slicing) and data characteristics (e.g., sparseness) leading to different storage layouts than we will present in this chapter [218]. In particular, SciDB does not natively support time series forecasting and forecast models, meaning that their storage is not directly optimized for this kind of calculations. In contrast, IBM Informix [62], TempoDB [233] and Splunk [20] are commercial time series databases that specifically target to natively support of time series data. They store time series as a first class citizen of their database providing native time series data types as well as suitable and efficient data models. The focus of these systems is clearly on an appropriate handling and querying of time series data as well as a convenient general storage of time series data in contrast to the non-beneficial storage in relational database system.

On the contrary to the special purpose systems above, the optimizations presented in this chapter specifically target to improve the most time-consuming operation in the forecasting process and thus, specifically acknowledges the characteristics of the forecast model parameter estimation. In particular, the access-pattern-aware time series storage introduced in this chapter is the first approach that optimizes the data storage of a data management system with respect to the specific access patterns of forecast models. As a result, our storage approach is not contrary but orthogonal to the techniques used in commercial time series database systems. Thus, these systems would greatly profit from complementing their storage approaches with our novel access-pattern-aware time series storage.

6.1.3 Summarizing comparison

In Table 6.1 we summarize the characteristics of the presented related work solutions and compare them to the capabilities provided by our pEDM system (enhanced with the storage approach presented below in this chapter). The first two characteristics deal with the general support for forecasting and storing time series data. It is obvious that most of the commercial time series databases and research approaches support the native storage of time series data. However, the special time

	Fa system	SciDB	Commer-cial	Skip-list	Splunk	pEDM
Native Forecasting	+	-	+	+	-	+
Native time series storage	o	o	+	+	+	+
Forecast process opt.	+	-	-	o	-	+
Model-aware storage	-	-	-	o	-	+
Accuracy preserving	-	-	-	-	-	+

Table 6.1 Comparing related work: time series storage approaches.
Legend: + supported, o partially, - not available/not applicable

series storage in this sense refers to an efficient storage with respect to memory efficiency and query processing in general. The reason is that natively supporting time series data does not automatically mean to natively support time series forecasting. In addition, offered time series support in most cases means to provide basic forecasting capabilities using some general-purpose forecasting techniques. Special optimizations of the forecasting process and a data storage that is specifically suited for the needs of an efficient forecasting (model-aware storage) is only partially supported by the presented research approaches—the Fa system (process optimization) and the skip-list approach (partial process optimization and model-aware storage). In particular, the research interest in such topics is growing in recent times, since time critical applications involving time series forecasting gain increasing importance (consider for example the use-cases described in our market analysis in Chapter 2). The last and very important characteristic is the focus on preserving accuracy in the face of applying optimization measures to the forecasting calculation. Both the Fa system as well as the skip-list approach sacrifice accuracy when applying their optimization. The commercial system, SciDB and Splunk do not natively support forecasting or any storage optimizations with respect to the forecasting process, which means that a comparison in this category is not applicable. Overall, with our pEDM system we target to significantly improve the efficiency of time series forecasting by optimizing the forecasting process as well as implementing additional optimizations on the time series storage level.

6.2 Creating an Access-Pattern-Aware Time Series Storage

Time series data in its most general form is a set of measurements exhibiting a strict sequential temporal order. One distinguishes between equidistant and non-equidistant time series, where equidistant time series exhibit a constant interval between its values (e.g., one value every 15 minutes) and non-equidistant time series contain measurements at arbitrary points in time. For the following approaches we are exclusively focusing on equidistant time series data, since meaningful forecasting in most cases can only be conducted on this kind of time series. Given their natural sequential temporal order, time series seem to be a perfect candidate for sequential main memory access. However, while some rather simple forecast models actually read time series values sequentially, most of the advanced and typically more accurate forecast models consider additional information such as seasonal behavior or measurements of external factors. Thus, they exhibit a much more complex access pattern to time series values. The core idea of our approach is to provide a time series storage that specifically exploits these more complex time series patterns and stores the time series values in a respective order. With that, we allow forecast models to access the time series values sequentially with respect to their specific data access pattern. In the following we start our description by investigating common time series access patterns, followed by the description of our general storage. We then describe how to adapt our time series storage to two real-world forecast models serving as representatives for their respective forecast model class.

6.2.1 Model Access Patterns

A first criterion when distinguishing different forecast model access pattern is to consider the two important forecast model classes—namely single-equation and multi-equation forecast models. Single-equation forecast models describe the entire behavior of a time series using only a single equation. Each relevant aspect of a time series is then directly modeled as part of the main equation by referencing for example past values of a time series or by using a separate components for each aspect. Important aspects that are part of single-equation models are among others the most recent time series values, trends as well as seasonal information. Common examples for single-equation models are the numerous variations of exponential smoothing models (typically using separate components) as well as Box-Jenkins models (e.g., ARIMA—typically using references in the equation) as introduced in Section 3.2. Figure 6.3(a) illustrates an example access pattern of a single equa-

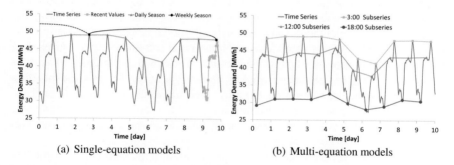

(a) Single-equation models   (b) Multi-equation models

Fig. 6.3 Access patterns for different forecast model types.

tion model that considers a daily and weekly season next to the actual time series values. Example 6.1 recalls the double seasonal variation of the exponential smoothing model as defined by Taylor et al. from Section 3.3 as an example model that corresponds to the presented access pattern.

Example 6.1. The double seasonal exponential smoothing models describes three aspects of a time series using separate components, where each components exhibits its own parameter (λ, δ, ω) determining its concrete influence. The values of the components calculated at the point in time t are stored in separate containers (e.g., in value arrays) and are only considered s_i steps later than they were calculated. The variable s_i represents the component-specific distance from the current point in time. In the example below $s_0 = 1$, $s_1 = $ day and $s_2 = $ week.

forecast

$$\hat{x}_t(k) = l_t + d_{t-s_1+k} + w_{t-s_2+k}$$
$$+ \phi^k(x_t - (l_{t-s_0} + d_{t-s_1} + w_{t-s_2}))$$

level

$$l_t = \lambda(x_t - d_{t-s_1} - w_{t-s_2}) + (1-\lambda)l_{t-s_0}$$

season 1

$$d_t = \delta(x_t - l_{t-s_0} - w_{t-s_2}) + (1-\delta)d_{t-s_1}$$

season 2

$$w_t = \omega(x_t - l_{t-s_0} - d_{t-s_1}) + (1-\omega)w_{t-s_2}$$

In contrast to single-equation models, multi-equation models decompose the time series into distinct time slots and assign a separate sub-model to each of them. Each sub-model is a separate instance of the given model equation exhibiting individual values for the included parameters. In most cases, the splitting of the time series is conducted along an observed season. In Section 3.3 we already introduced a very prominent representative of the multi-equation forecast model class—namely the EGRV forecast model introduced by Ramanathan et al. [197]. In this chapter we exemplarily use the EGRV model, but our approach can be applied to other multi-equation models as well. Figure 6.3(b) illustrates an example access pattern of a multi-equation model, where we split the time series along the daily season. For calculating forecasts each sub-model is mainly considering historic values with respect to their assigned time frame and accordingly is producing forecasts for this time only. Thus, the sub-model assigned to the time 8:00 am for example is basing its calculations mainly on the time series values corresponding to 8:00 am. However, some models enrich their calculations with additional information that are potentially independent of the time series decomposition (e.g., error correction terms), but this does not change the general access patterns with respect to the access behavior to the main time series.

The presented access patterns of single-equation and multi-equation models mainly represent two ways of accessing additional information such as trends or seasonal behavior. Single-equation models model the entire behavior of a time series including all additional information as part of their equation. In contrast, multi-equation models ease their modeling by decomposing the most relevant season. Accordingly, we are naming the observed access patterns *information modeling* and *season decomposition*. Both patterns might occur in combination, meaning that for example a season not decomposed in a multi-equation model might be included in the sub-models using the *information modeling* pattern.

Besides the two access patterns introduced above, there is also an additional pattern that can be applied to both of the aforementioned forecast model classes. In particular, single equation as well as multi-equation forecast models often enrich the information provided by the main time series with additional information about external factors. Such models use the correlation between the external factors and the main time series to draw more accurate conclusions about the future development of the main time series. We already illustrated the need for including these information especially when forecasting the energy production of renewable energy sources (compare especially Sections 5.2 and 3.1.3). The consideration of additional external factors leads to the fact that during the forecasting calculation the employed models access values from multiple time series rather than considering just one. This typically results in an access-pattern, where we can observe an alternating access between all considered time series. Thus, at a point in time t first the value of the main time series corresponding to t is read and afterwards the values at t from the additional series are accessed successively. In the following we refer to this access-pattern as *series alternation*. Since the *series alternation* access pattern equally occurs for single-equation and multi-equation models it is possible to create a combination of all three access patterns introduced so far. In the following example 6.2 we illustrate the combination of all introduced access pattern using the multi-equation model EGRV.

Example 6.2. Assuming the production power P of a renewable energy power plant including wind and solar power is modeled under the influence of the wind speed W and the sun duration S. P, W, S and $\hat{P}$ are time series with start time $t = 0$ and identical interval of length 1 (*series alternation*). The predicted value of the main time series is denoted as $\hat{P}$. The multi-equation EGRV model is divided into 24 sub-models M_i in accordance to the hourly data and the daily season (*season decomposition*) of the main time series and additionally considers the weekly season denoted as P_{t-168}^{ws} (*information modeling*). The estimation on a training dataset starts from $t = 168$, the sub-model M_0 first consumes the values P_{168}, P_0^{ws}, W_{168} and S_{168} and predicts the value $\hat{P}_{192}$. Afterwards it considers P_{192}, P_{24}^{ws}, W_{192} and S_{192} to forecast $\hat{P}_{216}$. The described value access is repeated until the end of the time series is reached. After finishing the calculation for sub-model M_0 the second sub-model M_1 starts at the subsequent index 169, following the exact same access pattern to approximate the value $\hat{P}_{169}$. The calculations are continued this way for all remaining sub-models M_2 to M_{23}.

$$M_0 : P_{168}, P_0^{ws}, W_{168}, S_{168} \rightarrow \hat{P}_{192}; P_{192}, P_{24}^{ws}, W_{192}, S_{192} \cdots$$
$$M_1 : P_{169}, P_1^{ws}, W_{169}, S_{169} \rightarrow \hat{P}_{193}; P_{193}, P_{193}^{ws}, W_{193}, S_{193} \cdots$$
$$\vdots$$
$$M_{23} : P_{191}, P_{23}^{ws}, W_{191}, S_{191} \rightarrow \hat{P}_{215}; P_{215}, P_{47}^{ws}, W_{215}, S_{215} \cdots$$

In this section we described three access pattern which deviate from the natural sequential order of time series—namely *information modeling*, *season decomposition* and *series alternation*. The access patterns cover a large range of commonly used forecast models, but their concrete implementation is model-specific. This means that the described access patterns might occur in arbitrary combinations and the concrete pattern of considered values is different for each model. Nevertheless, the three presented access patterns can be seen as general rules and the presented instantiations as examples of how forecast models are accessing time series values during forecasting.

6.2.2 Access-Pattern-Aware Storage

Based on the general access patterns described in the previous Section 6.2.1 our general idea is to optimize the storage of time series data considering the way forecast models are accessing time series values. The reason is that the data processing capabilities of in-memory systems are limited by main memory latency and bandwidth. As a result, similar to hard disks, sequential reading or writing in main memory is much faster compared to random access. In addition, requesting a particular value from main memory typically means that not only the requested single value is read, but a full block of values is fetched. The size of the block is hardware specific, but in many systems it is a so called cache line with a size of 64 byte (e.g., Intel Xeon, Intel Core i7). Thus, assuming the typical size of a double value of 8 bytes, 8 time series values are read and stored in the cache when accessing the main memory once. This strongly favors to store all required values close together to avoid reading unnecessary values and thus, to reduce the number of memory accesses. This is of utmost importance, since the time-consuming parameter estimation task involves a large number of iterations, where each iteration requires to read all necessary time series values. As a result, spatial locality in main memory emerges as the new optimization goal to unleash the full power of in-memory data analysis [22, 249].

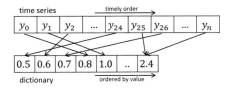

Fig. 6.4 Dictionary compression.

From a general point of view time series data is a perfect candidate for sequential memory access given the likewise sequential order of the values. However, given the access patterns identified in Section 6.2.1 most forecast models do not access the time series data in its given order. In addition, with respect to the limited size of main memory most in-memory DBMS sorted the data differently with the goal of providing optimal compression. One common strategy, not only used in in-memory DBMS, is dictionary compression. There, all distinct values of a table are stored in a dictionary in ascending or descending order and the actual values in the table are replaced with references to the entries in the dictionary. Figure 6.4 illustrates an example dictionary compression of an arbitrary series of values. While this can provide a reduced memory footprint also for time series data, it is less beneficial for accessing values in a specific order different than the order provided by the dictionary. Thus, for forecasting calculations the spatial locality of the values is relatively low, meaning that the data for most parts cannot be accessed sequentially. This results in a growing number of memory accesses and hence in an increased impact of the memory latency reducing the overall data processing performance. For this reason, we propose a special storage approach for time series data that specifically acknowledges the individual access patterns of the employed forecast models. In principal, the access-pattern-aware storage manages the time series values in an order that corresponds to the pattern a forecast model is accessing them. With that, we target to provide mainly sequential access to the considered time series values and thus, an increased performance when calculating forecasts. In Section 6.2.1 we identified three general access patterns that a large range of forecast models exhibit in different combinations and individual implementations. Accordingly, in the following we provide a blue print for a generic time series storage supporting different compositions of the access patterns that might be individually adapted to the specifics of the forecast models employed in a system. We start with describing the specific storage approach specifically suited for our three access pattern.

Multi-Series Storage

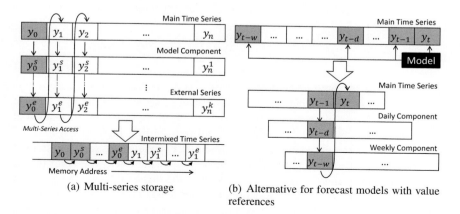

(a) Multi-series storage

(b) Alternative for forecast models with value references

Fig. 6.5 Access-pattern-aware storage for *information modeling* and *series alternation*.

The most common access pattern is *information modeling*, where in addition to the most recent measurements forecast models also include seasonal information and other additional factors. Thus, at a point in time t a forecast model may for example consider the most recent time series value x_t and additionally seasonal values with the distance of the respective season x_{t-s}; e.g., the daily and weekly season x_{t-d} and x_{t-w} (compare the *forecast* equation in Example 6.1). One common approach for including such additional information is to use individual forecast model components (compare *level, season 1, season 2* in Example 6.1) describing the individual influence of a specific factor that is varying over time. Accordingly, each component is maintained as an individual time series containing the influence values each for a specific point in time t. Thus, *information modeling* using additional components behaves very similar to the *series alternation* pattern, because in both cases a forecast model is equally considering multiple time series at the same time. For this reason, it is possible to create a storage layout that likewise suits both access patterns. The additional time series of components and external factors are typically stored in individual containers separate from the main time series, which means that they are most likely maintained in different areas of the main memory. Accordingly, when calculating a forecast, for each point in time t we need to consider values from all additional time series, requiring to separately access all individual containers as illustrated in the upper part of Figure 6.5(a). Additionally, in most cases only a single value is required from each container, but since data is read in blocks a large number of values contained in a fetched cache line is not necessary for the calculation. As a result, the naïve layout requires alternating access to multiple areas of the main memory, instead of allowing to sequentially read all necessary values. This is of special importance since the estimation of forecast models involves a large number of iterations, where a single iteration is calculating a lot of forecasts for different points in time of the training dataset.

The basic idea of a storage layout optimizing the memory access with respect to both access patterns—*information modeling* and *series alternation*—is to combine all considered additional time series with the main time series. The layout is illustrated at the bottom of Figure 6.5(a) and is in the following referred to as *multi-series storage* layout. As a result, instead of separate time series storage requiring an alternating access between the series, all relevant values needed at a point in time t are stored subsequently and thus, with a high spatial locality. Thus, we can access the values purely sequentially leading to a reduced number of memory accesses and an increased utilization of cache lines. The latter means that the number of unnecessary values stored in the different cache levels of the system significantly decreases, because all values needed for the current and following forecasting calculations are stored subsequently in main memory. Thus, each cache line contains a high number of values that are eventually considered by the forecast model. This substantially reduces the cache fragmentation and the number of cache misses.

For forecast models exhibiting the *information modeling* access pattern, but not using separate components for seasonal information, the above described multi-series storage layout is also applicable. In most cases such models directly use historic time series values in the distance of the respective seasons as illustrated in Figure 6.5(b). To provide all necessary values needed at point in time t at once, we create additional time series each containing shifted replicates of the main time series values corresponding to one season. These additional time series are then combined with the main time series as described for the *multi-series storage*. This in turn means however, that we increase the memory footprint of such time series. Thus, while this might be acceptable in principal, since models using separate components are increasing the footprint in a similar way, the employment of the *multi-series storage* for these kind of forecast models is use-case specific. The reason is that in some cases the main time series might already consume a large amount of memory (very fine-grained data) or a large number of time series is considered in the system. In general, as long as a higher memory footprint is acceptable and the system is able to provide the required resources one should exploit the increased performance of the improved memory layout. In addition, it is also possible to automatically decide about the employment of the *multi-series storage* on the fly given a constant monitoring of system resources or to activate it only for the most frequently used time series. Furthermore it is not necessary to permanently store the respective additional time series, but to delete them after successfully calculating the requested forecast.

Partitioned Storage

When dealing with the *season decomposition* access pattern the time series is accessed by multiple sub-models, where each sub-model is mainly considering the values of its specific time frame. This leads to our idea of a *partitioned storage* layout. The basic idea of the *partitioned storage* as illustrated in Figure 6.6 is to first partition the time series in main memory exactly in the way the time series is logically decomposed with respect to the selected season g. Thus, we create a number of partitions P_i that directly corresponds to the number of sub-models. Each partition P_i contains only the values of one specific time frame. Afterwards, we assign each partition P_i to its corresponding sub-model SM_i. In addition, we replicate the values that are commonly accessed by all sub-models (e.g., the component *Load*8 of the EGRV model) and store the replicates in the partitions as well. This ensures the independence of the partitions and the sub-models. Thus, the physical partitioning of the time series ensures that each sub-model physically accesses only the portions of the time series it needs for its own calculations. This avoids the con-

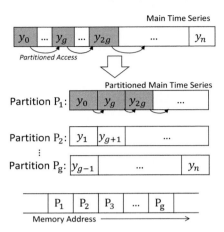

Fig. 6.6 Partitioned storage layout.

stant scanning of unnecessary additional values. In addition, the time series values of a partition are stored subsequently with a high spatial locality and can hence, be read fully sequentially. This tight data storage also reduces the number of memory accesses, since in each fetched block only values relevant for the respective sub-models are contained. As a result, the number of cache lines and memory pages read during a sub-model estimation decreases and thus, the number of cache and memory accesses. Finally, since each sub-model only needs to access its respective partition, the sub-models are fully independent, which is one important factor for improving the parallelization capabilities when estimating a full multi-equation model.

Combined General Storage

The identified access patterns typically do not occur isolated, but forecast models often exhibit a combination. When combining the *partitioned storage* and the *multi-series storage*, we first mix all considered time series as described for the *multi-series storage* and afterwards partition the resulting data structure with respect to the *season decomposition* pattern. The result can be seen as a three-dimensional data container as illustrated in Figure 6.7. In particular, each sub-model is considering its own partition containing a two-dimensional array with respect to the multi-series storage. Thus, the partitioning results in an additional third dimension compared to the pure *multi-series storage*. In memory, this structure results in a continuous sequential data storage with a high spatial locality as shown at the bottom of Figure 6.7. As a result, forecast models exhibiting the

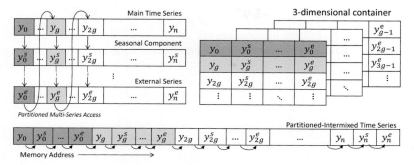

Fig. 6.7 Storage combining multi-series and partitioned layouts.

identified access patterns can access the necessary values fully sequentially. This substantially decreases the number of required separate memory accesses and thus, substantially increases the performance when estimating forecast models.

6.3 Applying the Access-Pattern-Aware Storage to Real-World Forecast Models

In the previous section we presented two storage approaches—*multi-series storage* as well as the *partitioned storage*—that provide efficient memory layouts for the three identified access patterns *information modeling*, *season decomposition* and *series alternation*. In addition, we also provided a combined storage approach that specifically targets forecast models exhibiting multiple access patterns at once. This combined storage approach may serve as a general blueprint for an access-pattern-aware storage. In this section, we demonstrate the concrete implementation of our storage for two examples forecast models representing single equations and multi-equation forecast models as well as different access-pattern combinations.

6.3.1 Optimized Storage for Single-Equation Models

We first describe the concrete application of our optimized time series storage to single-equation forecast models using the multi-seasonal implementation of exponential smoothing as introduced by Taylor [229] (compare double seasonal exponential smoothing in Section 3.3 and Example 6.1). This model exhibits the *information modeling* access pattern and employs a separate component for the considered time series factors. While Taylor is describing his exponential smoothing models for up to three seasons, we first generalize this model to support an arbitrary number of seasonal information and call the generalized model n-seasonal exponential smoothing (NSESM). The generalization of the model helps us to provide a storage scheme that is independent of the number of seasons considered in an exponential smoothing model.

N-Seasonal-Exponential-Smoothing

The original equation of the double seasonal exponential smoothing (DSESM) model is presented in Example 6.1. To abstract the components of DSESM, we substitute the weights λ, δ, ω with parameters p_i and the component coefficients l_t, d_t, w_t with $c_{i,t}$. The index $i \, (0 \leq i \leq N)$ refers to the specific component and s_i to the component specific distance. As a result, we arrive at:

$$\widehat{y}_t(k) = c_{0,t} + \sum_{i=1}^{N} c_{i,t-s_i+k} + \phi^k(\sigma_t)$$

$$c_{i,t} = p_i(\sigma_t + c_{i,t-s_i}) + (1 - p_i)c_{i,t-s_i} \qquad (6.1)$$

$$\sigma_t = x_t - \sum_{i=0}^{N} c_{i,t-s_i}.$$

For each additional component c_i the NSESM model stores an additional time series containing the influence values of the respective component. In contrast to the main time series the values of these time series are not fixed, but are determined during forecasting calculation. As shown in Equation (6.1) and in Example 6.1 when iterating over the time series we are calculating the influence of all components c_i for each specific point in time t. The calculation involves the current time series value adjusted for the influence of the other components (compare calculation of σ) and the former influence of the considered component $c_{i,t-s_i}$ with $(0 \leq i \leq N)$. It is important to note that for the actual forecasting calculation the influence values of most components are only considered s_i time steps later than the point in time t they were calculated. The length of this distance s_i depends on the time series aspect a specific component is representing. For example with respect to the daily season d_t the influence determined at point in time t is considered only 24 steps later at point in time $t + s_1$, where $s_1 =$ day assuming a time series in hourly granularity.

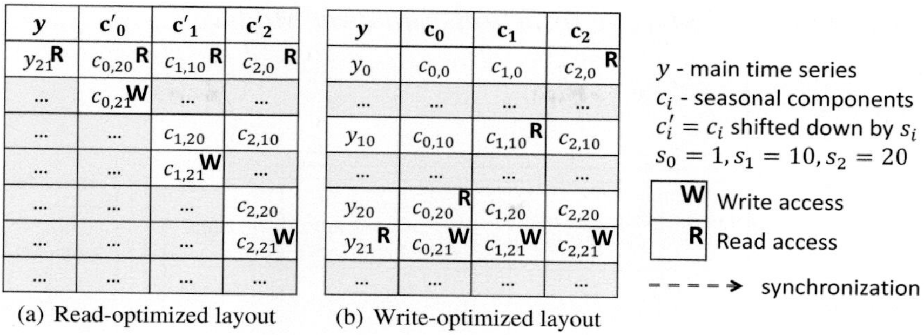

y	c'_0	c'_1	c'_2
y_{21} R	$c_{0,20}$ R	$c_{1,10}$ R	$c_{2,0}$ R
...	$c_{0,21}$ W	...	...
...	...	$c_{1,20}$	$c_{2,10}$
...	...	$c_{1,21}$ W	...
...	...	...	$c_{2,20}$
...	...	...	$c_{2,21}$ W
...	...	...	...

(a) Read-optimized layout

y	c_0	c_1	c_2
y_0	$c_{0,0}$	$c_{1,0}$	$c_{2,0}$ R
...	...	...	...
y_{10}	$c_{0,10}$	$c_{1,10}$ R	$c_{2,10}$
...	...	...	...
y_{20}	$c_{0,20}$ R	$c_{1,20}$	$c_{2,20}$
y_{21} R	$c_{0,21}$ W	$c_{1,21}$ W	$c_{2,21}$ W
...	...	...	...

(b) Write-optimized layout

y - main time series
c_i - seasonal components
$c'_i = c_i$ shifted down by s_i
$s_0 = 1, s_1 = 10, s_2 = 20$

W Write access

R Read access

- - - - → synchronization

Fig. 6.8 Read and write-optimized DSESM storage with highlighted accesses.

Applying the Optimized Storage to the NSESM Model

To provide an optimal storage for the NSESM model, we apply our *multi-series storage* layout. Thus, we create a logical two-dimensional array where each row represents a point in time t and the columns contain the main time series values x_t as well as the influence values of the different components $c_i (0 \leq i \leq N)$. Accordingly, at each point in time t the NSESM model can read all relevant values sequentially. However, since we calculate new influence values during each calculation step, we are required to also write these new values to our two-dimensional array. The issue is that for the NSESM model most of the calculated influence values are considered at later and component-specific points in time. In principal, the component time series c_i are shifted by their distance s_i with respect to the main time series x_t. As a result, while we provide an optimal way for reading values, we need to write each calculated value into a different part of the two-dimensional array, meaning that we need to access the main memory multiple times. This is illustrated in Figure 6.8(a), where we exemplarily show three components considered in addition to the main time series. Accordingly, we may also create a write-optimized layout, where we align the different time series in a way that it is possible to write all required values sequentially. However, due to the different distance factors of the components, this means in turn that we would need to separately read the values required for a single calculation (compare Figure 6.8(b)). In our experiments we found that the read-optimized layout is slightly advantageous for a small number of components, while the write-optimized layout provides a better performance with an increasing number of components considered in the model. The reason is that writing is a more complicated operation and thus, the more values we write to main memory the more increases the importance to optimize with focus on write accesses.

6.3.2 Optimized Storage for Multi-Equation Models

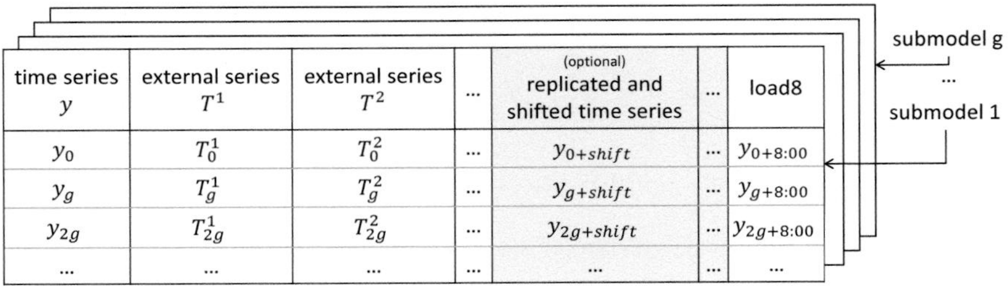

time series y	external series T^1	external series T^2	...	(optional) replicated and shifted time series	...	load8
y_0	T_0^1	T_0^2	...	$y_{0+shift}$	...	$y_{0+8:00}$
y_g	T_g^1	T_g^2	...	$y_{g+shift}$	...	$y_{g+8:00}$
y_{2g}	T_{2g}^1	T_{2g}^2	...	$y_{2g+shift}$	...	$y_{2g+8:00}$
...	...	...	...	...	...	...

Fig. 6.9 EGRV model storage.

To demonstrate the application of our storage layouts to multi-equation fore-cast models we use the EGRV forecast model (compare Section 3.3). The EGRV model is typically split with respect to one or multiple seasons. In the energy do-main this concerns in most cases the daily season (resulting in hourly models) as well as the weekly season (resulting in different hourly models for working days and weekends). In addition, the EGRV forecast model supports the inclusion of external information, which results in the need to access multiple time series dur-ing the forecasting calculation. To provide an optimal storage for the EGRV model we use our combined storage layout that includes the advantages of the partitioned and multi-series storage layouts. Below we illustrate one sub-model of an example EGRV model that considers the temperature, the wind speed, and the sun duration as external information.

$$HOUR1 = \alpha \cdot Deterministic + \beta \cdot Externals + \gamma \cdot Load8 + \delta \cdot Lags$$
$$Externals = \beta_1 \cdot temperature + \beta_2 \cdot windspeed + \beta_3 \cdot sunduration$$
$$Lags = \delta_1 x_{t-24} + \delta_2 x_{t-48} + \delta_3 x_{t-72} + \delta_4 x_{t-96} + \delta_5 x_{t-120}$$

Applying the Optimized Storage to the EGRV model

In principal, the sub-models of a multi-equation model refer to the external time se-ries in the same way they refer to the main time series. This means that EGRV has a *series alternating* access pattern. Accordingly, we partition all external time se-ries in the same way we are partitioning the main time series. In addition, for each sub-model we combine the partitions of all involved time series pursuant to our combined storage layout illustrated in Figure 6.7 resulting in one two-dimensional array per partition containing all relevant information for each point in time t in one row. This includes the special component *load8*, which denotes the previous time series value at 8:00 am and optionally also the *Lags* which are accessed in an *information modeling* manner. Together with the two-dimensional array we also store other sub-model-relevant data such as date information, to have all data as close as possible. The final storage layout for the EGRV model is illustrated in Figure 6.9. The combined storage layout applied to the EGRV forecast model allows for a sequential access to all required values.

Parallel Execution of Multi-Equation Forecast Models

We further optimize the parameter estimation of multi-equation models by exploiting the parallelization capabilities of modern multi-core hardware. Therefore, we assign all sub-models including their respective partitions to a number of threads that execute the parameter estimation of the sub-models in parallel. Due to the fact that memory throughput and latency can quickly become the limiting factors when using multi-core parallelization, the parallel estimation also profits from the access-pattern-aware storage. In addition, with the help of our partitioning we ensure that all model are independent of each other with respect to reading time series values. Ideally, the number of utilized threads would exactly match the number of involved sub-models, which would also bring the greatest benefit for the parallelization. However, in the real world the number of threads that can be directly executed in parallel on a specific system is limited. The number of these so called hardware threads is typically much smaller compared to the number of involved sub-models (e.g., 48, 96). Assigning more threads than available hardware threads typically does not create any additional benefit in our scenario, but rather induces additional costs due to overhead for thread scheduling and cache displacement issues. As a result, for the parallel execution of the sub-model estimation, we limit the number of parallel threads to the number of hardware threads available on the executing hardware system and thus, assign multiple sub-models to each thread for sequential estimation. The assignment of the sub-models to the threads is typically conducted using a task queue, where each thread picks the next sub-model as soon as it finished the previous parameter estimation. This leads to good load balance, even if time for estimating sub-models differs significantly.

	P1	P7	P8	P9	P12	P15	P16	P20
M11	0.5250	0.9991	0.9883	0.9990	0.3798	0.4762	0.3710	0.5355
M16	0.5511	0.9974	0.9633	0.8651	0.3445	0.3161	0.3530	0.5441
M17	0.9989	0.9078	0.9928	0.8645	0.3409	0.3857	0.3012	0.5523

Table 6.2 Parameter comparison of three example models.

Given the thread-local serial estimation of a subset of models, there is further optimization potential for the sequential estimation of the sub-models assigned to one thread. Due to the fact that some sub-models describe similar shapes, we assume that these models should also have similar parameter combinations. In a small experiment we compared the parameters between sub-models after their initial estimation and the results supported our assumption for the most part. Table 6.2 presents some example parameters for three example models M11, M16, and M17. While the assumption holds for most parameters, it does not for all. Some parameters still differ for sub-models we identified as similar (marked grey in Table 6.2). In our example, this concerns P1 and P7 for model M17 as well as P9 and P15 for model M11. Still, both models keep their relative similarity to model M16. As a result, the parameter combinations of similar models are a much better approximation of a good starting point for the parameter estimation, compared to starting from the origin. Thus, the basic idea of our improvement is to iteratively provide the result of the preceding parameter estimation, as the input (i.e., the starting value) for the estimation of the next sub-model. This *sequential start* approach typically reduces the number of necessary iterations for the subsequent optimization algorithms per thread, because only the first sub-model in each thread needs the full effort for the parameter estimation. All subsequent models then profit from better suited starting parameters, which results in a reduced runtime of the parameter estimation. It is important to note that the sequential start approach is most beneficially used, when no further advanced techniques for determining starting values such as the forecast model repository in our online forecasting process (compare Section 5.1 and Section 4.3) are employed. The reason is that these advanced techniques already provide very good starting points that in most cases lead to a very good execution time (number of iterations) and forecasting accuracy. As a result, in most cases it is not necessary to further improve those starting points, which means that we should see the sequential start approach of being orthogonal to other techniques that try to provide suitable starting points.

To guarantee a beneficial execution using the sequential start approach, we first cluster the most similar sub-models and afterwards assign each cluster to a thread. For this purpose, we measure the distances between the individual parameter values for all sub-models (e.g., $\text{dist}(\alpha_{M1}, \alpha_{M2})$, $\text{dist}(\alpha_{M1}, \alpha_{M3})$) determined during previous iterations. For this purpose we use the *euclidean distance* and combine the models with the least distance to each other into one cluster. The number of used clusters directly corresponds to the number of threads assigned to the estimation task of the multi-equation model at hand. In detail, we employ the *k-means clustering* approach using the following process:

1. We retrieve sub-model instances from the forecast model repository of the online forecasting process or the last forecasting calculation involving the model.
2. We assign random sub-models as centroids, where the number of centroids corresponds to the number of available threads.

3. We compute the euclidean distance between the centroids and the remaining sub-models.
4. We match the sub-models with the minimal distance to a centroid to the respective cluster. Models are equally distributed meaning that each thread receives the same or at least a similar number of sub-models. If a group is full newly arriving sub-models are assigned to the next best matching cluster.
5. The following steps are repeated until no sub-model changes thread anymore.

   - Incrementally compute new centroid from all sub-models per cluster.
   - Measure distance between new centroids and all sub-models.
   - Reorder models with respect to new distance measures.

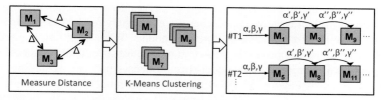

Fig. 6.10 Clustered parallelization with sequential start.

As soon as our clustering process is finished, we assign the clusters to the respective threads and execute sequential start parameter estimation for each thread. Figure 6.10 illustrates the parallelization process. Due to the stronger similarity between the sub-models within one thread, we can even further reduce the number of iterations conducted by the parameter estimation algorithms and thus, reduce the time needed to estimate all sub-models.

6.4 Evaluation

In this evaluation we substantiate the claims of our storage optimization approach and demonstrate that with the help of our time series storage layouts we are able to significantly decrease the execution time of the forecast model parameter estimation. Our evaluation compares the runtime of our storage layouts and is based on two forecast models and two real-world datasets. In our experiments, we employ the NSESM model as introduced in section 6.3.1 and the EGRV model. The parameters of both forecast models are estimated using the Nelder Mead downhill simplex algorithm [177] and L-BFGS Search [42]. We used the real-world datasets National Grid D1 and MeRegio D2. The dataset D2 was accomplished by external influences from the Deutscher Wetterdienst (DWD) and comprise information about air- and ground temperature, cloud cover, wind speed, pressure, humidity, and sun duration [66] (Each series contains 5,808 values).

For the evaluation we used a Quad-Core Intel(R) Core(TM) i7 870 (2.93 GHz, Hyperthreading), 16 GB RAM, Windows 7. Our test suite is written in C++ (GCC 4.6.1) and uses Intel TBB 4.1-2 [135] for the parallelization. Our approaches were implemented as part of the pEDM prototype.

We compare our access-pattern-aware storage layouts applied to single equations models (compare Section 6.3.1) and multi-equation models (compare Section 6.3.2) to a dictionary compressed storage as used in many DBMS and a naïve sequential storage layout. The dictionary sorts all distinct values of a time series in ascending order. The values are accessed using a list of references translating the original position of a value in the time series to the position in the dictionary. The naïve sequential storage layout simply preserves the given sequential order of a time series. Both alternative approaches are completely model independent and thus can be used with all kinds of forecast models. When applying our access-pattern-aware storage approach to a forecast model, we specifically adapt the storage layouts with respect to the model-specific access pattern. Accordingly, the eventual layouts we employ for the NSESM forecast model (representing single-equation forecast models) are different from the layouts we use for the EGRV forecast model (representing multi-equation forecast models). This means that for the NSESM model we separately compare the runtime benefits of the read and write optimized storage layouts. For the EGRV model we evaluate different partitioned layouts and the combined layout. In particular, we present a partitioning that only considers the main time series as well as an evolvement that also includes external series into the partitioning. The additionally evaluated combined storage integrates the multi-series storage for all involved time series leading to a high spatial locality providing efficient sequential access for the EGRV model.

It is important to note that the concrete execution time of the parameter estimation depends on the used optimization algorithm as well as on the model and dataset. In this context, the main influence is the number of parameter combinations evaluated during the parameter estimation. Since our storage optimization is independent from the number of evaluations, we normalize our results and compare the runtime in milliseconds per thousand evaluations. As a side note a typical parameter estimation may require up to multiple million evaluations depending on the size of the parameter search space.

6.4.1 Single-Equation Models

Figure 6.11 illustrates the results for the NSESM forecast model involving the base level component, the daily and the weekly season (2 seasons) as well as addition-

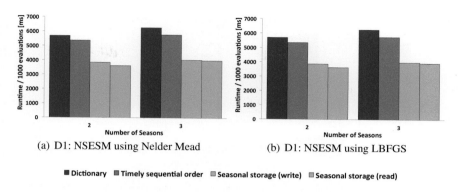

(a) D1: NSESM using Nelder Mead   (b) D1: NSESM using LBFGS

■ Dictionary ■ Timely sequential order ■ Seasonal storage (write) ■ Seasonal storage (read)

Fig. 6.11 NSESM on dataset D1 using Nelder Mead and LBFGS.

ally the annual season (3 seasons). Since the MeRegio dataset is smaller and does not provide enough data for an annual season, the NSESM model on this dataset only includes the base level component, the daily season (1 season) and the daily and weekly season (2 seasons). As expected the sorted dictionary required the longest runtime, since for nearly each value a separate cache line is fetched. In contrast, the sequential access is faster, because at least directly subsequent values can be read together in one cache line. However, our seasonal storages achieve the lowest runtime since they provide the highest spatial locality and thus, the least number of memory accesses. Overall, our access-pattern-aware storage was able to reduce the runtime by up to 40% (MeRegio, 2 seasons, LBFGS). Both the read and write-optimized storage layouts provide on par results, with a slight advantage for the read-optimized version. The results for the Nelder Mead and the LBFGS algorithms are almost identical, confirming the independence of our approach from the optimization algorithm. On the MeRegio dataset our storage layouts achieved very similar results as illustrated in Figure 6.12(a). In particular, the relative benefits of the different storage layouts are almost identical. For the MeRegio dataset we omitted a separate figure for the Nelder Mead results, since we already illustrated the independence of the results from the search strategy.

To provide additional information on the differences of the read and write-optimized layout, we also evaluated the runtime of both layouts with an increasing number of additional components. In this experiment, we omitted the execution of optimization algorithms and directly compared the runtime when evaluating the same parameter combination 1000 times. Figure 6.12(b) illustrates the runtimes for up to ten components, where we added additional seasons to the exponential smoothing model. The results show that the read-optimized and write optimized storage provide an almost identical performance. The read-optimized storage is only very slightly faster for up to three seasons. This is mainly reasoned by the

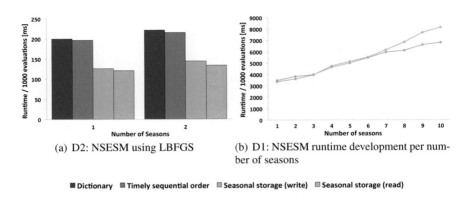

(a) D2: NSESM using LBFGS

(b) D1: NSESM runtime development per number of seasons

■ Dictionary ■ Timely sequential order ▨ Seasonal storage (write) ▨ Seasonal storage (read)

Fig. 6.12 Further experimental results for the NSESM forecast model.

fact that we need to read one more value than we are writing (compare Figure 6.8(a)), which increases the importance to optimize the read access in the first place. However, for a higher number of components the write-optimized version is steadily improving its benefit over the read-optimized layout. This is based on the fact that write access is a slightly more costly operation. Thus, with increasing amount of write operations it gets more and more important to provide a storage layout that is optimized for writing values. In this experiment the additional costs for reading the additional value matches the increasing costs of the writing operation at the point of including four components. Accordingly, at this point the read and write-optimized layouts provide on par results. For a further increasing number of components the costs for writing the values outweigh the costs for reading the additional value and thus, a write-optimized layout is providing more beneficial results.

Giving a general recommendation, one should use the write-optimized storage for forecast models exhibiting a larger number of components that require to write the calculated values to the main memory. For a smaller number of components (such as triple seasonal exponential smoothing) the read-optimized storage provides a very slight advantage.

6.4.2 Multi-Equation Models

Figure 6.13 illustrates the results for the EGRV model. Since the National Grid dataset does not contain external data series, in Figure 6.13(a) we do not distinguish different partitioning options. Similar to the NSESM experiments, the dic-

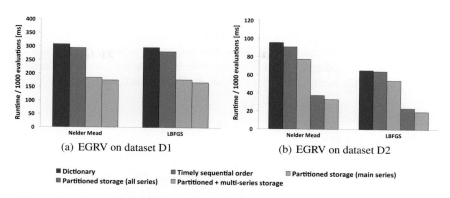

(a) EGRV on dataset D1   (b) EGRV on dataset D2

■ Dictionary   ■ Timely sequential order   ■ Partitioned storage (main series)
■ Partitioned storage (all series)   ■ Partitioned + multi-series storage

Fig. 6.13 EGRV on both datasets using Nelder Mead and LBFGS.

tionary storage performs worst and the temporal sequential order provides only little improvement. The difference between the dictionary compression and the naïve storage is relatively small. We account most of the difference between both storage layouts to the fact that the dictionary is providing an indirect access to the time series values, while the naïve storage allows to directly access the values. The partitioned storage for the time series provides a significant improvement of the runtime. In particular, comparing the results for both datasets, we can see that the relative improvement of the partitioned storage layout is larger for the MeRegio dataset. The reason is that the MeRegio dataset includes multiple time series from external information. Applying our partitioned storage layouts to all involved time series at the same time, we substantially increase the benefit of the optimized storage. In Figure 6.13(b) we can see that only partitioning the main time series provides a significantly worse runtime (Nelder Mead: 77.28 ms) compared to partitioning all time series (Nelder Mead: 32.93 ms). Beyond that, when adding the multi-series storage and thus, creating the combined layout we can observe a further runtime improvement leading to an eventual runtime decrease of up to 70% (LBFGS). The runtime improvement of the combined layout is caused by additionally combining all time series and components and thus, enabling to read all required values sequentially. In particular, the combined storage reduces the runtime by additional 15% (LBFGS: Partitioned storage: 23.43 ms – Combined storage: 19.45 ms). Considering the National Grid dataset, the combined storage including partitioned and multi-series storage also provides the highest runtime improvement reducing the runtime by 43% (LBFGS) compared to the dictionary compression. However, the improvement of the combined storage towards the pure partitioned storage is slighter (only 5.5% using LBFGS), since no external time series are involved and thus, the number of components that are combined is greatly reduced.

Overall, our access-pattern-aware storage significantly improves the runtime of the forecast model parameter estimation. In the most beneficial case we were able to reduce the required runtime by 70%. It is important to note that our storage approach does not influence the calculation rule of the forecast models, meaning that we provide the runtime benefits without sacrificing the forecasting accuracy.

Cache Utilization

	# L3 Misses	% L3 Hits	# L2 Misses	% L2 Hits
Non-optimized storage	206.850 Mio.	93%	8034.014 Mio.	2%
Access-pattern-aware storage	0.237 Mio	99%	7.245 Mio.	96%

Table 6.3 Test results: cache misses per storage approach.

Besides the pure runtime experiments, we also present the cache utilization when using our access-pattern-aware storage in conjunction with multi-equation forecast models. For this purpose, we exemplarily compare the effect of our partitioned storage with a sequential time series storage (non-optimized storage), since all optimized storage approaches result in the same effects. The partitioned storage was applied to a multi-equation EGRV model considering in this case only a single time series. For the purpose of measuring the cache utilization, we used the Intel Performance Counter Monitor that evaluates the values of the Performance Management Unit located directly on modern Intel CPUs. With the help of this tool we measured the number of cache misses that occurred in 20 seconds while running the estimation of an EGRV model. The used Intel Core i7-2635QM with 4 cores provides a 6 MB L3 cache and 256kB L2 cache per core. Our test dataset contained 122,736 values, which resulted in a size of roughly 1MB. This means that the complete test dataset can be cached in the L3 cache and thus, we expect high L3 cache hit rates in all cases. The results are presented in Table 6.3. As expected, all cases exhibit a very high L3 cache hit rate. The only difference we observed is about the total number of cache misses, which is significantly higher for the non-optimized storage. We account this difference to the fact, that in the non-optimized case a larger number of cache lines must be fetched from the L3 cache, since each cache line only contains one value required for a single calculation step. For the L2 cache we observed that the non-optimized storage exhibits a very low L2 hit rate of only 2%. In contrast the partitioned storage provides a hit rate of almost 100%. This means that densely storing the necessary values with a high spatial locality results in a better cache utilization, meaning in more required values persisted in the L2 cache and thus, to less cache misses.

Clustered Parallelization with Sequential Start

In our last experiment, we showcase the benefits of our clustered sequential start approach (compare section 6.3.2) when estimating the sub-models of an EGRV forecast model in parallel. In particular, we compare our clustering approach with a standard strategy that does not optimize the parallel execution of a parameter estimation (No Sequential Start) and a strategy that uses the sequential start approach, but simply picks the sub-models from a task queue rather than assigning them with respect to their similarity (Sequential Start). For this purpose, we measure the number of iterations when re-estimating the parameters of an initial EGRV model instance using Nelder Mead or LBFGS as local optimization algorithms. The initial instance is provided by either an estimation from scratch or using our online forecasting process (compare Section 4.3). The from scratch estimation starts a global optimization that estimates the parameters of an EGRV model using simulated annealing. In contrast, the online forecasting process provides a previously used EGRV model instance that is retrieved from the forecast model repository. The experiment was conducted using the dataset D1 with half-hourly data. Accordingly, the EGRV model exhibits 48 sub-models. Thus, given our test system with 8 hardware threads (4 CPU cores + hyperthreading), each thread has to estimate 6 sub-models. From the dataset D1 we used the years 2002 to 2008 for the initial estimation using the from scratch strategy and for initializing our online forecasting process. During the year 2009 we executed the local optimization using Nelder Mead and LBFGS at distinct evaluation points, where we exemplarily selected December 1st 2009 at 23:30 for presentation. For all other evaluation points that are not presented, we observed similar results. It is important to note that the number of iterations directly corresponds to the required runtime of the parameter estimation.

Figure 6.14 illustrates the results of our experiment. When estimating the parameters from scratch our clustered sequential start approach was able to significantly reduce the number of required iterations for both employed algorithms—Nelder Mead and LBFGS—at all times (i.e., for all evaluation points). In conjunction with the Nelder Mead algorithm our clustering approach only needed 183266 iterations compared to 349164 iterations when estimating the parameters without optimizing the parallel execution. This means a reduction by almost 50%. When using the LBFGS algorithm we were able to reduce the number of iterations by around 1/3 (no sequential start: 22325749, clustered sequential start: 14154719). The sequential start approach without using clustering always provided results that

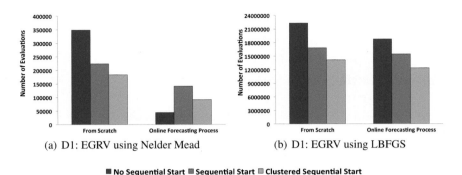

(a) D1: EGRV using Nelder Mead   (b) D1: EGRV using LBFGS

■ No Sequential Start ■ Sequential Start □ Clustered Sequential Start

Fig. 6.14 Number of iterations for parallelization strategies.

are in between the results of the two other strategies. In particular, it reduced the number of required iterations by around 35% (Nelder Mead) and 25% (LBFGS) respectively. The results for the parameter estimation using our online forecasting process are mixed. Considering the estimation using LBFGS our sequential start approach was again able to decrease the number of iterations by 35% for the clustered and 18% for the non-clustered execution. However, for the Nelder Mead algorithm our clustered sequential start approach required around twice the number of iterations (non sequential start: 44035, clustered sequential start: 91365). Even worse, without using the clustering the number of iterations were more than tripled (sequential start: 141276). These results show the risk of our approach when used in conjunction with other approaches for determining appropriate starting points such as the forecast model repository of the online forecasting process. In this case, the forecast model repository already provided a very good starting point, reducing the number of iterations compared to the from scratch estimation by around 90%. In such a setting our sequential start approach poses the risk of moving away from an already very good initial solution towards a slightly inferior starting point. This issue was observed for around half the evaluation points and for both evaluated optimization algorithms.

Overall, optimizing the parallel estimation of an EGRV model by exploiting the similarities between the different sub-models substantially reduces the efforts required for the parameter estimation process. This is especially true when estimations are started from scratch using global optimization algorithms. However, when used in conjunction with other techniques for determining appropriate starting points our sequential starting approach should be used with care, since in some situations it might increase the number of required iterations. Nevertheless, even in such cases the number of iterations is reduced compared to an estimation from scratch.

6.5 Conclusion

In our pEDM system we complement the logical optimization introduced in Chapter 5 with additional optimization on the physical layer. In particular, we exploit an emerging trend in database technology by storing and processing time series data directly within the main memory. Thus, data is not read from disk anymore avoiding the additional I/O overhead. While such in-memory systems bare the potential to substantially increase the forecasting calculation performance, optimizing the data layout to limit the influence of memory latency and bandwidth emerges as a new optimization goal.

For this purpose we introduced a novel access-pattern-aware storage for time series. In particular, we propose to layout time series data in the main memory with respect to the patterns the employed forecast models are accessing time series values. With this approach we significantly increase the spatial data locality and thus, allow to read the time series values sequentially instead of requiring random access to them. In this chapter we identified three typical access patterns for the two common forecast model classes—namely single-equation and multi-equation forecast models. The access patterns are *information modeling*, *season decomposition* and *series alternation*. These patterns led to the development of the *multi-series* as well as the *partitioned* storage layouts. Since in most cases the presented access patterns do not occur isolated, but in combination, we additionally combined the two single layouts forming the more general *combined* storage layout. We further demonstrated the application of our access-pattern-aware storage layouts to both model classes, using an n-seasonal variation of exponential smoothing (NSESM) as a representative for single-equation models and the EGRV forecast model representing the multi-equation model class. In addition, we presented our clustered parallelization concept to optimize the parallel estimation of the sub-models contained in a multi-equation model. The clustered parallelization provides the potential to significantly reduces the number of iterations required during the parameter estimation process of a multi-equation forecast model.

In our evaluation we showcased the potential of our novel time series storage approach on two real-world datasets. With the help of our access-pattern-aware storage layouts we were able to significantly reduce the runtime required for estimating the forecast model parameters by up to 70 %. We further demonstrated the improved cache utilization we reached with the help of our improved storages. A very important fact of our optimized storage is that we do not influence the data granularity or the calculation of the forecast models. Thus, we do not influence the resulting accuracy of the predictions. Overall, the proposed optimized time series storage is the first approach that optimizes the data storage of a database system with respect to the specific access patterns of forecast models. In addition, the inner-parallelization approach for multi-equation forecast models was able to significantly reduce the number of iterations required for the parameter estimation when no suitable starting points where present. It is important to note that in contrast to our storage optimizations, the clustered parallelization slightly influences the accuracy of the resulting forecast model.

Chapter 7
Conclusion and Future Work

In the energy domain forecasting is a fundamental prerequisite for the balancing of energy demand and supply and thus, for the stability of the energy grid. While large number of accurate forecast models already exist, new developments in the electricity markets of different countries worldwide pose new requirements on the forecasting calculation process. The electricity market changed from a static one-day ahead market to a more flexible and dynamic trading in real-time. In this markets the number of market participants substantially increased and deals can be closed shortly before the target fulfillment date of the negotiated contract. In addition, the utilization of renewable energy sources significantly increased. In contrast to conventional energy sources, e.g. based on fossil fuel and nuclear, the production of renewable energy sources can not be planned and their output is not dispatchable. Thus, while up until recently it was sufficient to directly match the production with respect to the predicted demand, more sophisticated real-time balancing concepts are required today. The challenge of real-time balancing is addressed using a large number of novel concepts such as energy routing in the grid, demand-response systems, or automatic generation control. All of these concepts motivate among other things forecasting capabilities that are tightly integrated into the energy management systems to foster quick and autonomous decisions on changing grid situations.

In this book, we proposed a novel forecasting concept that is capable of rapidly providing accurate forecasts at any point in time. The *online forecasting process* follows an iterative concept, where an initial, already accurate forecast is provided as a first solution that is afterwards iteratively refined over time. Applications can pick up these improved forecasts by subscribing to the forecasting process. Thus, instead of simply providing a single forecast at the end of the entire time-consuming forecasting process, we allow applications to specifically decide upon the acceptable runtime of the forecasting process and the target accuracy of the calculated forecast. This means that we support applications that require both forecasts after a certain amount of time as well as a specific accuracy. Furthermore, the online forecasting process allows to define runtime constraints and accuracy targets with providing the forecasting request and thus, we enable applications to directly adapt the progression of the calculation process to their needs. The online forecasting process takes advantage of optimizations on the logical and on the physical layer.

Logical optimizations target to enhance the process of calculating forecasts, without depending on a certain forecast model, optimization algorithms, or data organization. The most important optimization on the logical layer is to exploit the fact that in the energy domain most of the time series context, i.e., external factors influencing the progression of the main time series, are observable. Thus, we can use these information to optimize the selection of forecast models and forecast model instances. For this purpose, the online forecasting process utilizes our novel *Context-Aware Forecast Model Repository* to preserve and reuse previously employed forecast model instances. In particular, the repository stores forecast model instances in conjunction with information about the time series context the instances were used in. Assuming that in similar time series context states similar instances are producing accurate results, we use the time series context as one of our major selection criteria for choosing the most appropriate forecast model instance for the current time series development. In our evaluation we showed that the time series context is a beneficial selection criteria optimizing both the time needed for the selection process as well as the quality of the selected instance.

Besides using the time series context as a decision criterion we can also consider these information as part of our forecast model to improve the forecasting accuracy. This is especially useful when forecasting energy supply from renewable energy sources, since they greatly depend on external influences. However, the naïve approach of directly integrating external information into the forecast models bares the risk of substantially increasing the runtime of the forecasting calculation process. The reason is that for each considered external information we need to add additional parameters to the forecast model, which significantly increases the parameter search space. To relax this issue, we introduce our *framework for an efficient integration of external information*. The framework proposes to create a separate model that includes the forecast model components referring to external information. Since both models exhibit different update cycles for their included components, we can maintain them at different points in time. Thus, when requesting a forecast in most cases we can reuse an already optimized external information model, meaning that for the parameter estimation of the actual model, we do not need to consider further components. We further optimized the separate external information model using dimension reduction techniques. With the help of the presented framework we were able to significantly reduce the additional runtime needed for the parameter estimation, with the result, that we almost do not need any additional time compared to the case were no external information is included.

The final optimization on the logical layer concerns forecasting of hierarchical time series. As described in Chapter 2, the European electricity market is hierarchically organized, including market participants responsible for the balancing of energy demand and supply on the upper levels of the hierarchy. Our novel *efficient hierarchical forecasting* approach exploits the fact that smart meters are more and more deployed, meaning that we can expect the usage of smart meters in most consumer entities (industrial and private) in the near future. We propose to utilize the calculation capabilities of these smart meters and to directly integrate forecasting functionality. Thus, besides measuring the current energy consumption, smart meters will also calculate forecasts for their respective entity. Higher-level entities may then aggregate the calculated forecast models to directly receive a global forecast model without the need for conducting a costly parameter estimation. With the help of these techniques we were able to reduce the required time for creating a global forecast models by several orders of magnitudes. In addition, end-users and companies may likewise profit from the new forecasting capabilities, since they can be used to optimize emerging techniques such as smart houses and price-optimized usage.

In addition, to the optimizations on the logical layer, the physical layer likewise offers great optimization potential. Physical optimizations directly target the execution environment, the data organization as well as optimizing specific forecast models and optimizers. One direction of increasing the forecasting efficiency is to deeply integrate forecasting into the employed data management system. For this purpose we provided a concept that describes the direct integration of the data storage with the forecasting process. A tight integration allows forecast algorithms to directly access the required time series data and avoids copying data between the database and the analytical application. In addition, we may use the enhanced data processing capabilities of the typically highly developed database systems. This is especially true when employing in-memory databases that provide the potential so significantly speed up query execution and algorithmic calculations on the data. However, such systems bare special optimization potential to limit the influence of memory latency and bandwidth. For this purpose, we provided a storage approach that significantly increases the spatial memory locality of time series data. Our concept exploits the fact that forecast models exhibit certain access patterns to the time series data. Thus, providing time series values in an order that specifically acknowledges these access patterns, allows forecast models to mostly access their required time series values fully sequentially. In our evaluation we demonstrated that with the help of our access-pattern-aware storage we were able to significantly reduce the time required for the forecast model parameter estimation by up to 70%.

Overall, with the help of our concept we were able to significantly improve the way forecasts are calculated in the sense of increasing the forecasting efficiency and accuracy as well as adding important aspects such as application-awareness.

Future Work

In this book we provided a novel forecasting calculation process including a number of additional optimizations on the logical as well as on the physical layer. However, the research field of efficiently providing accurate forecasts especially with respect to energy demand and supply is not exhausted and provides a number of additional research questions.

First and foremost, creating a database system with sophisticated and tightly integrated time series support is a comprehensive and complicated task. Thus, besides applying concepts such as at the online forecasting process or our access-pattern-aware storage it is necessary to also deal with more general issues. Among other things this comprises the questions:

- How to efficiently store time series with respect to memory consumption and query processing times?
- What grammar shall I apply to likewise allow an exhaustive query functionality, but at the same time keep it understandable for the user?
- What helper structures (indexes) do I need to allow an efficient access to time series data with respect to multiple different applications and algorithms?

A database system with tightly integrated analytics and especially predictive analytics capabilities will be of great value for research and industry.

Following up on our developed concepts, there are also options to further enhance these optimizations. Currently the online forecasting process only deals with a single time series and only provides the in-sample error calculated during the forecast model optimization to the user. Thus, with respect to the online forecasting process, the following research questions arise:

- How to efficiently handle multiple time series at the same time?
- How to efficiently provide probabilistic forecasts or single-point forecasts including sophisticated information about the confidence interval?
- Is it possible to design an interface that allows customers to define their own forecast models?

Also the optimizations on the logical layer may be further improved. The context information used in the context-aware forecast model repository could be further used to more specifically determine the direction of the parameter estimation. In addition, for the hierarchical forecasting, we currently only support the same forecast models on all hierarchical layers. It should be investigated if it is possible to also support a synchronization between heterogen forecast models. Overall, we provide the following research questions for future work in these areas:

- How could one use time series context information to more efficiently determine a beneficial point in time for conducting a global maintenance search?
- How could our framework for an efficient integration of external information be used in conjunction with a physical meteorological weather model?
- Is there a way to synchronize heterogenous models within a hierarchy using our efficient hierarchical forecasting approach?

Finally our physical approaches and especially our access-pattern-aware time series storage can be further optimized. Currently, our storage approach targets to provide a separately stored time series for each employed forecast model. This could be for example optimized by providing physical index structures providing the respective access-pattern-aware storage instead of physically sorting the data within the main memory. However, it is necessary to substantially evaluate the impact of using an index rather than a physical organization. The following question provide a direction for future work:

- How could a general multi-purpose database system with integrated forecasting capabilities realize the access-pattern-aware storage?
- Is it possible to provide an access-pattern-aware storage using a physical index structure rather than a direct sorting within the main memory? What are the implications on runtime and storage?
- How could we better synchronize multiple parallel accesses to the time series with respect to reusing values? Is there potential to further optimize the main memory and the cache with respect to these parallel requests?

In this book we specifically focused on time series in the energy domain. However, many of these concept are supposed to be applicable in general or at least adaptable to other application domains. This could be a further general research direction, that we are currently pursuing. We are further in the process of integrating the presented concepts into an industrial in-memory database solution that is already rolled out to customers. This opens up a wide field of additional research questions.

References

[1] Aamodt, A., Plaza, E.: Case-based reasoning; foundational issues, methodological variations, and system approaches. AI Communications **7**(1), 39–59 (1994)

[2] Adya, M., Collopy, F.: How effective are neural networks at forecasting and prediction? A review and evaluation. Journal of Forecasting **17**(5-6), 481–495 (1998)

[3] Agrawal, D., Chen, D., Lin, L., Shanmugasundaram, J., Vee, E.: Forecasting high-dimensional data. In: Proceedings of the 2010 ACM SIGMOD International Conference on Management of data, pp. 1003–1012 (2010)

[4] Ahlstrom, M.: Wind and solar energy: Forecasting and integrating variable generation (2013). URL http://www.windlogics.com/wp-content/uploads/2014/03/Wind-and-Solar-Energy-IEEE-MAW-112213.LR_.pdf. (Last checked: 2014-08-05)

[5] Ahlstrom, M., Zavadil, R.: The role of wind forecasting in grid operations and reliability. In: Proceedings of the 2005 Transmission and Distribution Conference and Exhibition: Asia and Pacific (IEEE/PES), pp. 1–5 (2005)

[6] Ahmed, N.K., Atiya, A.F., Gayar, N.E., El-Shishiny, H.: An empirical comparison of machine learning models for time series forecasting. Econometrics Reviews **29**(5), 594–621 (2010)

[7] Akaike, H.: A new look at the statistical model identification. IEEE Transaction on Automatic Control **19**(6), 716–723 (1974)

[8] Alfares, H.K., Nazeeruddin, M.: Electric load forecasting: Literature survey and classification of methods. International Journal of System Science **33**(1), 23–34 (2002)

[9] Ashley, K.D.: Modeling legal argument: Reasoning with cases and hypotheticals. MIT Press (1990)

[10] Asmus, P.: The value of real-time wind power forecasting (2010). URL http://www.peterasmus.com/journal/2010/7/24/the-value-of-r

eal-time-wind-power-forecasting.html. (Last checked: 2014-08-05)

[11] Bacher, P., Madsen, H., Nielsen, H.A.: Online short-term solar power forecasting. Solar Energy **83**(10), 1772–1783 (2009)

[12] Balakrishnan, S.V.: Fast incremental adaptation using maximum likelihood regression and stochastic gradient descent. In: Proceedings of the 8th European Conference on Speech Communication and Technology (EUROSPEECH), pp. 1521–1524 (2003)

[13] Barroso, J.M.: The european union and energy: Looking to the future. EU Focus **September**(1), 1–8 (2006)

[14] Berndt, E., Hall, B., Hall, R., Hausman, J.: Estimation and inference in nonlinear structural models. Annals of Economic and Social Measurement **3**(4), 653–665 (1974)

[15] Berndt J. Donald, J.C.: Using dynamic time warping to find patterns in time series. In: Proceedings of the 1994 AAAI Workshop on Knowledge Discovery in Databases, pp. 359–370 (1994)

[16] Berthold, H., Boehm, M., Dannecker, L., Rumph, F.J., Pedersen, T.B., Nychtis, C., Frey, H., Marinsek, Z., Filipic, B., Tselepis, S.: Exploiting renewables by request-based balancing of energy demand and supply. In: Proceedings of the 11th IAEE European Conference (2010)

[17] Berthold, H., Savinov, A., Šikšnys, L., Pedersen, T.B., Jensen, C.S., Frey, H., Nychtis, C., Konsman, M., Rumph, F.J., Bobnar, M., Marinšek, Z., Cerne, G., Filipic, B., Böhm, M.: Micro-request-based aggregation, forecasting and scheduling of energy demand, supply and distribution: State of the art report and initial draft of the role model. Tech. rep., MIRABEL Project (2010). URL https://wwwdb.inf.tu-dresden.de/miracle/fi les/deliverables/M6/D1.1.pdf. (Last checked: 2014-08-05)

[18] Bessa, R., Miranda, V., Botterud, A., Wang, J.: 'Good' or 'bad' wind power forecasts: a relative concept. Wind Energy **14**(5), 625–636 (2011)

[19] Beyerer, J., Wernstedt, J.: Essay: Energienutzung in der Zukunft. Essay, Fraunhofer-Institut Informations- und Datenverarbeitung IITB (2006). URL https://www.iosb.fraunhofer.de/servlet/is/2369/ visIT_03_06.pdf. (Last checked: 2014-08-05)

[20] Bitincka, L., Ganapathi, A., Sorkin, S., Zhang, S.: Optimizing data analysis with a semi-structured time series database. In: Proceedings of the 3rd Workshop on Managing systems via log analysis and machine learning techniques (SLAML), pp. 1–9 (2010)

[21] Boehm, M., Dannecker, L., Doms, A., Dovgan, E., Filipic, B., Fischer, U., Lehner, W., Pedersen, T.B., Pitarch, Y., Siksnys, L., Tusar, T.: Data management in the mirabel smart grid system. In: Proceedings of the 15th EDBT/ICDT Workshops, pp. 95–102 (2012)

[22] Borkar, S.Y., Mulder, H., Dubey, P., Pawlowski, S.S., Kahn, K.C., Rattner, J.R., Kuck, D.J.: Platform 2015: Intel processor and platform

evolution for the next decade. Tech. rep., Intel Corporation (2005). URL https://epic.hpi.uni-potsdam.de/viewfile/Home/TrendsAndConceptsII2010?filename=HW_Trends_borkar_2015.pdf. (Last checked: 2014-08-05)

[23] Botterud, A., Wang, J., Miranda, V., Bessa, R., Keko, H., Akilimali, J.: Wind power forecasting and electricity market operations. In: 32nd Int. Association for Energy Economics (IAEE) Int. Conference, pp. 1–13 (2009)

[24] Botterud, A., Zhou, Z., Wang, J., Bessa, R.J., Keko, H., Mendes, J., Sumaili, J., Miranda, V.: Use of wind power forecasting in operational decisions. Tech. rep., Argonne National Laboratory (2011). URL http://www.dis.anl.gov/pubs/71389.pdf. (Last checked: 2014-08-05)

[25] Box, G.E.P., Jenkins, G.M., Reinsel, G.C.: Time Series Analysis: Forecasting and Control, 4th edn. John Wiley & Sons Inc. (2008)

[26] Branting, L.K.: Exploiting the complementarity of rules with reciprocity and fairness. In: Case-Based Reasoning Workshop, pp. 39–50 (1991)

[27] Braspenning, P., Thuijsman, F., Weijters, A.: Artifical Neural networks: An Introduction to ANN Theorey and Practice. Springer Verlag Inc. (1995)

[28] Brettschneider, P., Ritter, S.: Energy data management in liberalized markets. Tech. rep., Fraunhofer Application Center System Technology AST (2010). URL http://www.iosb.fraunhofer.de/servlet/is/28395/. (Last checked: 2014-08-05)

[29] Brockwell, P.J., Davis, R.A.: Introduction to Time Series and Forecasting, 1 edn. Springer Verlag Inc. (2002)

[30] Brown, P.G.: Overview of SciDB: Large scale array storage, processing and analysis. In: Proceedings of the 2010 ACM SIGMOD International Conference on Management of data, pp. 963–968 (2010)

[31] Broyden, C.: The convergence of a class of double-rank minimization algorithms. Journal of the Institute of Mathematics and Its Applications **6**(1), 76–90 (1970)

[32] Broyden, C.G.: A class of methods for solving nonlinear simultaneous equations. Mathematics of Computation **19**(92), 577–593 (1965)

[33] Bundesministerium für Umwelt, Naturschutz und Reaktorsicherheit: Erneuerbare Energien in Zahlen: Nationale und Internationale Entwicklung (2009). URL http://www.eta-energieberatung.de/upload/downloads/Erneuerbare%20Energien%20in%20Zahlen%20-%20Nationale%20und%20internationale%20Entwicklung%20-%20BMU%202012.pdf. (Last checked: 2014-08-05)

[34] Bundesministerium für Umwelt, Naturschutz und Reaktorsicherheit: Renewable energy source in figures: National and international development (2009). URL http://www.folkecenter.dk/mediafiles/folkecenter/Renewable-Energy-in-Figures.pdf. (Last checked: 2014-08-05)

[35] Bundesministerium für Umwelt, Naturschutz und Reaktorsicherheit: Energiekonzept für eine umweltschonende, zuverlässige und bezahlbare Energieversorung (2010). URL `http://www.bundesregierung.de/Con tentArchiv/DE/Archiv17/_Anlagen/2012/02/energiekonzept-fin al.pdf`. (Last checked: 2014-08-05)

[36] Bundesnetzagentur: Smart Grid und Smart Market: Eckpunktepapier der Bundesnetzagentur zu den Aspekten des sich verändernden Energiever- sorgungssystems (2011). URL `http://www.bundesnetzagentur.de/S haredDocs/Downloads/DE/Sachgebiete/Energie/Unternehmen_Ins titutionen/NetzzugangUndMesswesen/SmartGridEckpunktepapier /SmartGridPapierpdf.pdf`. (Last checked: 2014-08-07)

[37] Bundesnetzagentur: Annual report 2011 (2012). URL `http://www.bund esnetzagentur.de/SharedDocs/Downloads/EN/BNetzA/PressSecti on/ReportsPublications/2012/AnnualReport2011pdf.pdf`. (Last checked: 2014-08-07)

[38] Bundesnetzagentur, Bundeskartellamt: Monitoringbericht 2012 (2012). URL `http://www.bundesnetzagentur.de/SharedDocs/Download s/DE/Allgemeines/Bundesnetzagentur/Publikationen/Bericht e/2012/MonitoringBericht2012.pdf`. Copyright Bundesnetzagentur 2015, (Last checked: 2014-08-07)

[39] Bunn, D.W., Farmer, E., eds.: Comparative models for electric load fore- casting. John Wiley & Sons Inc. (1985)

[40] Bunnoon, P., Chalermyanont, K., Limsakul, C.: A computing model of arti- ficial intelligent approaches to mid-term load forecasting: a state-of-the-art survey for the researcher. International Journal of Engineering and Tech- nology $2(1)$, 94–100 (2010)

[41] Burges, C.J.C.: Dimension reduction: A guided tour. Foundations and Trends in Machine Learning $2(4)$, 275–365 (2009)

[42] Byrd, R.H., Lu, P., Nocedal, J., Zhu, C.: A limited memory algorithm for bound constrained optimization. SIAM Journal on Scientific Computing 16, 1190–1208 (1995)

[43] Byrd, R.H., Nocedal, J., robert B. Schnabel: Representations of quasi- newton matrices and their use in limited memory methods. Mathematical Programming $63(1-3)$, 129–156 (1994)

[44] Cailliau, M., Ogando, J.A., Egeland, H., Ferreira, R., Feuk, H., Figel, F., Jensen, S.G., Karas, J., Kawann, C., Villar, C.M., McManus, J., Naletto, S., Nosei, H., Poullikkas, A., Sundell, J., Vrolijk, R., Walter, B., Zoglauer, M.: Integrating intermittent renewable sources into the EU electricity system by 2020: Challenges and solutions. Tech. rep., Eurelectric: Electricity for Eu- rope (2011). URL `http://www.eurelectric.org/media/45254/res_ integration_paper_final-2010-030-0492-01-e.pdf`. (Last checked: 2014-08-10)

[45] Cancelo, J.R., Espasa, A., Grafe, R.: Forecasting the electricity load from one day to one week ahead for the spanish system operator. International Journal of Forecasting **24**(4), 588 – 602 (2008)

[46] Cano, R., Sordo, C., Gutierrez, J.M.: Applications of bayesian networks in meteorology. Advances in Bayesian Networks **1**, 309–327 (2004)

[47] Center for Renewable Energy Sources: (2011). URL `http://www.cres.g` `r/`. (Last checked: 2014-08-07)

[48] Cofino, A.S., Cano, R., Sordo, C., Gutierrez, J.M.: Bayesian networks for probabilistic weather prediction. In: In Proceedings of the 15th Eureopean Conference on Artificial Intelligence (ECAI), pp. 695–699 (2002)

[49] Cohen, J., Dolan, B., Dunlap, M., Hellerstein, J.M., Welton, C.: Mad skills: New analysis practices for big data. PVLDB **2**(2), 1481–1492 (2009)

[50] Corana, A., Marchesi, M., Martini, C., Ridella, S.: Minimizing multimodal functions of continuous variables with the "simulated annealing" algorithm. ACM Transactions on Mathematical Software **13**(3), 262–280 (1987)

[51] Cottet, R., Smith, M.: Bayesian modeling and forecasting of intraday electricity load. Journal of the American Statistical Association **98**, 839–849 (2003)

[52] Council of European Energy Regulators: ERGEG fact sheet - The electricity regional initiative: Making progress towards a single European market (2007). URL `http://www.ceer.eu/portal/page/portal/EER` `_HOME/EER_PUBLICATIONS/FACTSHEETS/Tab5/E05-ERF-03-06B_ERI` `_FS-05-02-22.PDF`. (Last checked: 2014-08-10)

[53] Crabtree, G., Misewich, J.: Integrating renewable electricity on the grid: A report by the aps panel on public affairs. Tech. rep., American Physical Society (2011). URL `http://www.aps.org/policy/reports/popa-rep` `orts/upload/integratingelec.pdf`. (Last checked: 2014-08-07)

[54] Daneshi, H., Daneshi, A.: Real time load forecast in power system. In: Proceedings of the 3rd International Conference on Electric Utility Deregulation and Restructuring and Power Technologies (DRPT), pp. 689–695 (2008)

[55] Dannecker, L., Boehm, M., Lehner, W., Hackenbroich, G.: Forecasting evolving time series of energy demand and supply. In: Proceedings of the 15th International Conference on Advances in Databases and Information Systems (ADBIS), pp. 302–315 (2011)

[56] Dannecker, L., Boehm, M., Lehner, W., Hackenbroich, G.: Partitioning and multi-core parallelization of multi-equation forecast models. In: Proceedings of the 24th Scientific and Statistical Database Management Conference (SSDBM), pp. 106–123 (2012)

[57] Dannecker, L., Gaumnitz, G., Roesch, P., Lehner, W., Hackenbroich, G.: Fisor: A storage advisor for high-speed in-memory time series forecasting.

In: Proceedings of the VLDB Endowment (PVLDB) (to be published 2015). (handed in for review)

[58] Dannecker, L., Lorenz, R., Rösch, P., Lehner, W., Hackenbroich, G.: Efficient forecasting for hierarchical time series. In: Proceedings of the 22nd ACM International Conference on Information and Knowledge Management (CIKM), pp. 2399–2404 (2013)

[59] Dannecker, L., Rösch, P., Fischer, U., Gaumnitz, G., Lehner, W., Hackenbroich, G.: pEDM: Online-forecasting for smart energy analytics. In: Proceedings of the 22nd ACM International Conference on Information and Knowledge Management (CIKM), pp. 2411–2416 (2013)

[60] Dannecker, L., Schulze, R., Boehm, M., Lehner, W., Hackenbroich, G.: Context-aware parameter estimation for forecast models in the energy domain. In: Proceedings of the 23rd Scientific and Statistical Database Management Conference (SSDBM), pp. 491–508 (2011)

[61] Dannecker, L., Vasilyeva, E., Böhm, M., Lehner, W., Hackenbroich, G.: Efficient integration of external information into forecast models from the energy domain. In: Proceedings of the 16th International Conference on Advances in Databases and Information Systems (ADBIS), pp. 139–152 (2012)

[62] Dantale, V.S., Hays, T., Nair, A., Roy, J.: Solving Business Problems with Informix TimeSeries. IBM Redbooks (2012). URL http://www.redbooks.ibm.com/abstracts/sg248021.html. (Last checked: 2014-08-11)

[63] Darbellay, G.A., Slama, M.: Forecasting the short-term demand for electricity: Do neural networks stand a better chance? International Journal of Forecasting **16**(1), 71–83 (2000)

[64] Das, S., Sismanis, Y., Beyer, K.S., Gemulla, R., Haas, P.J., McPherson, J.: Ricardo: Integrating R and Hadoop. In: Proceedings of the 2010 ACM SIGMOD International Conference on Management of data, pp. 987–998 (2010)

[65] Davidon, W.: Variable metric method for minimization. SIAM Journal on Optimization **1**(1), 1–17 (1991)

[66] Deutscher Wetterdienst: CDC - Climate Data Center. http://www.dwd.de (2012). (Last checked: 2014-08-08)

[67] Directorate-General for Energy, European Commision: Quarterly report on european electricity markets (2012). URL http://ec.europa.eu/energy/observatory/electricity/doc/qreem_2012_quarter2.pdf. (Last checked: 2014-08-08)

[68] Directorate-General for Research: European technology platform smart grids: Vision and strategy for Europe's electricity networks of the future. Tech. rep., European Commission (2006). URL http://ec.europa.eu/research/energy/pdf/smartgrids_en.pdf. (Last checked: 2014-08-10)

[69] Dordonnat, V., Koopman, S., Ooms, M., Dessertaine, A., Collet, J.: An hourly periodic state space model for modelling french national electricity load. International Journal of Forecasting **24**(4), 566 – 587 (2008)

[70] Duan, S., Babu, S.: Processing forecasting queries. In: Proceedings of the 33rd International Conference on Very large data bases (VLDB), pp. 711–722 (2007)

[71] Dunn, D.M., Williams, W.H., DeChaine, T.L.: Aggregate versus subaggregate models in local area forecasting. Journal of the American Statistical Association **71**(353), 68–71 (1976)

[72] Dvorak, P.: IBM has big-data ideas to improve forecasting, production of wind and solar. Windpower: Engineering & Development (2013). URL http://www.windpowerengineering.com/featured/business-new s-projects/ibm-has-big-data-ideas-to-improve-forecasting-f or-wind-and-solar/. (Last checked: 2014-08-08)

[73] EC - Commision of the European Communities: Second strategic energy review: An eu energy security and solidarity action plan (2008). URL http://eur-lex.europa.eu/legal-content/EN/TXT/?q id=1407503221882&uri=CELEX:52008DC0781. (Last checked: 2014-08-08)

[74] EC - Commision of the European Communities: Energy infrastructure priorities for 2020 and beyond - A blueprint for an integrated European energy network (2011). URL http://ec.europa.eu/energy/publications/d oc/2011_energy_infrastructure_en.pdf. (Last checked: 2014-08-11)

[75] Edison Project Consortium: Edison Project (2013). URL http://www.ed ison-net.dk. (Last checked: 2014-08-05)

[76] EnBW Energie Baden-Württemberg AG: Annual report 2011 (2011). URL https://www.enbw.com/company/investors/events/finance-cal ender/2012.html. (Last checked: 2014-08-10)

[77] ENTSO-E - European Network of Transmission System Operators for Electricity: The harmonized electricity market role model (2011). URL https://www.entsoe.eu/fileadmin/user_upload/edi/librar y/role/role-model-v2011-01.pdf. (Last checked: 2014-08-10)

[78] ENTSO-E - European Network of Transmission System Operators for Electricity: Scenario outlook and system adequacy forecast 2011 - 2025 (2011). URL https://www.entsoe.eu/publications/system-devel opment-reports/adequacy-forecasts/soaf-2011-2025/Pages/de fault.aspx. (Last checked: 2014-08-10)

[79] ENTSO-E - European Network of Transmission System Operators for Electricity: 10-year network development plan 2012 (2012). URL https://www.entsoe.eu/fileadmin/user_upload/_library/SDC/T YNDP/2012/TYNDP_2012_report.pdf. (Last checked: 2014-08-10)

[80] ENTSO-E - European Network of Transmission System Operators for Electricity: UCTE operation handbook (2012). URL https://www.entsoe.eu/publications/system-operations-r eports/operation-handbook/Pages/default.aspx. (Last checked: 2014-08-10)

[81] E.ON SE: Annual report 2011 (2011). URL http://www.eon.co m/en/about-us/publications/annual-report/archive.html. (Last checked: 2014-08-10)

[82] Ernst, B., Oakleaf, B., Ahlstrom, M., Lange, M., Moehrlen, C., Lange, B., Focken, U., Rohrig, K.: Predicting the wind. Power and Energy Magazine, IEEE 5(6), 78–89 (2007)

[83] EU - The European Parliament and the Council: Regulation (EC) No 713/2009: Establishing an agency for the cooperation of energy regulators (2009). URL http://eur-lex.europa.eu/LexUriServ/LexUriServ.d o?uri=OJ:L:2009:211:0001:0014:EN:PDF. (Last checked: 2014-08-10)

[84] EU - The European Parliament and the Council: Regulation (EC) No 714/2009: On conditions for access to the network for cross-border exchanges in electricity and repealing (2009). URL http://eur-lex.europa.eu/LexUriServ/LexUriServ.do?uri=OJ: L:2009:211:0015:0035:EN:PDF. (Last checked: 2014-08-10)

[85] European Commision - Directorate-General for Energy: EU energy trends to 2030 (2009). URL http://ec.europa.eu/energy/observatory/ trends_2030/doc/trends_to_2030_update_2009.pdf. (Last checked: 2014-08-11)

[86] European Energy Exchange: Press release: EEX review of 2011 (2012). URL http://cdn.eex.com/document/103018/20120112_EEX_Jahres zahlen_2011.pdf. (Last checked: 2014-08-10)

[87] European Energy Exchange: Press release: EEX review of 2012 (2013). URL https://www.eex.com/blob/53944/59efc5ddff9ee4ea1fd8c 9badf78bf3e/20130114-eex-jahresrueckblick-data.pdf. (Last checked: 2014-08-10)

[88] EWEA - The European Wind Energy Association: EU energy policy to 2050 (2011). URL http://www.ewea.org/fileadmin/ewea_document s/documents/publications/reports/EWEA_EU_Energy_Policy_to_ 2050.pdf. (Last checked: 2014-08-10)

[89] Faerber, F., Cha, S.K., Primsch, J., Bornhoevd, C., Sigg, S., Lehner, W.: SAP HANA Database - Data management for modern business applications. SIGMOD Record 40(4), 45–51 (2011)

[90] Fan, J.Y., McDonald, J.D.: A real-time implementation of short-term load forecasting for distribution power systems. Transactions on Power Systems 9(2), 988–994 (1994)

[91] Feinberg, E.A., Genethliou, D.: Load forecasting. In: Power Electronics and Power Systems, pp. 269–285. Springer Inc. (2005)

[92] Ferreira, C., Gama, J., Matias, L., Botterud, A., Wang, J.: A survey on wind power ramp forecasting. Tech. rep., Argonne National Laboratory (2011). URL http://www.dis.anl.gov/pubs/69166.pdf. (Last checked: 2014-08-10)

[93] Fischer, U., Boehm, M., Lehner, W., Pedersen, T.B.: Optimizing notification of subscription-based forecast queries. In: Proceedings of the 24th International Conference on Scientific and Statistical Database Management (SSDBM), pp. 449–466 (2012)

[94] Fischer, U., Böhm, M., Lehner, W.: Offline design tuning for hierarchies of forecast models. In: Proceedings of the 14th GI-Fachtagung für Datenbanksysteme in Business, Technology und Web (BTW), pp. 167–186 (2011)

[95] Fischer, U., Dannecker, L., Siksnys, L., Rosenthal, F., Boehm, M., Lehner, W.: Towards integrated data analytics: Time series forecasting in DBMS. Datenbank-Spektrum 13(1), 45–53 (2013)

[96] Fischer, U., Rosenthal, F., Lehner, W.: F2DB: The flash-forward database system. In: Proceedings of the 28th IEEE International Conference on Data Engineering (ICDE), pp. 1245–1248 (2012)

[97] Fischer, U., Rosenthal, F., Lehner, W.: Sample-based forecasting exploiting hierarchical time series. Proceedings of the 16th International Database Engineering & Applications Sysmposium (IDEAS) pp. 120–129 (2012)

[98] Fischer, U., Schildt, C., Hartmann, C., Lehner, W.: Forecasting the data cube: A model configuration advisor for multi-dimensional data sets. In: Proceedings of the 29th IEEE International Conference on Data Engineering (ICDE), pp. 853–864 (2013)

[99] Fletcher, R.: A new approach to variable metric algorithms. Computer Journal 13(1), 317–322 (1970)

[100] Fletcher, R.: Practical methods of optimization. John Wiley and Sons (1987)

[101] Fletcher, R., Powell, M.J.D.: A rapid convergent descent method for minimization. Computer Journal 6(2), 163–168 (1964)

[102] Fletcher, T.: Support vector machines explained. Tech. rep., University College London (2008). URL http://www.tristanfletcher.co.uk/SVM%20Explained.pdf. (Last checked: 2014-08-10)

[103] Fliedner, G.: Hierarchical forecasting: Issues and use guidelines. Industrial Management & Data Systems 101(1), 5–12 (2001)

[104] Friedman, J.H., Bentley, J.L., Finkel, R.A.: An algorithm for finding best matches in logarithmic expected time. ACM Transactions on Mathematical Software 3(3), 209–226 (1977)

[105] Frontier Economics and Consentec: Blowing in the wind - Measuring and managing the costs of renewable generation in Europe. Tech. rep., Frontier Economics Ltd (2009). URL http:

`//www.energinorge.no/getfile.php/FILER/Om%20Energi%20N`
`orge/IN%20ENGLISH/Frontier%20Blowing%20in%20the%20wind.pdf.`
(Last checked: 2014-08-10)

[106] Gao, F., Han, L.: Implementing the nelder-mead simplex algorithm with adaptive parameters. Computation Optimization and Applications **8**(1), 1–19 (2010)

[107] Gardner Jr., E.S.: Exponential smoothing: The state of the art - Part II. International Journal of Forecasting **22**(4), 637–666 (2006)

[108] Ge, T., Zdonik, S.: A skip-list approach for efficiently processing forecasting queries. In: Proceedings of the 34th International Conference on Very large data bases (VLDB), pp. 984–995 (2008)

[109] GE Energy: Western wind and solar integration study. Tech. rep., National Renewable Energy Laboratory (2010). URL `http://www.nrel.gov/doc s/fy13osti/55588.pdf`. (Last checked: 2014-08-11)

[110] General Secretariat of the Council: European Council 4th February 2011: Conclusions. Governmental publication, European Commission (2011). URL `http://www.consilium.europa.eu/uedocs/cms_data/ docs/pressdata/en/ec/119175.pdf`. (Last checked: 2014-08-10)

[111] Genoese, F., Klobasa, M., Wietschel, M.: Zukünftige Entwicklung von erneuerbaren Energien in Deutschland und Anforderungen an das Energiesystem. Umweltwirtschaftsforum (UWF) **17**(4), 307–312 (2009)

[112] Ghofrani, M., Hassanzadeh, M., Etezadi-Amoli, M., Fadali, M.: Smart meter based short-term load forecasting for residential customers. In: Proceedings of the 2011 North American Power Symposium (NAPS), pp. 1–5 (2011)

[113] Gibbels, R., Futch, M.: Smarter energy: Optimizing and integrating renewable energy resources. White paper, IBM Sales and Distribution: Energy and Utilities (2012). URL `http://www-01.ibm.com/common/ssi/cgi -bin/ssialias?infotype=SA&subtype=WH&htmlfid=EUW03067USEN`. (Last checked: 2014-08-10)

[114] Giebel, G., Brownsword, R., Kariniotakis, G., Denhard, M., Draxl, C.: The state-of-the-art in short-term prediction of wind power: A literature overview. Project deliverable, EU FP6 Project: ANEMOS. plus (2011). URL `http://www.prediktor.dk/publ/GGiebelEtAl-StateOfTheArt InShortTermPrediction_ANEMOSplus_2011.pdf`. (Last checked: 2014-08-10)

[115] Giebel, G., Landberg, L., Kariniotakis, G., Brownsword, R.: State-of-the-art on methods and software tools for short-term prediction of wind energy production. In: Proceedings of the 2003 European Wind Energy Conference (2003)

[116] Gnauk, B., Dannecker, L., Hahmann, M.: Leveraging gamification in demand dispatch systems. Proceedings of the 15th EDBT/ICDT Workshops pp. 103–110 (2012)

[117] Goldberg, D.E.: Genetic Algorithms in Search, Optimization, and Machine Learning. Addison-Wesley Professional (1989)

[118] Goldfarb, D.: A family of variable metric updates derived by variational means. Mathematics of Computation **24**(1), 23–26 (1970)

[119] Gooijer, J.G.D., Hyndman, R.J.: 25 years of time series forecasting. International Journal of Forecasting **22**(3), 443–473 (2006)

[120] Grosse, P., Lehner, W., Weichert, T., Faerber, F., Li, W.: Bridging two worlds with RICE. In: Proceedings of the 37th International Conference on Very Large Data Bases (VLDB), pp. 1307–1317 (2011)

[121] Gül, T., Stenzel, T.: Variability of wind power and other renewables. IEA report, International Energy Agency (2005). URL http://www.uwig.org /iea_report_on_variability.pdf. (Last checked: 2014-08-10)

[122] Gunn, S.R.: Support vector machines for classification and regression. Tech. rep., University of Southampton (1998). URL http://users.ecs.soton. ac.uk/srg/publications/pdf/SVM.pdf. (Last checked: 2014-08-11)

[123] Hahn, H., Meyer-Nieberg, S., Pickl, S.: Electric load forecasting methods: Tools for decision making. European Journal of Operational Research **199**(3), 902 – 907 (2009). URL http://www.sciencedirect.com/science/article/B6VCT-4VYX MKW-1/2/4c07e825afa512dbb8485bd6c8c2c30f

[124] Henseler, J.: Artifical Neural networks: An Introduction to ANN Theorey and Practice, chap. 2. Back Propagation, pp. 37–66. Springer Verlag Inc. (1995)

[125] Hippert, H., Pedreira, C., Souza, R.: Neural networks for short-term load forecasting: A review and evaluation. Power Systems **16**(1), 44–55 (2001)

[126] Hobbs, B., Jitprapaikulsarn, S., Konda, S., Chankong, V., Loparo, K., Maratukulam, D.: Analysis of the value for unit commitment of improved load forecasts. Power Systems, IEEE Transactions on **14**(4), 1342–1348 (1999)

[127] Holt, C.C.: Forecasting seasonals and trends by exponentially weighted moving averages. International Journal of Forecasting **20**(1), 5–10 (2004 (Original: 1957, O.N.R Memorandum 52))

[128] Holttinen, H., Miettinen, J., Sillanpää, S.: Wind power forecasting accuracy and uncertainty in finland. Tech. rep., VTT Technical Research Centre of Finland (2013). URL http://www.vtt.fi/inf/pdf/technology/2013/ T95.pdf. (Last checked: 2014-08-11)

[129] Holyoak, K.J., Morrision, R.G. (eds.): The Cambridge Handbook of Thinking and Reasoning. Cambridge University Press (2005)

[130] Hooke, R., Jeeves, T.: Direct search solution of numerical and statistical problems. Journal of the ACM **8**(2), 212–229 (1961)

[131] Hyndman, R.J.: Another look at forecast-accuracy metrics for intermittent demand. Foresight: The International Journal of Applied Forecasting **4**, 43–46 (2006)

[132] Hyndman, R.J., Ahmed, R.A., Athanasopoulos, G.: Optimal combination forecasts for hierarchical time series. Tech. rep., Monash University (2007). URL http://robjhyndman.com/papers/hierarchical/. (Last checked: 2014-08-11)

[133] Hyndman, R.J., Koehler, A.B., Snyder, R.D., Grose, S.: A state space framework for automatic forecasting using exponential smoothing methods. International Journal of Forecasting **18**(3), 439–454 (2002)

[134] Inman, R.H., Pedro, H.T., Coimbra, C.F.: Solar forecasting methods for renewable energy integration. Progress in Energy and Combustion Science **39**(6), 535 – 576 (2013)

[135] Intel Corporation: Intel® Threading Building Blocks (Intel® TBB). URL http://threadingbuildingblocks.org/. (Last checked: 2014-08-11)

[136] IRENA Secretariat: IRENA remap 2030: Doubling the global share of renewable energy - A roadmap to 2030. Tech. rep., International Renewable Energy Agency (2013). URL http://www.irena.org/menu/index.aspx?mnu=Subcat&PriMenuID=36&CatID=141&SubcatID=290. (Last checked: 2014-08-11)

[137] Jennrich, R.I., Moore, R.H.: Maximum likelihood estimation by means of nonlinear least squares. In: Proceedings of the Statistical Computing Section, pp. 57–65. American Statistical Association (1975)

[138] Jeon, J., Taylor, J.W.: Using conditional kernel density estimation for wind power density forecasting. Journal of the American Statistical Association **107**(497), 66–79 (2012)

[139] Jolliffe, I.: Principal Component Analysis, 2nd edn. Springer Series in Statistics. Springer Verlag Inc. (2002)

[140] Kalaitzakis, K., Stavrakakis, G., Anagnostakis, E.: Short-term load forecasting based on artificial neural networks parallel implementation. Electric Power Systems Research **63**, 185–196 (2002)

[141] Karan, M.B., Kazdagli, H.: Financial aspects in energy: A European perspective, chap. The development of energy markets in Europe. Springer Verlag Inc. (2011)

[142] Kashani, M.H., Jahanshahi, M.: Using simulated annealing for task scheduling in distributed systems. In: In Proceedings of the 1st International Conference on Computational Intelligence, Modelling and Simulation (CIMSim), pp. 265–269 (2009)

[143] Kempton, W., Dhanju, A.: Electric vehicles with V2G: Storage for large-scale wind power. Windtech International **2**(2), 18–21 (2006)

[144] Kim, C., Chhugani, J., Satish, N., Sedlar, E., Nguyen, A.D., Kaldewey, T., Lee, V.W., Brandt, S.A., Dubey, P.: FAST: Fast architecture sensitive tree search on modern cpus and gpus. In: Proceedings of the 2010 ACM SIGMOD International Conference on Management of data, pp. 339–350 (2010)

[145] Kirkpatrick, S., Jr., C.D.G., Vecchi, M.P.: Optimization by simulated annealing. Science. New Series **220**(4598), 671–680 (1983)

[146] Klotz, J.H.: Updating simple linear regression. Statistica Sinica **5**(1), 399–403 (1995)

[147] Kordon, A.: Applying Computational Intelligence: How to Create Value. Springer Inc. (2010)

[148] Koton, P.: Using experience in learning and problem solving. Ph.D. thesis, Massachusetts Institute of Technology (1988)

[149] Kriesel, D.: Ein kleiner Überblick über Neuronale Netze. URL http://www.dkriesel.com/science/neural_networks (2007). (Last checked: 2014-08-11)

[150] Krohn, S., Morthorst, P.E., Awerbuch, S.: The economics of wind energy. (data from Risoe DTU), The European Wind Energy Association (2009). URL http://www.ewea.org/fileadmin/files/library/publications/reports/Economics_of_Wind_Energy.pdf. (Last checked: 2014-08-11)

[151] Krollner, B., Vanstone, B., Finnie, G.: Financial time series forecasting with machine learning techniques: A survey. In: Proceedings of the 18th European Symposium on Artificial Neural Networks - Computational Intelligence and Machine Learning (ESANN), pp. 94–100 (2010)

[152] Krzanowski, W.J.: Principles of Multivariate Analysis: A User's Perspektive, revised edn. Oxford University Press (2000)

[153] Kyriakides, E., Polycarpou, M.: Short term electric load forecasting: A tutorial. In: K. Chen, L. Wang (eds.) Trends in Neural Computation, *Studies in Computational Intelligence*, vol. 35, pp. 391–418. Springer Berlin Heidelberg (2007)

[154] Lahtinen, J., Myllymäki, P., Silander, T., Tirri, H.: Empirical comparison of stochastic algorithms in a graph optimization problem. In: Proceedings of the 2nd Nordic Workshop on Genetic Algorithms and their Applications, pp. 45–59 (1996)

[155] Lei, M., Shiyan, L., Chuanwen, J., Hongling, L., Yan, Z.: A review on the forecasting of wind speed and generated power. Renewable and Sustainable Energy Reviews **13**(4), 915 – 920 (2009)

[156] Levenberg, K.: A method for the solution of certain non-linear problems in least squares. The Quarterly of Applied Mathematics **2**(2), 164–168 (1944)

[157] Lew, D., Milligan, M., Jordan, G., Piwko, R.: The value of wind power forecasting. In: Proceedings of the 91st American Meteorological Society

Annual Meeting at the Second Conference on Weather, Climate, and the New Energy Economy, pp. 1–10. National Renewable Energy Laboratory (2011)

[158] Liu, D.C., Nocedal, J.: On the limited memory BFGS method for large scale optimization. Mathematical Programming **45**(3), 503–528 (1989)

[159] Lorenz, R., Dannecker, L., Rösch, P., Lehner, W., Hackenbroich, G.: Forecasting in hierarchical environments. In: Proceedings of the 25th Scientific and Statistical Database Management Conference (SSDBM), pp. 37–40 (2013)

[160] Mann, J.W., Smith, G.D.: A comparison of heuristics for telecommunications traffic routing. In: R.S. et al (ed.) Modern Heuristic Search Methods. John Wiley and Sons (1996)

[161] Marquardt, D.W.: An algorithm for least-squares estimation of nonlinear parameters. Journal of the Society for Industrial and Applied Mathematics **11**(2), 431–441 (1963)

[162] McCrone, A.: Global trends in renewable energy investment 2012. Tech. rep., Frankfurt School - UNEP Collaborating Center for Climate and Sustainable Energy Finance, Bloomberg New Energy Finance (2012). URL `http://fs-unep-centre.org/sites/default/files/publicat ions/globaltrendsreport2012.pdf`. (Last checked: 2014-08-11)

[163] McLeod, A.I., Sales, P.R.H.: Algorithm as 191: An algorithm for approximate likelihood calculation of arma and seasonal arma models. Journal of the Royal Statistical Society. Series C (Applied Statistics) **32**(2), 211–223 (1983)

[164] Melard, G.: Algorithm as 197: A fast algorithm for the exact likelihood of autoregressive-moving average models. Journal of the Royal Statistical Soci- ety. Series C (Applied Statistics) **33**(1), 104–114 (1984)

[165] Mendes, J., Bessa, R.J., Hrvoke, Sumaili, J., Miranda, V., Ferreira, C., Gama, J.: Development and testing of improved statistical wind power forecasting methods. Tech. rep., Argonne National Laboratory (2011). URL `http://www.dis.anl.gov/pubs/71390.pdf`. (Last checked: 2014-08-11)

[166] MeRegio Project Consortium: MeRegio Project (2012). URL `http://ww w.meregio.de/en/`. (Last checked: 2014-08-05)

[167] Metropolis, N.: Equation of state calculations by fast computing machines. Journal of Chemical Physics **21**(6), 1087–1092 (1953)

[168] Microsoft Corporation: SQL Server 2008 - Analysis services overview. White paper, SQL Server Development (2007). URL `http://download.microsoft.com/download/B/F/2/BF2FFE31-C C84-4FA0-A3D6-1F3102187AFE/Microsoft%20SQL%20Server% 202008%20Analysis%20Services%20Overview.pdf`. (Last checked: 2014-08-11)

[169] Microsoft Inc: SQL Server 2008 - Predictive analysis with SQL Server. White paper, SQL Server Development (2008). URL http://download.microsoft.com/download/1/D/0/1D0AA2A5-E 2FB-4F72-B41D-04548D25A9D5/SQL%20Server%202008%20R2%20D ata%20Mining%20Whitepaper%20Overview.docx. (Last checked: 2014-08-11)

[170] MIRABEL Project Consortium: MIRABEL Project (2013). URL http://www.mirabel-project.eu. (Last checked: 2014-08-05)

[171] Monteiro, C., Bessa, R., Miranda, V., Botterud, A., Wang, J., Conzelmann, G.: Wind power forecasting: State-of-the-art 2009. Tech. rep., Argonne National Laboratory (2009). URL http://www.dis.anl.gov/pubs/65613.pdf. (Last checked: 2014-08-11)

[172] Morales, J.M., Conejo, A.J., Madsen, H., Pinson, P., Zugno, M.: Renewable energy sources: Modeling and forecasting. In: Integrating Renewables in Electricity Markets, *International Series in Operations Research & Management Science*, vol. 205, pp. 15–56. Springer US (2014)

[173] Möst, D., Jochem, P., Fichtner, W.: Dezentralisierung der Energieversorgung: Herausforderungen an die Systemanalyse und -steuerung. Technikfolgenabschätzung - Theorie und Praxis **19**(3), 22–29 (2010)

[174] Möst, D., Müller, T., Schubert, D.: Herausforderungen und Entwicklungen in der deutschen Energiewirtschaft - Auswirkungen des steigenden Anteils an erneuerbarer Energien auf die EEG-Umlagekosten und die Versorgungssicherheit. In Jörg Radtke, Bettina Henning: Die deutsche "Energiewende" nach Fukushima, Metropolis Verlag (2013)

[175] Müller, K.R., Smola, A.J., Rätsch, G., Schölkopf, B., Kohlmorgen, J., Vapnik, V.: Predicting time series with support vector machines. In: Proceedings of the 7th International Conference on Artificial Neural Networks, pp. 999–1004 (1997)

[176] Nationalgrid UK: Metered half-hourly electricity demands (2010). URL http://www2.nationalgrid.com/uk/Industry-information/e lectricity-transmission-operational-data/. (Last checked: 2014-08-11)

[177] Nelder, J., Mead, R.: A simplex method for function minimization. The Computer Journal **7**(4), 308–313 (1965)

[178] Neumann, G.A., Finkler, T.F., Cardozo, N.S.M., Secchi, A.R.: Parameter estimatin for lldpe gas-phase reactor models. Brazilian Journal of Chemical Engineering **24**(2), 267–275 (2007)

[179] NIST/SEMATECH: e-handbook of statistical methods. Tech. rep., National Institute of Standards and Technology (2010). URL http://www.itl.ni st.gov/div898/handbook/. (Last checked: 2014-08-11)

[180] Nocedal, J.: Updating quasi-newton matrices with limited storage. Mathematics of Computation **35**(151), 773–782 (1980)

[181] Nocedal, J., Wright, S.J.: Numerical Optimization. Springer Verlag Inc. (1999)

[182] Oracle Corp.: Oracle product brief: Oracle solutions of utilities. Tech. rep., Oracle Utilities (2012). URL http://www.oracle.com/us/industries /utilities/024459.pdf. (Last checked: 2014-08-11)

[183] Oracle Corporation: Driving strategic planning with predictive modeling. White paper, Oracle Crystal Ball (2008). URL http://www.oracle.com/us/solutions/ent-performance-bi/ performance-management/064129.pdf. (Last checked: 2014-08-11)

[184] Page, A.J., Keane, T.M., Naughton, T.J.: Multi-heuristic dynamic task allocation using genetic algorithms in a heterogeneous distributed system. Journal of Parallel Distributed Computing **70**(7), 758–766 (2010)

[185] Pai, P.F., Hong, W.C.: Support vector machines with simulated annealing algorithms in electricity load forecasting. Energy Conversion and Management **46**(17), 2669–2688 (2005)

[186] Palpanas, T., Vlachos, M., Keogh, E., Gunopulos, D., Truppel, W.: Online amnesic approximation of streaming time series. In: Proceedings of the 20th IEEE International Conference on Data Engineering (ICDE), pp. 339–349 (2004)

[187] Park, D., El-Sharkawi, M., II, R.M., Atlas, L., Damborg, M.: Electric load forecasting using an artifical neural network. Power Systems **6**(2), 442–450 (1991)

[188] Pearson, K.: I. Mathematical contributions to the theory of evolution. III. Regression, heredity, and panmixia. Philosophical Transactions of the Royal Society **A**(187), 253–318 (1896)

[189] Pearson, K.: On lines and planes of closest fit to systems of points in space. Philosophical Magazine **2**(6), 559–572 (1901)

[190] Pearson, K.: Notes on the history of correlation. Biometrika **13**(1), 25–45 (1920)

[191] Pelland, S., Remund, J., Kleissl, J., Oozeki, T., Brabandere, K.D.: Photovoltaic and solar forecasting: State of the art. Tech. rep., International Energy Agency (2013). URL http://www.iea-pvps.org/index.php?id =1&eID=dam_frontend_push&docID=1690. (Last checked: 2014-08-11)

[192] Pineda, I., Wilczek, P.: Creating the interal energy market. Industrial analysis and report, EWEA - European Wind Energy Association (2012). URL http://www.ewea.org/uploads/tx_err/Internal_ene rgy_market.pdf. (Last checked: 2014-08-10)

[193] Pinson, P.: Wind energy: Forecasting challenges for its operational management. Statistical Science **28**(4), 564–585 (2013)

[194] Porter, B.W., Bareiss, R.E.: Protos: An experiment in knowledge acquisition for heuristic classification tasks. In: Proceedings of the 1st International Meeting on Advances in Learning, pp. 159–174 (1986)

[195] Porter, B.W., Bareiss, R.E., Holte, R.C.: Concept learning and heuristic classification in weak-theory domains. Artifical Inteligence **45**(1–2), 229–263
(1990)

[196] Rademaekers, K., Slingenberg, A., Morsy, S.: Review and analysis
of EU wholesale energy markets: Historical and current data analysis of EU wholesale electricity, gas and co2 markets. Report to
the european commission, ECORYS Nederland BV (2008). URL
http://ec.europa.eu/energy/gas_electricity/studies/doc/
2008_eu_wholesale_energy_market_historical.pdf. (Last checked:
2014-08-11)

[197] Ramanathan, R., Engle, R., Granger, C.W., Vahid-Araghi, F., Brace, C.:
Short-run forecasts of electricity loads and peaks. International Journal of
Forecasting **13**(2), 161–174 (1997)

[198] Reimann, C., Filzmoser, P., Garrett, R., Dutter, R.: Statistical Data Analysis
Explained: Applied Environmental Statistics with R. John Wiley & Sons
Inc. (2008)

[199] RWE AG: Annual report 2011 (2011). URL https://www.rwe.com/we
b/cms/en/634422/rwe/investor-relations/reports/2011/. (Last
checked: 2014-08-11)

[200] Sample, N., Haines, M., Arnold, M., Purcell, T.: Optimizing search strategies in k-d trees. In: Proceedings of 5th WSES/IEEE World Multiconfer-
ence on Circuits, Systems, Communications & Computers (CSCC) (2001)

[201] SAP SE: SAP Solutions in detail - Energy data management
with SAP utilities. White paper, SAP Utilities (2009). URL
http://global.sap.com/uk/solutions/bestrunnow/pdfs/BRN_
4_1_EnergyDataManagement.pdf. (Last checked: 2014-08-11)

[202] SAP SE: SAP solution brief: Turn smart meter data into powerful insights
and actions. White paper, SAP Smart Meter Analytics (2011). URL
http://www.saphana.com/servlet/JiveServlet/previewBody/
3598-102-1-7482/Smart%20Meter%20Solution%20Brief.pdf

[203] SAP SE: Smart grid analytics: Understanding the data latency problem
- and how to solve it. White paper, SAP Smart Grid Solutions (2011).
URL http://www.ngueurope.com/media/whitepapers/SAP-Thought
Leadership.pdf

[204] SAP SE: SAP IS-U-EDM documentation (2013). URL https:
//help.sap.com/erp2005_ehp_05/helpdata/en/7d/a0023b288d
d720e10000000a114084/frameset.htm. (Last checked: 2014-08-11)

[205] SAP SE: SAP HANA Platform (2014). URL http://www.sap.com/pc/t
ech/in-memory-computing-hana/software/overview/index.html.
(Last checked: 2014-08-11)

[206] Schank, R.C.: Dynamic Memory: A Theory of Remining and Learning in
Computers and People. Cambridge University Press (1983)

[207] Scharff, R.: On distributed balancing of wind power forecast deviations in competitive power systems. Ph.D. thesis, KTH School of Electrical Engineering Sweden (2012)

[208] Schiffer, H.W.: Quo Vadis Energiemarkt? In: Jahresmitgliederversammlung des Vereins deutscher Elektrotechniker (2011)

[209] Sedgewick, R.: Algorithms. Addison-Wesley (1988)

[210] Shanno, D.F.: Conditioning of quasi-newton methods for function minimization. Mathematics of Computation **24**(1), 64–656 (1970)

[211] Sharma, N., Sharma, P., Irwin, D., Shenoy, P.: Predicting solar generation from weather forecasts using machine learning. In: 2011 IEEE International Conference on Smart Grid Communications (SmartGridComm), pp. 528–533 (2011)

[212] da Silva, A.P.A., Ferreira, V.H., Velasquez, R.M.: Input space to neural network based load forecasters. International Journal of Forecasting **24**(4), 616 – 629 (2008)

[213] Singh, V., Vaibhav, K., Chaturvedi, D.: Solar power forecasting modeling using soft computing approach. In: Proceedings of the 2012 International Conference on Engineering (NUiCONE), pp. 1–5 (2012)

[214] Smith, E.E., Medin, D.L.: Categories and Concepts. Harvard University Press (1981)

[215] Smola, A.J., Schölkopf, B.: A tutorial on support vector regression. Tech. rep., NeuroCOLT2 - ESPRIT Working Group (1998). URL `http://svms.org/tutorials/SmolaScholkopf1998.pdf`. (Last checked: 2014-08-11)

[216] Soares, L.J., Medeiros, M.C.: Modeling and forecasting short-term electricity load: A comparison of methods with an application to brazilian data. International Journal of Forecasting **24**(4), 630 – 644 (2008)

[217] Song, K.B., Ha, S.K., Park, J.W., Kweon, D.J., Kim, K.H.: Hybrid load forecasting method with analysis of temperature sensitivites. Transactions on Power Systems **21**(2) (2006)

[218] Soroush, E., Balazinska, M., Wang, D.: Arraystore: A storage manager for complex parallel array processing. In: Proceedings of the 2011 ACM SIGMOD International Conference on Management of data, pp. 253–264 (2011)

[219] Sotiropoulos, D., Stavropoulos, E., Vrahatis, M.: A new hybrid genetic algorithm for global optimization. Nonlinear Analysis, Theory, Methods and Applications **30**(1), 4529–4538 (1997)

[220] Souza, R.C., Barros, M., de Miranda, C.V.C.: Short term load forecasting using double seasonal exponential smoothing and interventions to account for holidays and temperature effects. Tech. rep., Pontifícia Universidade Católica do Rio de Janeiro (2007). URL

`http://www.tlaio.org.mx/EventosAnteriores/TLAIOII/T2_10_`
`A34iRCS-EfectosTemperatura.pdf`. (Last checked: 2014-08-11)

[221] Spearman, C.: The proof and measurement of association between two thins. American Journal of Psychology **15**(1), 72–101 (1904)

[222] Steckler, N., Florita, A., Zhang, J., Hodge, B.M.: Analysis and synthesis of load forecasting data for renewable integration studies. In: Proceedings of the 12th International Workshop on Large-Scale Integration of Wind Power Into Power Systems. National Renewable Energy Laboratory (2013)

[223] Stergiou, C., Siganos, D.: Neural networks. Tech. rep., Imperial College London (1996). URL `http://www.doc.ic.ac.uk/~nd/surprise_96/` `journal/vol4/cs11/report.html`. (Last checked: 2014-08-11)

[224] Suhr, D.D.: Principal component analysis vs. exploratory factor analysis. In: Proceedings of the 30th SAS Users Group International Conference (SUGI), pp. 1–11 (2005)

[225] Tanenbaum, A.S.: Modern Operating Systems, 3rd edn. Prentice Hall (2007)

[226] Taylor, J.W.: Short-term electricity demand forecasting using double seasonal exponential smoothing. Journal of Operational Research Society **54**(8), 799–805 (2003)

[227] Taylor, J.W.: Density forecasting for the efficient balancing of the generation and consumption of electricity. International Journal of Forecasting **22**(4), 707–724 (2006)

[228] Taylor, J.W.: An evaluation of methods for very short-term load forecasting using minute-by-minute british data. International Journal of Forecasting **24**(4), 645 – 658 (2008)

[229] Taylor, J.W.: Triple seasonal methods for short-term electricity demand forecasting. European Journal of Operational Research **204**(1), 139–152 (2009)

[230] Taylor, J.W.: Short-term load forecasting with exponentially weighted methods. Transactions on Power Systems **27**(1), 458–464 (2012)

[231] Taylor, J.W., McSharry, P.E.: Short-term load forecasting methods: An evaluation based on european data. Power Systems **22**(4), 2213–2219 (2007)

[232] Taylor, J.W., de Menezes, L.M., McSharry, P.E.: A comparison of univariate methods for forecasting electricity demand up to a day ahead. International Journal of Forecasting **22**(1), 1–16 (2006)

[233] TempoDB Inc.: TempoDB (2014). URL `https://tempo-db.com`. (Last checked: 2014-08-05)

[234] Tomić, J., Kempton, W.: Using fleets of electric-drive vehicles for grid support. Journal of Power Sources **168**(20), 459–468 (2007)

[235] Tsymbal, A.: The problem of concept drift: Definitions and related work. Tech. rep., Department of Computer Science Trinity College Dublin

(2004). URL `https://www.cs.tcd.ie/publications/tech-reports/reports.04/TCD-CS-2004-15.pdf`. (Last checked: 2014-08-11)

[236] Tulving, E.: Episodic and semantic memory. In: Organization of Memory, pp. 381–403. New York: Academic Press (1972)

[237] Ulbricht, R., Fischer, U., Lehner, W., Donker, H.: Rethinking energy data management: Trends and challenges in today's transforming markets. In: Proceedings of the 15th GI-Fachtagung für Datenbanksysteme in Business, Technology und Web (BTW), pp. 421–440 (2013)

[238] Vattenfall AB: Annual report 2011 (2011). URL `http://www.vattenfall.com/en/file/2011_Annual_Report.pdf_20332206.pdf`. (Last checked: 2014-08-11)

[239] Venayagamoorthy, G.K., Rohrig, K., Erlich, I.: One step ahead: Short-term wind power forecasting and intelligent predictive control based on data analytics. Power and Energy Magazine, IEEE **10**(5), 70–78 (2012)

[240] Visalakshi, P., Sivanandam, S.N.: Dynamic task scheduling with load balancing using hybrid particle swarm optimization. International Journal of Open Problems in Computer Science and Mathematics **2**(3), 475–488 (2009)

[241] Wang, J., Botterud, A., Miranda, V., Monteiro, C., Sheble, G.: Impact of wind power forecasting on unit commitment and dispatch. In: Proceedings of the 8th International Workshop on Large-Scale Integration of Wind Power into Power Systems (2009)

[242] Weron, R., Misiorek, A.: Modeling and forecasting electricity loads: A comparison. In: Proceedings of the 2004 International Conference on the European Electricity Market (EEM), pp. 135–142 (2004)

[243] Wetter, M., Wright, J.: A comparison of deterministic and probabilistic optimization algorithms for nonsmooth simulation-based optimization. Building and Environment **39**(8), 989–999 (2004)

[244] Wilkes, J., Moccia, J., Dragan, M.: Wind in power: 2011 European statistics. Industrial analysis and report, EWEA - The European Wind Energy Association (2012). URL `http://www.ewea.org/fileadmin/files/library/publications/statistics/Wind_in_power_2011_European_statistics.pdf`. (Last checked: 2014-08-10)

[245] Winter, R., Kostamaa, P.: Large scale data warehousing: Trends and observations. In: Proceedings of the 26th IEEE International Conference on Data Engineering (ICDE), p. 1 (2010)

[246] Winters, P.R.: Forecasting sales by exponentially weighted moving averages. Management Science **6**, 324–342 (1960)

[247] Wittgenstein, L.: Philosophical Investigations. Basil Blackwell (1953)

[248] Woll, O., Weber, C.: Hybride Ansätze zur Preismodellierung im Kontext von Portfoliomanagement und Kraftwerksbewertung. In: VDI: Optimierung

in der Energiewirtschaft, VDI Reports 2157, pp. 93–104. Verein Deutscher Ingenieure (2011)

[249] Wulf, W.A., McKEE, S.A.: Hitting the memory wall: Implications of the obvious. Computer Architecture News **23**(1), 20–24 (1995)

[250] Yeo, T., Byles, D., Gardiner, B., Lavery, I., Lee, P., Owen, A., Pincher, C., Robertson, J., Sandys, L., Smith, R., Witehead, A.: A European super-grid. Tech. rep., Energy and Climate Change Committee - House of Commons (2011). URL http://www.publications.parliament.uk/pa/cm 201012/cmselect/cmenergy/1040/1040.pdf. (Last checked: 2014-08-11)

[251] Zavadil, R.: Renewable generation forecasting: The science, applications, and outlook. In: Proceedings of the 46th Hawaii International Conference on System Sciences (HICSS), pp. 2252–2260 (2013)

[252] Zellner, A., Tobias, J.: A note on aggregation, disaggregation and forecasting performance. Journal of Forecasting **19**(5), 457–469 (2000)

[253] Zhang, C., Sun, S., Yu, G.: A bayesian network approach to time series forecasting of short-term traffic flows. In: Proceedings of the 7th IEEE International Conference on Intelligent Transportation Systems (ITSC), pp. 216–221 (2004)

[254] Zliobaite, I.: Learning under concept drift: An overview. Tech. rep., Vilnius University (2009). URL http://sites.google.com/site/zliobaite/ Zliobaite_CDoverview.pdf. (Last checked: 2014-08-11)